JOHN POYER

JOHN POYER

the Civil Wars in Pembrokeshire
and the British Revolutions

LLOYD BOWEN

UNIVERSITY OF WALES PRESS
2020

www.uwp.co.uk

British Library Cataloguing-in-Publication Data
A catalogue record for this book is available from the British Library.

ISBN   978-1-78683-654-0
eISBN   978-1-78683-655-7

The right of Lloyd Bowen to be identified as author of this work has been asserted
in accordance with sections 77, 78 and 79 of the Copyright, Designs and Patents
Act 1988.

MIX
Paper from
responsible sources
FSC® C013604

Typeset by Marie Doherty
Printed by CPI Antony Rowe, Melksham

For Nicki, Tal and Osian,
and in memory of my mother and father

'I don't want to achieve immortality through my work; I want to achieve immortality through not dying'.

Woody Allen

Contents

Map

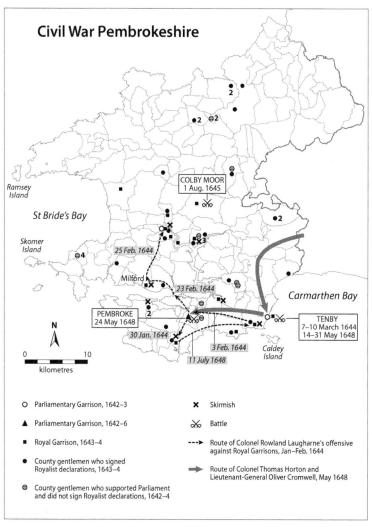

Civil War Pembrokeshire

Ramsey Island

St Bride's Bay

Skomer Island

COLBY MOOR
1 Aug. 1645

25 Feb. 1644

Milford

23 Feb. 1644

Carmarthen Bay

PEMBROKE
24 May 1648

N

30 Jan. 1644

3 Feb. 1644

11 July 1648

Caldey Island

TENBY
7–10 March 1644
14–31 May 1648

0   10
kilometres

○   Parliamentary Garrison, 1642–3

▲   Parliamentary Garrison, 1642–6

■   Royal Garrison, 1643–4

●   County gentlemen who signed Royalist declarations, 1643–4

⊖   County gentlemen who supported Parliament and did not sign Royalist declarations, 1642–4

✕   Skirmish

⚔   Battle

- - -▶   Route of Colonel Rowland Laugharne's offensive against Royal Garrisons, Jan–Feb. 1644

➡   Route of Colonel Thomas Horton and Lieutenant-General Oliver Cromwell, May 1648

Adapted with permission from D. W. Howell (ed.), *An Historical Atlas of Pembrokeshire* (Pembrokeshire County History, 5, 2019).

Abbreviations

BL	British Library, London
Bodl. Lib.	Bodleian Library, Oxford
CJ	*Journals of the House of Commons*
HMC	Historical Manuscripts Commission Reports
Leach, *Pembrokeshire*	A. L. Leach, *The History of the Civil War (1642–1649) in Pembrokeshire and on its Borders* (London, 1937)
LJ	*Journals of the House of Lords*
NLW	National Library of Wales, Aberystwyth
Pembs. Co. Hist.	Brian Howells (ed.), *Pembrokeshire County History Volume III: Early Modern Pembrokeshire, 1536–1815* (Haverfordwest, 1987)
PJLP	Wilson H. Coates, Anne Steele Young and Vernon F. Snow (eds), *The Private Journals of the Long Parliament* (3 vols, New Haven and London, 1982–92)
TNA	The National Archives, Kew
Whitelocke, *Memorials*	Bulstrode Whitelocke, *Memorials of the English Affairs* (4 vols, Oxford, 1853)
Worc. Coll.	Worcester College, Oxford
WWHR	*West Wales Historical Records*

Acknowledgements

I am most grateful to the staff of the libraries and archives who have helped me research this volume. My thanks to the ever professional and efficient staff at The National Archives, The National Library of Wales, Lambeth Palace Library and the Bodleian Library. Particular thanks are due to Mark Bainbridge of Worcester College Library in Oxford who assisted me in accessing the Clarke papers and answered my many enquiries with speedy good grace. James Kirwan and Sandy Paul of Trinity College, Cambridge, were also very helpful in providing me with a copy of a unique Poyer text at lightning speed.

I am very lucky in being part of a supportive academic community in the Department of History at Cardiff University. My colleagues have sustained my spirits and provided a stimulating environment in which to think about and discuss the British Civil Wars despite the many challenges our Department faces. Particular thanks are due to Mark Williams and Keir Waddington for their unstinting support and assistance. The book was shaped by conversations with Stephanie Ward who did not fall asleep when discussing something other than misery in the 1930s, and I am very grateful for her encouragement. David Doddington was always good for the LOLs.

The research for this volume arose out of a conference on the memory of the civil wars I organised with Mark Stoyle. Mark's encouragement, enthusiasm, historical acuity and practical advice and assistance have been invaluable in thinking about and writing this volume. His has been the most important intellectual stimulus for this work, and I am enormously grateful for his wonderful good humour, support and friendship. Andy Hopper, Ismini Pells and David Appleby are splendid colleagues on our AHRC project investigating civil war petitions, and I am most appreciative of their stimulating company and assistance.

The staff at the University of Wales Press have been the model of efficient support and I am thankful for their diligent professionalism. Llion Wigley has been impressively patient with the various iterations of this project. He did not panic when the initial 'small pamphlet' became something rather different, and I am very appreciative of his help.

My friends have been tiresomely but predictably absent in the researching and writing of this book. Dar remains a slave to the Caribbean all-inclusive, while Dark Skies' fixation with ocelot breeding and *Exchange and Mart* means he is rarely available for comment. Dids went to the spectacular lengths of dying so he would not have to read this book; *chwarae teg*.

My family has been an inexhaustible source of support, humour and distraction. I am so very grateful to my wife Nicki and our sons Taliesin and Osian for helping me research and write this book. One of this triumvirate has tremendous patience and generosity, which have been so important for me. My boys are just remarkable, and their plans for world-domination through Poyer studies, or Juan Sweener, remain viable. I am very sorry my parents did not live to see this book published, but they contributed to it as much as anyone, so thank you mam and dad.

Preface

Most books examining the British civil wars (*c*.1642–51) have an entry in their index: 'Poyer, John'. It usually is only a single entry, however, denoting a brief mention of John Poyer's role in an insurrection against parliamentary rule in 1648. Poyer rebelled against the parliament which had been victorious in the first civil war (1642–6) and his actions helped to initiate a series of uprisings and provincial revolts which, along with the invasion of the Scottish Covenanters in the summer of 1648, are collectively known as 'The Second Civil War'. His rebellion is sufficient to justify his inclusion in such texts, but this book's aim is to provide a richer context for, and more detailed analysis of, his revolt, and also to suggest that Poyer had a fascinating history before April 1648 which not only repays deeper enquiry, but which can also help us better understand his motivations and actions during that tumultuous spring and summer.

John Poyer's was a fascinating life. He was essentially a nobody; born into an obscure family in a run-down town 'in a nooke of a little county', as one contemporary put it, on the western periphery of the British mainland.[1] Yet he became a leading light of the parliamentarian war effort in this part of the country in the early 1640s and held out as mayor in his bastion of Pembroke as the royalist tide swept up to the town's walls. Poyer was a charismatic and capable individual who managed to mobilise the local population behind him in some desperate times. His early declaration for parliament should have left him in an enviable position after the king's defeat in 1646. Many parliamentarians were rewarded with offices and positions of local power as the new order needed trusted servants to implement its policies in the provinces. This was not to be Poyer's fate, however. Although he remained governor of Pembroke, he was crossed by local gentry enemies who had opposed him during the 1640s. These were men who initially supported King Charles I, but who later found their way into parliament's camp. As one Poyer supporter put it at the time, 'in our distresse [they] were our greatest enemies and successe onlie induced [them] to profess our frindshippe'.[2]

Despite Poyer's steadfast support of parliament, then, the aftermath of the civil war saw him effectively 'frozen out' of local government as his enemies rose to positions of authority through their productive friendships with powerful figures in parliament and its New Model Army. Estranged, isolated and impoverished by his wartime service, Poyer looked for support from a parliament that increasingly did not favour him. His marginalisation eventually led to outright resistance, and Poyer rebelled against parliament and the New Model Army in early 1648. He soon declared his support for the imprisoned Charles I and sought aid and assistance from the exiled Prince of Wales. This royalist revolt spread quickly through south Wales but was ruthlessly suppressed, and parliament sent down Lieutenant General Oliver Cromwell to besiege Poyer and his recalcitrant royalists in Pembroke. After a long and attritional siege Poyer surrendered to parliament's mercy in July 1648. He and two of his fellow rebels were put on trial in Whitehall shortly after King Charles I was beheaded. They were found guilty and sentenced to death, but it was decided to show mercy so that only one of their number would die. A child drew lots on their behalf, and the unlucky Poyer was given a blank piece of paper which meant his death. He was executed by firing squad in Covent Garden on 25 April 1649.

This, then, was a life full of incident and interest. Poyer is an intriguing figure, but he is also a paradoxical and quixotic one. Although he was a man who could inspire considerable loyalty and allegiance, even his staunchest admirers saw him as an irascible and splenetic individual who was difficult to like and to admire. It was a parliamentarian who wrote that Poyer 'would find any occasion to pick a quarrel'.[3] His enemies seem truly to have hated and reviled him and made sure they told the world how they felt. We here encounter a central problem with trying to write about Poyer, and it is one which many historians have not sufficiently recognised: that we often look at him through his adversaries' hostile gaze.[4] Poyer is not an individual who bequeathed reams of correspondence which reveal his innermost thoughts and motivations. Indeed, he only left behind a handful of letters and petitions, and all of these are 'official' in nature. As a result, we often have to fall back on hostile reports and pamphlets about Poyer which are written with a very jaundiced eye. The principal author of such accounts was Poyer's *bête noire*, John Eliot of Amroth (Pembrokeshire), a skilled author and publicist and Poyer's implacable antagonist. Eliot was adept at inserting his partial and prejudiced view of Poyer (often anonymously) into many forms of print, and historians have often treated such pieces uncritically. The present volume is no apologia for John Poyer. However, it does argue that we need a much more critical and evaluative eye when it comes to our evidence for Poyer's actions and motivations than has been the case in previous discussions. In fact, an argument can be made that our modern view of Poyer often comes uncomfortably close to reproducing the perspective promulgated by John Eliot in the mid-seventeenth century. This volume acknowledges that Poyer was a divisive and contentious figure who remains something of a mystery because of the nature of our evidence. Nonetheless, it suggests that we should be more aware of the difficulties Poyer faced in trying to remain faithful to a parliament which was increasingly, in its local iterations at least, seeking to engineer his ruin.

In tackling some of these issues, this volume has brought to light many new sources from which we can better reconstruct and understand Poyer's background, actions and entanglements during the 1640s. These include numerous pamphlets which have never been utilised by historians before, many of which only exist as single copies. Only the ghosts of some of these texts remain, however, in the form of answers to pamphlets which have not survived (such as Poyer's first published work, *The Relation* from 1645) or as manuscript transcriptions rather than the printed texts themselves, which have disappeared. These pamphlets have offered a significant new evidential corpus for studying Poyer and Pembrokeshire's politics during the 1640s. One important discovery has been the manner in which Poyer's *Declaration* for the king in April 1648 was instrumentalised and distributed as a form of associative text or oath in south Wales and beyond. This helps to explain how his rising quickly snowballed from a minor army mutiny into a major provincial rising which required the mobilisation of a significant New Model force to address it.

In addition, the volume has made more extensive use than any previous study of Poyer and Pembrokeshire of the periodical literature which grew to be such a feature of political life in the 1640s. Much can be revealed by examining copies of the dense weekly propaganda sheets which emerged from the partisan presses of London and Oxford. John Eliot's capacity for contributing anonymous anti-Poyer copy into these newsbooks is just one of the discoveries such an analysis has provided. In addition, this book makes use of extensive new archival finds in The National Archives, the Huntington Library, Worcester College, Oxford, and the Bodleian

Library. These have helped, for example, to locate Poyer within the orbit of the Pembroke gentleman John Meyrick in his early years, and have provided a much fuller understanding of the context in which Poyer's *Vindication* was published shortly before his death in 1649.

The evidential problems of seeing Poyer through his enemies' eyes perhaps help to explain why few historians have tried to unravel the conundrum of this high-profile 'turncoat', or sought to better understand his motivations and actions.[5] He is not an attractive individual and certainly ended up on the wrong side of history. Commentators also prefer careers of straightforward commitment; there is something unsavoury about a man who changes his allegiance and shifts his positions. However, it is one of this book's arguments that Poyer was, in fact, a consistent politician. This was one of his problems: that he failed to adapt to the shifting politics of his times and ended up before a firing squad because of his inflexibility. Rather than seeing Poyer's royalist declaration in 1648 as an aberration, a shift from his earlier public politics, this volume argues that we need to take Poyer's own words more seriously, that in 1648 he 'still continue[d] to [his] . . . first principles'.[6] Poyer considered that parliament had become a radical body which had fallen away from its original undertaking to seek moderate reformation and an accommodation with the king; it had departed from him rather than vice versa.

This volume, then, seeks to better understand and contextualise Poyer within his milieu and the local and national politics of his times. It argues that Poyer needs to be located within the bitter factional politics of civil war Pembrokeshire, and that we should pay greater attention than we have hitherto to the connections these factions made with figures at Westminster. This study is the first to explore in any depth Poyer's background, and it reveals that he was an intimate of the Meyrick family of Monkton near Pembroke. This helps place him within the orbit of the influential earl of Essex, leader of parliament's army in 1642. His brother-in-law and fellow parliamentarian soldier Rowland Laugharne was close to Essex, as was Poyer's sometime 'master', the Pembroke MP, Sir Hugh Owen of Orielton. On the other side of this factional divide we can locate Poyer's enemies, principal among them being the Lorts of Stackpole and their allies John Eliot and Griffith White. The factional politics of civil war Pembrokeshire is a murky business which no previous study has satisfactorily explored or understood. For example, the role of John White, MP for Southwark, and Richard Swanley, the parliamentarian vice admiral, in assisting the Lorts and frustrating Poyer's requests for promotion and payment of his arrears, is discussed here for the first time. Chapters 3 and 4 offer a sustained analysis of the ways in which such political connection and factional confrontation were important in shaping Poyer's civil war experience.

A discussion of Poyer's life during the 1640s, then, reveals something important about the conduct of provincial politics in the transformed circumstances of civil war. The capacity to make and sustain political connections at the centre was crucial in obtaining and maintaining parliament's good graces. In this, Poyer's enemies were more adept and agile than he and his associates were, and the appointment of John Eliot as Pembrokeshire's 'agent' at Westminster in early 1645 is shown here to be a crucial development in a manner which has not been sufficiently appreciated. Through an analysis of Poyer's experiences, then, this volume offers more general insights into the conduct of political business in the aftermath of war and the means by which local power was acquired and preserved.

In examining the operation of political connection across the 1640s, this book also offers a case study of the ways in which the fissures within the post-war parliamentary coalition were transmitted into the provinces. The rise of the New Model Army and of political Independency after 1646 offered a rich set of opportunities for the Lorts and their allies. Poyer, Laugharne and their associates, by contrast, looked to the more moderate Presbyterian political bloc to represent and defend their interests. Thus it was that the factional differences within Pembrokeshire's parliamentary politics assumed a more overt ideological form, although issues of power, money and authority were always present in these confrontations. This is not to say that ideological divisions within the parliamentary phalanx in Pembrokeshire were not present before, but rather that they were instrumentalised, weaponised and adopted new forms when the immediate business of fighting the royalists was done. In their political alignments, however, the Lorts had chosen a more potent set of allies than Poyer. The earl of Essex died in September 1646, and although Poyer and his associates still had some political successes such as the election of his Presbyterian ally Arthur Owen to the Pembrokeshire constituency seat, the Presbyterians lost ground rapidly to their Independent opponents both centrally and locally as 1647 progressed.

Poyer's presence among these Presbyterians places him as something of a political moderate, but the discussion here reveals that he was a

religious conservative also. Somewhat unusually among precocious parliamentarians, Poyer was not a thoroughgoing puritan who had advanced
ideas about Protestant reform. He was certainly anti-Catholic, and his first
emergence into public view was as a bulwark against the Catholic rising
in Ireland in 1642. However, this activism did not translate into radical
religious positions, and he seems to have remained from first to last a
supporter of the Established Church and its liturgy. It is probable that he
wished to see a degree of reform within the Church, but this would probably have been only to remove the corruptions which had built up during
Charles I's reign. In 1645 he made the ideologically freighted gesture
of bequeathing large communion chalices to Pembroke's two churches,
and was described by his enemies as a 'stiffe maintainer of the Booke of
Common-prayer'.[7] Recognising his 'episcopalianism' helps us to better
understand the basis of his declaration for the king in April 1648. By this
time parliament had become transformed from a body seeking moderate
reform in Church and state to an institution contemplating radical change
in these areas. As a 'prayer book Protestant', in 1648 Poyer found more
in common with the king's party than with the Lorts's Independents.
Indeed, it is a core argument of this book that, although Poyer's antipathy
to parliament initially revolved around questions of arrears and indemnity,
previous commentators are incorrect in seeing him as simply being driven
by 'self-interest', or that his insurrection was a spasm of mere opportun-
ism. Rather, this volume contends that there was a political and ideological
consistency which Poyer articulated at several points between February
1648 and his death in April 1649. Thus, it is argued, his 'royalism' should
be understood as a genuine reflection of his core beliefs, rather than as a
mere disingenuous and dissembling posture intended to conceal greedy
self-interest, as is so often claimed.

Important, too, in the wider themes revealed by Poyer's life and civil
war experience, is the use of the new mass media of print. Attention to
the role of political print has been a growing area of research in recent
years, and this study offers a modest contribution to this scholarship. Poyer
and his associates utilised print to make their case for better treatment by
parliament and to lobby against their enemies' nefarious designs. This was
an important means for the relatively distant and isolated Pembrokeshire
Presbyterians to communicate with the centre. However, this study suggests that their print campaigns were often relatively limited in scope
and were sometimes 'fronted' by individuals such as Poyer himself who

distributed texts such as his *Relation* personally to influential power brokers in Westminster. In this battle of the printed word, it seems that Poyer's enemies had a much more effective and influential instrument in the shape of John Eliot. Eliot was able to publish responses to Poyer and his associates quickly and effectively, and his position in Westminster seems to have helped him in this regard. He evidently had friends and associates in the newsbook world who allowed him to slip copy into their news-sheets when occasion required. He was also aligned with the growing power of the Army interest, and material such as his list of grievances against Poyer, which he sent to the commander of the New Model Sir Thomas Fairfax in late 1647, soon found its way into a newsbook sympathetic to the army. Although we can understand much about Poyer through printed works, then, we must be aware that a good deal of this evidence was produced with the explicit purpose of ruining his reputation and undermining his position. His public persona was highly partial; we should be wary that our histories do not follow suit.

Shortly before he died, John Poyer said, 'I have had experience of changes; though I was once low, yet I came to be very high'.[8] This book follows his journey through these changes not only to understand his role in them, but also to place Poyer and his struggles in their local and national contexts. Although Poyer is a minor figure in the civil wars, he is an individual whose life and career help illuminate many aspects of the rapidly changing world of the 1640s. This volume offers a more thorough and developed analysis of his attempts to navigate these changes than has been provided hitherto, but it also offers a discussion which provides new insights into the dynamics of provincial politics in the 1640s and the origins of the Second Civil Wars. Poyer's story is, ultimately, a compelling one of human ambition and tragedy. His life ended in Covent Garden with two bullets in his heart. How things came to this pass is a tale of faction and hubris, but also one of conviction and bravery. This book traces that journey and begins with a humble glover in a small town in south-west Wales.

CHAPTER 1

The Setting: John Poyer and Early Stuart Pembrokeshire, *c*.1606–1640

John Poyer's origins are lowly and unremarkable. In this he resembles his opponent at the siege of Pembroke in 1648, Oliver Cromwell. However, where Cromwell was a 'by birth a gentleman, living neither in any considerable height, nor yet in obscurity', Poyer could not even boast a gentlemanly lineage or minor status among the landed men of his native Pembrokeshire.[1] Indeed, Poyer's background was so lowly that we cannot even be certain of his parentage. Rather he was a man who worked for his living: in other words, the very definition of what a gentleman was not in this period, and his enemies would make much of his 'mechanic' origins and low social rank. As we shall see, he began his working life in a local gentleman's household before becoming a glover and a merchant. He even tried his hand as a fuller, or one who dealt with the cleaning of wool before its processing. All accounts agree that Poyer's origins, and indeed the vast majority of his relatively short life, are located in and around the borough of Pembroke. Before we consider Poyer's early life and his activities prior to the civil wars, then, we need to consider the environment in which he operated and the nature of the society in which he moved.

Pembroke was the county town of Pembrokeshire in south-west Wales and commanded a position over a branch of the sprawling Milford Haven estuary. Originally of Norman foundation, the town's most notable feature was its imposing castle, which was largely constructed during the late-twelfth and early-thirteenth centuries. The town was the administrative centre for the medieval earldom of Pembroke, a role which helped sustain its local importance.[2] Pembroke was famous as the birthplace of Henry VII who had landed near the town in 1485 at the head of the successful invasion force that took the crown from Richard III and founded the Tudor dynasty. This was a matter of considerable local pride, with one antiquarian writing that Henry's Pembroke origins caused locals to 'greatly rejoice'.[3] As a recognition of special favour towards his birthplace, King Henry VII bestowed upon Pembroke a charter of incorporation in the first year of his reign, organising the borough's government around its chief officer, the mayor, alongside a council composed of two bailiffs and twelve other chief burgesses.

Yet despite such favours from its most famous local son, early modern Pembroke was much reduced from its medieval heyday. The author who wrote of Pembroke's delight in Henry VII's origins, George Owen, was a Pembrokeshire man with considerable local knowledge. In the guise of a traveller roaming around the county during the reign of Queen Elizabeth I, he cast his eye over the borough of Pembroke, observing,

> your ancient shire town . . . though now greatly decayed, yet still does it carry the show of a good town, loving people and courteous, very civil and orderly. The decay of that town, being the head of your shire, and which was in such estimation as it has been in your country in times past, made my heart sorry.[4]

The Jacobean cartographer, John Speed, was rather less forgiving in his assessment of the borough. He described Pembroke as 'more ancient in shewe than it is in yeeres, and more houses without inhabitants than I saw in any one city throughout my survey [of Great Britain]'.[5] The place seemed to him an imposing shell, with impressive buildings hiding a malaise within. Its population at this time was somewhere between 1,000 and 1,500 souls.[6]

Pembroke's rather sorry state by the early seventeenth century reflected a decline in its economic significance. It had retained its position as the shire town of Pembrokeshire, the new county created by the Acts of Union (1536–42). This gave it a degree of prestige and importance and also bestowed the privilege of sending an MP to parliament. It was also the case, however, that the neighbouring town of Haverfordwest was becoming increasingly prosperous and influential at Pembroke's expense.[7] The shire town's rather sorry state in the decades before the civil wars was caused by an economic downturn and the decline of its trading and mercantile sectors. The principal 'industry' of south Pembrokeshire, in addition to the farming of oats and wheat, was wool and sheep. The trading of finished woollen goods had been crucial to the local economy in the fourteenth and fifteen centuries, but by the end of Elizabeth I's reign the export of raw, unfinished, wool dominated.[8] Our Elizabethan antiquarian, George Owen, observed that the inhabitants of southern Pembrokeshire 'vent and sell their wool to Bristol men, Barnstaple and Somersetshire, which come twice every year to the country to buy the wool'.[9] This connection with south-west England helps to explain how we find the surname Poyer in Somerset as well as Pembrokeshire during the seventeenth century, although the exact relationship between these far-flung families is difficult to establish.[10]

The shift from the trade in finished wools to the export of the raw product, however, was linked to Pembroke's economic troubles. The powerful body of local law and administration, the Pembrokeshire justices of the peace, wrote in 1607 how the decline of 'townes in thies partes hath chiefelie growen by the losse and discontinuance of the trade of clothinge', which they attributed to the underhand practices of illicit traders. These men, they claimed, took locally produced wool into

> secreate and obscure places and there uttered and soulde underhand unto strangers who carrie and convaye away the same out of the countrye so as the . . . townes . . . are not imployed or sett on worcke . . . as in former tymes they have bin, to the hindrance and decaie of the . . . townes.[11]

Before the civil war, the powerful local gentleman – who would later become an important associate of Poyer – Hugh Owen of Orielton, was elected mayor of Pembroke in 1632.[12] He took the office partly, he wrote, to advance plans for encouraging the business of wool manufacture in the area as well as 'raysinge of trade which is now decayed'.[13] As we will see, John Poyer was involved in the wool business before the civil wars, perhaps in an attempt to further such schemes for local rejuvenation. However, the recent economic shifts which left his home of Pembroke with so many empty houses, also produced a difficult situation for a merchant and trader to make his way in the world.

Despite Pembroke's empty properties in the seventeenth century, contemporaries agreed that it remained an impressive military site. Although wars had not troubled the area for many decades, Pembroke's imposing medieval castle, thick town walls and advantageous strategic position, made it a strong potential bastion even in the face of modern artillery. This defensive strength would be crucial to its role in the civil war and to Poyer's importance as its mayor and the commander of its garrison. It is therefore worth spending a moment or two considering contemporary descriptions of the town's defences. The cartographer John Speed, who also provided our best visual image of the seventeenth-century town in his 1611 publication *The Theatre of the Empire of Great Britain*, noted that the walls around the town stretched for 880 paces, but at this time they were 'indifferent for repaire'.[14] He was impressed, however, by the 'large castle' at the west end of the town which dominated its prospect.[15]

A fuller description of the town and castle was drawn up by George Owen in the 1590s. Owen was a good Protestant Elizabethan and, like the rest of the country, at this time was concerned about the Catholic threat from abroad. This was the era of the Armada and the nation was on high alert and was particularly worried about coastal security. Pembrokeshire was especially important in this regard because of its proximity to Ireland. Ireland possessed a majority Catholic population, despite the best efforts of English monarchs to settle Protestants and Protestantism there. And Ireland loomed large and forbidding in the imaginations of men like George Owen. Anxiety about a possible Catholic invasion through the defensive weak point of Milford Haven was a concern in the 1590s and would resurface in a manner that energised John Poyer in 1641–2. Partly because of these worries, Owen drew up a memorandum about the defensive status of Milford Haven for the earl of Pembroke who sat on the nation's governing Privy Council. As part of this 'pamflett', Owen turned his attention to Pembroke as an important link in the area's defensive network.[16] Although his description was rather outdated by Poyer's time, it nonetheless provides the best near-contemporary account we have of his home and its defensive capacities, which would be vital in his resistance efforts during the civil wars.[17]

Owen observed that Pembroke was 'all one streete in length without any crosse streetes' and was 'walled about with a stronge wall of lyme and stone'. It was, moreover,

> compassed on each side with a branche of Milford . . . as a stronge mote, floweinge at every tyde in such sorte that noe accesse by horse or foote

is permitted to the town but over two bridges, the town haveinge three gates onlye and the towne walles being strongly defended with 6 flancker towres in such sorte as out of them the whole walles may be scoured and defended from approach of enemies.

He then considered the castle, which he described as 'faire, stronge and large . . . standing strongelye walled with a mightie thicke wall all buylt of lyme & stone'. The castle contained inner and outer courtyards with numerous flank towers covering the approaches. The castle's strength lay not only in its thick walls, he continued, but also in its location:

seated upon a high mayne rocke of 30 and in most places 40 foote high, naturally steepe in most places and the rest easily to be made in such sorte, that if the castle walles might be battered, as most thereof cannot be, yet were it not possible to ascend upp the said rocke to enter the breach.

This inaccessibility was augmented by the waters flowing at the rock's base along with the 'owse [ooze] and slyme' deposited there which 'mightilye defend' the town from any potential enemies. In addition, the town and the castle had several sources of its own spring water which would assist in any siege. It also possessed the 'greate' Wogan's Cave underground which was able 'to receave a greate multitude of people, being a place free from all assaults', and was furnished with its own water supply. Owen concluded that the castle 'is thought allmost impregnable', an assessment echoed half a century later by a participant in the siege of Pembroke in 1648 who described the town as 'the strongest place that ever we sat down before, and the castle even impregnable'.[18]

We can see, then, why Pembroke was such a potential prize in any conflict, and particularly in a civil war such as that which broke out in 1642. A formidable defensive redoubt, the town and castle of Pembroke became Poyer's base of operations. It was a place to which he could retreat when forces turned against him, and from which he could sally out and attack enemies when in a position of strength. Crucially, the town and castle could also be supplied from the estuary, and this would prove vital when Poyer's enemies encompassed him on land in the early 1640s. In addition to his positive assessment of the town and castle's defensive potential, however, Owen also observed that both were 'unfortified', which he considered 'very perilouse'. Speed's assessment of Pembroke's walls as 'indifferent for repaire' also reflected many years of benign neglect. Much of the county armour was adjudged to be defective or inadequate; the area simply was not geared up for war, and the efforts of local gentlemen, like the puritan Sir James Perrot, to enhance the defences of Milford Haven and Pembroke in the 1620s had negligible results.[19] However, Owen stressed that if steps were not taken adequately to fortify Pembroke, a hostile party could take the town 'and [it] would be by them soe fortified and defended as it would be the losse of manye lyves to remove them from thence'. So it would prove in the 1640s, and, as discussed in later chapters, it was Poyer who took a good deal of the initiative to repair and augment Pembroke's defences. The assessment of Pembroke Castle as 'allmost impregnable' would be proven correct. It seems that no military force managed to shift John Poyer from his Pembroke bolt hole during the first civil war. Crucial here, however, is the qualifying 'allmost', because despite a resolute defence in 1648, the refortified town, and Poyer along with it, would eventually fall before the onslaught of Oliver Cromwell and the New Model Army.

The town of Pembroke sat within the 'Englishry' of early modern Pembrokeshire. This was the southern part of the county which had been settled by Normans and Flemings during the medieval period. As a result of their influence, a sharp cultural division had grown up between the English-speaking inhabitants of the south (where all the county's major boroughs – Haverfordwest, Tenby and Pembroke – were located) and the Welsh-speaking populations of the north. This difference was captured most memorably once again by George Owen, who wrote of these two communities as separate 'nations'. In his late-Elizabethan 'Description' of the county, Owen related how the inhabitants of southern Pembrokeshire 'appear by their names, manners and language, speaking altogether the English, and differing in manners, diet, buildings and tilling of the land from the Welshmen [of northern Pembrokeshire]. And although this be now well near 500 years past, yet do these two nations keep each from dealings with the other, as mere strangers'.[20]

Although Owen probably exaggerated the separation of the two communities somewhat, it is nonetheless striking that Poyer's narrative, and that of the civil war in the county more generally, almost exclusively involves figures from the English-speaking south. This fact was noted by Arthur Leach in his history of the 1640s in Pembrokeshire written more than eighty years ago. Leach observed that beyond the Englishry 'not a shot was fired, not a sword drawn throughout the war . . . The war was fought in the Englishry: its issues apparently divided only the English-speaking Pembrokians, and their Welsh compatriots took no ascertainable part in it'.[21] Like Owen, Leach rather overstates his case, and it does not seem credible that the inhabitants of northern Pembrokeshire were either ignorant of the issues involved in the civil war or were wholly uninvolved in its events. There are suggestions, for example, that northern Pembrokeshire might have been more concerned with developments in Cardiganshire, which themselves are obscure and poorly documented, rather than issues in the Englishry.[22] It is the case, however, that contemporary records make hardly any reference to campaigns in the Welshry or to any mobilisation of men and resources from the north of the county. The most detailed contemporary narrative of the civil wars in the county, for example, makes no mention of personalities from beyond the Englishry.[23] Poyer's battles were fought out between neighbours who occupied his own, largely English-speaking, cultural and geographical community. It may be conjectured that southern Pembrokeshire's readier access to news, information and controversy in the English language might have helped inform and animate them politically, and probably encouraged them to forge links with political and military figures in Bristol, London and elsewhere in southern England. Contemporaries from southern Pembrokeshire made no mention, disparaging or otherwise, of the disposition and activities of those from the north of the county. Because of this evidential black hole, it would be dangerous to speculate too much about the reasons for the absence of north Pembrokeshire from the story of the civil war. Nonetheless, it is striking that Poyer's narrative can be told almost exclusively with reference to actors from the Englishry.

One of the aspects of Poyer's story that makes it so compelling is that he was an ordinary subject living in a quiet outpost of the realm who was thrust into the limelight by the extraordinary convulsions of the civil wars during the 1640s. An important thread of the civil war narrative more generally is the capacity of these upheavals to elevate individuals from the lower social classes into positions of prominence and influence that they almost certainly otherwise would not have achieved. In many ways Poyer is emblematic of such processes, but this also makes it difficult to trace his pre-war life in the way we could for an aristocrat or a gentleman. One scholar has claimed that 'nothing is known of Poyer's . . . younger years', but this is, in fact, far from true.[24] We have testimony regarding his background from himself and his enemies, but the polemical nature of such sources makes it hard to assess and verify. There is not much independent corroborating evidence, although some glimpses of Poyer in less controversial sources can be had on occasion.

His name points to origins among the Normans who had settled in south Pembrokeshire. The nineteenth-century local antiquarian Richard Fenton maintained that John Poyer hailed from Grove House near Narberth, which is situated some distance to the north-east of Pembroke.[25] He gives no authority for this claim, however, and there is no evidence to support it, although Poyers were in residence there in the later seventeenth century. Looking back after the first civil war, Poyer's enemies described him as 'borne to nothing, sprung up from a turn-spit to a glover'.[26] On another occasion he was derided as 'a man of meane birth and education, brought up by Master John Meyrick, Customer of Milford, first a boy in his kitchin, then groome of his stable, after in the trade of a glover'.[27] Or again, that he was 'a poore ragged boy which was hired to run to and fro on errands'.[28] Indeed one scurrilous tract averred that Poyer's 'mother is generally famed in the . . . town to be worse than [a whore]'.[29] It is telling that in his printed response to these jibes, Poyer stated 'I boast not of my parents', but gave no further details about his background.[30] Indeed, although we know of a few Poyers who lived in Pembroke in the early seventeenth century, we cannot identify John's parentage confidently. We know from depositions he gave in lawsuits before the civil wars in which he stated his age that Poyer was born around 1606.[31] This means it is very unlikely that he was the John Poyer, son of John Poyer, weaver, who died in Pembroke in early 1605, although this child was a minor at the time and there is a possibility that he was a newborn.[32] Beyond that, we simply do not know with any confidence.

For all their biting venom, his enemies' claim that he was a glover before the wars is clearly true. In a deposition he gave before commissioners for the High Court of Chivalry in January 1636, Poyer self-identified as a 'skinner' of St Mary's parish, Pembroke, that is, a man who dealt in leather, the raw material from which finished gloves would be made.[33] He then described himself a 'glover' before Exchequer commissioners in Pembroke in the autumn of 1639.[34] John Poyer, 'glover', was appointed as one of Pembroke's bailiffs in 1633.[35] We do not have sufficient records to ascertain the economic profile of the town in Poyer's time, but in 1688 the borough contained seven glovers, which suggests a fairly robust (albeit modest) local industry built on earlier foundations.[36] Near a stream to the south of the town were several tanyards which were leased from the corporation for the treating of animal hides, and Poyer may well have been one such lessee in the 1630s.

Although Poyer had a background in manufacture and trade rather than landed wealth and lineage, his interests may nonetheless have become fairly substantial. Although we need to take his own testimony with a pinch of salt as it was designed to counter his antagonists' assertions of his lowly origins, Poyer was emphatic that he was a significant Pembroke figure before the war. He claimed that the best gentleman in Pembroke apprenticed his son to him (which, incidentally, acknowledges that Poyer was master of a trade such as that of glover). Poyer continued that 'my dealings being in wooll, corn, skins, butter, and tallows . . . is well known . . . I dealt in these commodities with the merchants of Bristol for many thousands yeerly, and have given them full satisfaction in all things'.[37] Here was a much more significant and diverse trading portfolio than that which was suggested by Poyer's enemies, and it contains some details which are worthy of closer examination. By Poyer's own admission he dealt with skins for his trade as a glover. He also acknowledged his interest in wool, one of the main exports of south Pembrokeshire and which, as we will see in a moment, we know from other sources he was involved with in the 1630s. Tallow was a by-product of the skinning industry, and butter, another major export of south Pembrokeshire, would also have derived from his interests in the local market for cattle.[38] Export of corn involved a rather different sector of the economy, but Castlemartin, the hundred of south Pembrokeshire in which the town of Pembroke was situated, was involved in the export of these grains to Ireland and the south-west of England when there was a surplus.

Poyer's claim that he dealt with Bristol merchants for 'many thousands yeerly' needs to be viewed sceptically, although we should note that he later requested reimbursement from parliament for thousands of pounds of loans as well as his own money which he had spent in establishing and provisioning the parliamentary garrison at Pembroke.[39] This money had evidently come from somewhere. Moreover, in 1639 he had occasion to note that he was witness to bonds worth several hundred pounds which a fellow Pembroke man, Richard Gwillim, had made with Bristolian trad-ers.[40] This indicates that he was certainly moving in circles which had connections with the great hub of the western coasting trade, and gives some weight to his claims that these connections were substantial ones.

One of the several commercial interests Poyer mentioned in response to his enemies was that of woollens, and we know from a separate source that before the civil wars he did indeed try his hand in a business venture concerning wool manufacture. The interest in wool seems to have related to philanthropic initiatives for resuscitating the clothing industry in south Pembrokeshire in the early 1630s. Poyer's involvement in this initiative also brings into view two local families who will be important in tracing his connections and activities during the civil wars: the Meyricks of Monkton and the Owens of Orielton.

Our evidence of his involvement in the woollen industry comes from a lawsuit brought in the Court of Exchequer in the spring of 1639.[41] This related how a Pembroke widow, Lucy (or 'Luce') Meyrick came into pos-session of a corn mill and a fulling mill at Upton, a few miles north-west of Pembroke, following the death of her husband, John. In October 1634, the month in which John Meyrick died,[42] so the bill of complaint ran, John Poyer approached Lucy requesting that he might become the new tenant of the dilapidated fulling mill. Fulling was the first stage of pro-cessing raw wool into cloth in which the wool was thickened, softened and cleaned using water and fuller's earth (or sometimes urine). The process also involved compacting the raw fibres with water-powered wooden ham-mers in a building known as a fulling mill.[43] It was this treated wool which would be shipped to places like Bristol and the South West for further processing and onward sale. In the bill of complaint, Lucy Meyrick main-tained that Poyer informed her that he would 'repaire and amend' the mill 'and make it fitt for a fullinge . . . pretendinge that there was a great want of one thereabouts, and that hee hoped it would bee very beneficiall unto him'. It was alleged that Poyer took over the mill on a ten-year lease at an annual rent of thirty shillings along with an undertaking to repair the building. This agreement, however, was made in private 'when fewe or none were present', and 'was not put into wrytinge'. As a result, the contract proved difficult to enforce. The venture collapsed and recrimi-nations began to fly. In addition to breach of contract, Meyrick alleged that Poyer did not repair the structure as he had promised, but rather had 'pulled downe and carryed away and converted to his owne use the whole or greatest parte of the frame and timber of the roofe and lefte nothinge but the wheeles and water trough, soe as [the building] . . . is utterly ruinated and demolyshed'.

In his answer to these allegations, 'John Poyer of Pembroke, fuller', maintained that he leased the mill only on a year-to-year basis, 'to try whether hee could doe any good of it', and that 'if [it] soe bee that hee upon the said triall could make it advantadgious that then hee . . . would take some certen terme' of lease. He claimed that this allowed him to return it to Lucy Meyrick at short notice 'if hee did not like the same'. Poyer asserted that he *had* attempted to repair the mill, building a house at the site and repairing the wheels and 'other necessary parts' at a considerable charge. However, the fuller he employed, 'whoe hadd beter skill' than Poyer, told him that he could 'make noe good profitt or advantage thereof'. As a result, Poyer claimed, he ended the trial period as he was entitled to do and passed the property back to Lucy Meyrick. Unfortunately, we do not know the outcome of the case or whose version of events was determined to be correct.

Several points emerge from this previously unknown chapter of Poyer's pre-war life. The lawsuit affirms his involvement with the local woollen industry, but also positions him as an entrepreneur rather than only a trader. Additionally, it confirms Poyer as a man of some substance by this time as he must have had ready resources and a modicum of capital to contemplate taking on the fulling mill. There is also the suggestion that Poyer was a rather canny businessman who was testing the water with the new venture rather than over-committing himself. It would be dangerous to accept entirely the view that he simply ransacked the mill for his own profit. Cases such as this are often framed in the starkest terms by litigants but were usually grounded in some version of the truth. This being the case, it is quite possible that Poyer left the investment with little loss and tried to recoup some of his outlay by removing parts of the structure which he himself had repaired.

Some of Poyer's language in his answer to Meyrick's bill also suggests that his repairing of the fulling mill may have been part of the wider philanthropic scheme for generating employment and addressing economic decline through initiatives for reviving the local woollen industry. It was alleged in the Exchequer suit that Poyer had claimed 'there was a great want' of a fulling mill in the locality, and that it would be 'very beneficiall' to repair the Upton mill. The benefits of reinvigorating the local woollen industry were at this time being promoted by a number of prominent local gentlemen who believed that it would help in 'setting of the poore on worke'. Pembrokeshire justices received the support of the Privy Council for their schemes in 1631. Although this was framed as a charitable endeavour to assist in local employment, it was also something of a ploy to boost the economy of local towns. This would, of course, also help line the pockets of merchants such as John Poyer. The design to 'raise certaine manufactures in [Pembrokeshire] by the woulls growing there', involved a plan to restrict the wool sales to the open markets of Tenby, Haverfordwest and Pembroke.[44] This was an attempt to address the illicit trade in wool, mentioned by the justices as far back as 1607, and which was seen as a prime cause of urban decay, the reduction of customs incomes, and the rise in the number of landless poor and vagrants. Poyer himself would later claim 'I imployed more poor on work in making of cloth than any man in that country [of Pembrokeshire]'.[45] While such a statement has no hard evidence to back it up and was certainly an exaggeration, it does indicate that Poyer was involved in such charitable initiatives, and suggests that the case of the Upton fulling mill may have been part of a wider attempt to bolster the local woollen industry.

This connection with the Pembrokeshire woollens scheme perhaps also casts some light on Poyer's appointment as one of Pembroke's bailiffs in 1633. Bailiff was the second most senior position in the town oligarchy after the mayoralty, and in 1633 the mayor was Hugh Owen of Orielton. This was Owen's second consecutive term of office, and officials at the Council in the Marches of Wales, a powerful executive branch of government with particular competencies over the Welsh counties, observed that 'by direction from the Lords of the [Privy] Councell, the business of manufacture [of wools] in that cuntry is to goe on. And for the furtherance thereof and the raysinge of trade which is now decayed, hee [i.e. Hugh Owen] was chosen mayor'.[46] That he remained in post for a second term suggests that he continued to oversee or drive on this initiative. Owen would become Poyer's close ally in the early 1640s, with the latter being described as Owen's 'servant'. Poyer's appearance as bailiff to Owen's mayor, then, further advances the argument that he was involved in the philanthropic woollens initiative.

A final noteworthy element of the Upton case is the evidence it provides of Poyer's connection with the Meyrick family. It is arresting that Poyer was able to make the agreement about the fulling mill with Lucy

Meyrick in private and, essentially, on a promise. This suggests a degree of intimacy and close connection between Poyer and Meyrick which is important for our understanding of his local connections and also for his wartime associations. Lucy Meyrick was the wife of John Meyrick of the Fleet, Monkton, which lay just across the water from Pembroke. John Meyrick was a scion of a powerful local family and the son of an Elizabethan bishop of Bangor.[47] John's eldest brother, Sir Gelly Meyrick, had been the trusted lieutenant and man of business of Elizabeth I's sometime favourite, Robert Devereux, second earl of Essex.[48] Sir Gelly was caught up in Essex's Rebellion against Elizabeth in 1601 and was hanged at Tyburn for treason. The younger brother, John, led a slightly more sedate life in Pembrokeshire, although, importantly for our purposes, he was also an intimate member of the county's Essex faction. The second earl appointed him as clerk of the peace of the Pembrokeshire quarter sessions, which made him the chief official of the county's main administrative body. He also became Customer of Milford, a post which involved collecting customs duties throughout the Milford region, which included Pembroke, Tenby and Haverfordwest. In 1602 John, along with his then vigorous wife Lucy as well as a posse of local friends and associates, set upon a preacher who had come to Pembroke from Ireland and made critical remarks about the earl of Essex while drinking in one of the town's inns.[49] This connection between Meyrick and the Essex clan continued across the generations, and, in 1628, John Meyrick was one of those empowered by the third earl of Essex to make leases on his lands in south-west Wales.[50] Meyrick also leased the manor of Monkton from the earl as well as the tithes of St Mary's Pembroke (where Poyer lived) and other properties in Pembrokeshire.[51] This connection with the Devereux family would remain an important political connection in Pembrokeshire's civil war politics and would also become significant for Poyer. Indeed, it is possible that Poyer's service with John Meyrick introduced him to the local gentry who were connected with the third earl of Essex.

As we have seen, one of Poyer's wartime opponents subsequently maintained that Poyer was 'brought up by Master John Meyrick, Customer of Milford, first a boy in his kitchin, then groome of his stable, after in the trade of a glover'. Such a connection would help to explain the ready intimacy between Poyer and Lucy Meyrick which allowed him to take the lease of the fulling mill in a private conversation, although the menial nature of his service is more difficult to establish. That there is more than a grain of truth to this scurrilous pamphlet's claims, however, is indicated by John Meyrick's will, which was composed in 1633, although he died in late 1634. As he lay sick, John Meyrick appointed his faithful wife Lucy to be his executrix. At the end of this important document, he added a brief additional clause: 'I doe desire my cozen Henry Bolton and John Poyer, glover, when my . . . executrix shall have any occasion to use them, or any one of them, to follow her busines they wilbe very carefull, for I always found them to be just and honest unto me'.[52] This is a fascinating note, which indicates that Poyer was indeed a trusted intimate of the Meyrick family, and that he had even been recommended to Lucy Meyrick to help discharge the estate after John Meyrick's death. The Upton case was brought against Poyer by the overseers of Meyrick's will, Thomas Butler and Roger Pritchard, and it seems that we are dealing with a case in which Poyer overstepped the proper boundaries of assisting the widow, but that such an arrangement had been encouraged by John Meyrick. The nature and tone of the clause in Meyrick's will gives credence to the claim that Poyer was a onetime member of his household, and perhaps some kind of servant or man-of-business. Poyer was bequeathed nothing in the will, but Meyrick evidently trusted him and had experience of his services.

Poyer's connection with the Meyrick family can also be traced in another hitherto unused source.[53] In November 1635 Rowland Meyrick, John's son, brought a case in the High Court of Chivalry against another Pembroke man, George Catchmay. The High Court of Chivalry was an ancient court, recently revived by Charles I, which dealt with matters of honour between gentlemen.[54] It was particularly concerned with matters of slander ('giving the lie') which were seen to be provocative of a duel. The court's intervention, its supporters claimed, reduced violence and arbitrated matters of honour between the powerful landed gentry of England and Wales. Rowland Meyrick claimed that in December 1634 Catchmay, who was then serving as Pembroke's mayor, had addressed him as 'thou rogue' and said he would spend £200 to remove him as Customer of Milford, the position he had recently inherited from his father.[55] Again, in March 1635, while he was at a Pembroke inn, Meyrick alleged that Catchmay had called him 'a base rogue'.[56] For his part, Catchmay said that Rowland Meyrick, along with his brother John, called him 'base mayor', and sat above him in St Mary's church, Pembroke, providing a very public statement that they believed themselves to be Catchmay's social superiors. The court investigated these claims through a commission of local gentlemen which heard witnesses for Meyrick at a Pembroke inn between 18 and 20 January 1636. John Poyer, skinner, of St Mary's Pembroke, aged about thirty, gave evidence on Rowland Meyrick's behalf. He noted that he had known the plaintiff and his father John for some twenty years. This would mean since the age of ten, and thus adds to our body of evidence suggesting that Poyer was indeed a member of Meyrick's household from an early age; perhaps even that he was the 'kitchin boy' and subsequently 'groome' his opponents claimed.

As we might expect given his close connection with the family, Poyer's testimony was wholly supportive of Rowland Meyrick's case. He deposed that he had heard that Rowland's grandfather had been bishop of Bangor, providing clear evidence of his elevated status and lineage, but that Catchmay's father was a merely a Pembroke innkeeper and 'baselie descended and borne'.[57] Moreover, he claimed to have witnessed Catchmay meeting Meyrick near Pembroke gaol, who 'in a deriding and scornefull' manner asked '"Sirra, will thou goe into the gaole?"' The terms of address used here, 'sirra' and 'thou' were generally only employed towards social inferiors and were thus operating as terms of abuse. Poyer concluded that Catchmay's speeches 'were delivered in a provoking base opprobrious and disgracefull maner'; in other words, Poyer was indicating to the court that he considered Catchmay's speech to constitute an illegal provocation to a duel. This brief window on Poyer's life before the civil war, then, reveals him as an intimate of the Meyrick family and a man willing to support their case against the town's recent mayor. It helps to tie him into the circle of this influential local family, a family who, as we shall see, still had close connections with the earl of Essex.

A final civil war pamphlet, this time not from one of Poyer's enemies, repeats the social critique of the others and adds another intriguing detail. It described Poyer as moving 'from a groome then a glover and after a searcher in the customes, and at best a constant taker and sure holder fast of what so ever fish that came into his net'.[58] This is an image of a man who was on the make, someone who had his eye to the main chance and was looking to get ahead, which agrees with the version of Poyer that emerges from the Upton mill case. The mention of Poyer operating as searcher of customs has not been noticed before. It is certainly within the realms of possibility that John Meyrick, as the Customer of Milford, managed to secure his 'servant' a potentially lucrative office in local government. The searcher inspected goods to ensure that the correct duties were being paid on imports and exports. In addition to the fee from the office, it is likely that opportunities abounded for kickbacks and palm greasing.[59] However, there is no record that Poyer was appointed searcher. The man who officially held the post was William Hinton, who was appointed in 1632, and whom Poyer knew well.[60] Hinton would go on to become a Poyer supporter in the first civil war, but abandoned him when Poyer turned on his parliamentary masters.[61] There is no sign that Hinton ever gave up this position and no other appointee was mentioned. It is possible that Poyer paid Hinton a fee and discharged the duties himself, but the absence of any other reference to his acting as searcher means we should be sceptical about the claim that he held the post.

The Upton fulling mill case demonstrated that Poyer's relationship with the Meyricks was not necessarily smooth or straightforward. The Exchequer suit was brought against Poyer in the spring of 1639, and there are some rather obscure references which indicate that this was the prelude to a falling out between the family and a period of some violence and disruption involving Poyer. These references are to be found in notes of cases brought before the Court of the Council in the Marches of Wales in the 1630s. These are, however, very brief and often raise as many questions as they can answer. The first entry, dated 14 September 1639, lists John Meyrick as plaintiff against John Poyer for 'affray', with the additional notation 'sine die & noe fine', meaning an indefinite adjournment of any decision and no fine to be imposed.[62] John Meyrick was Rowland Meyrick's elder brother, the heir of Poyer's sometime master and friend. In December 1639, the casebooks list Poyer as defendant in another case of affray, this time brought by one Richard Browne. Browne married Bridget Meyrick who was Rowland and John Meyrick's cousin.[63] The note to this entry read, 'And continue till the defendant [i.e. Poyer] be out of prison'. A later hearing on 14 December 1640 dismissed the case against him without costs.[64] In January 1640 Poyer himself brought a case for wrongful imprisonment against one Edward Thomas, who remains unidentified, and the import of this case is unclear; it was noted that Thomas should be fined £20 unless just cause could be shown. Finally, in March 1640 it was Poyer who brought a suit against Rowland Meyrick and others, who were not named, apart from Richard Hinton, a clergyman in Pembroke who had deposed on Rowland Meyrick's behalf in 1636, and who was probably related to the Milford searcher, William. This was merely listed as a case of 'Ryott', and eight (unnamed) defendants were convicted and fined a substantial total of £150, while others were dismissed without costs.[65]

We do have another scrap of evidence which can help us a little with these suits, and which confirms that the brief Ludlow entries concern the Pembrokeshire protagonists. On 18 August 1640, Thomas Skyrme, a man from a Pembrokeshire family but apparently employed as an official in the Council in the Marches of Wales, gave evidence before the great sessions court at Haverfordwest.[66] He testified that he had read the information exhibited by John Poyer against Rowland Meyrick at the Council, and an indictment exhibited at the Haverfordwest great sessions. They concerned Meyrick's (and others') 'affray & misdemenors' which had occurred on 21 July 1638, and for which Meyrick had been fined 100 marks at the Council in the Marches. Skyrme informed the court, however, that Poyer's Haverfordwest suit and the one at Ludlow were 'one & the selfe same causes'. This seems to refer to the 'ryott' prosecution concluded in the Council in the Marches in March 1640. It seems that Poyer was trying to prosecute Meyrick twice for the same offence in two separate jurisdictions, which would not have been allowed after the case was determined in the superior court.

This is a confused and fragmentary picture offered up by partial and decontextualised sources. As a result, it is difficult to make any confident claims about what was happening here, although some clear inferences can be drawn. It is evident that a significant breach had opened up between Poyer and his onetime friends and associates among the Meyrick family. This was clearly a division which involved multiple members of the Meyrick clan, while Poyer always appears alone as plaintiff or defendant. It is also evident that this dispute was fairly extensive and that it involved violence. At one point in these confrontations Poyer was incarcerated. The prosecution of Rowland Meyrick for 'ryott' was serious and would have involved both multiple actors and violence or at least the threat of violence. The steep fine imposed on Poyer's opponents argues that this incident was indeed seen by the authorities as a grave breach of the peace. One scenario which might account for the entries found in these court books was that Poyer's actions over the Upton fulling mill were interpreted as a heinous betrayal of their father's and mother's trust by John Meyrick's sons and their wider family. In the claustrophobic setting of Pembroke's local politics, accusations and counteraccusations probably escalated readily into confrontation and ultimately violence. This is only conjecture, of course, but it is consistent with the piecemeal evidence of Poyer's activities in the later 1630s.

The evidence of these lawsuits also points to aspects of Poyer's personality which would receive greater attention from his enemies, and even his supporters, during the civil wars: his abrasiveness (or 'impudent rudenesse' in his enemies' estimation)[67] and his capacity for alienating would-be allies. Although it is impossible to attribute blame in these instances or to judge whether Poyer was more sinned against than sinning, these scattered notes depict a bullish and, in all likelihood, impulsive individual. There is a final dimension to these records which is worth noting also. Poyer's confrontation with Rowland and John Meyrick is that of a man escaping his background. While it is not clear whether he was a menial servant as a young man, it does appear that he served in John Meyrick's household. The court books, however, show an individual who was prepared to face down the second generation of this powerful family. This was no longer a servant, then, but an independent merchant with the means and resources to bring a case to judgment against the Meyricks in a national court. The kind of boldness and self-confidence which allowed him later to claim that he spent thousands a year in his trading with Bristol and that he had done more than any man to employ the Pembrokeshire poor in clothmaking, can perhaps be glimpsed in his willingness to confront his onetime patrons.

Another aspect of Poyer's life before the civil wars which is important to consider is his emergence as a member of Pembroke's town government. Although, as we have established, Pembroke was a small settlement in this period and one which faced some serious economic problems, it was nonetheless the basis of Poyer's power and authority throughout the 1640s. In 1649 Poyer claimed that 'for sixteen yeers together I was thought worthy to have the command of the trained bands of the town of Pembroke, wherein I gained the love of those inhabitants generally'.[68] The trained bands were the local militia, a kind of home guard of non-professionals who should have been supplied with arms and drilled regularly, although it was often the case that such bodies were in a rather sorry state in the early seventeenth century.[69] The trained bands would have been important for somewhere as strategically significant as Pembroke. Problematically for his claim, however, a militia list drawn up shortly before the civil wars showed that the captain of Pembroke's trained band was, in fact, Thomas Adams.[70] The Adamses were a prominent local family, one of whom had represented the borough in parliament in the late Elizabethan period.[71] Thomas was certainly a more likely head of the trained band than Poyer, and it seems probable that Poyer was trying to make more of his military experience than was actually the case. It is also possible, however, that Adams's position as captain of the Pembroke trained bands was largely an honorific one, and that Poyer acted as his deputy, and undertook the hands-on role of drilling the local militia. Whatever the case, it is doubtful that Poyer's claim was entirely fictional, indeed, it was one he subsequently repeated.[72] It seems likely, then, that he did obtain this role by 1642, even if he had not held it for the years previously as he claimed. Certainly, it is clear that he felt his position as head of Pembroke's militia presented him in a good light as a man with experience of military leadership and as a popular individual within the borough.

It would seem that Poyer counted these sixteen years of service from the time of his writing the pamphlet, which would date his appointment to around 1632 or 1633, when he was aged twenty-six or twenty-seven. Whatever the truth of his claims about his military position, it was at this point that he emerged for the first time in the town's oligarchy as one of the two bailiffs to mayor Hugh Owen. This demonstrates that Poyer, the glover and merchant, was sufficiently wealthy and influential to secure this important post. Other members of the Poyer family whose relationship with our John Poyer are uncertain, had served in this role earlier in the seventeenth century, but none had obtained the chief office of mayor. Poyer would go on to secure this crucial position in October 1641.

Poyer also maintained that before the wars he was a substantial taxpayer in Pembroke and a high collector of the parliamentary taxes voted in 1640–1.[73] However, being the collector for the parliamentary subsidy was a modest post indeed; one of the subsidies voted in 1640 raised the underwhelming sum of just £8 6s 0d from the town.[74] This once more underlines how Poyer was a comparative nobody in the world of pre-civil-war politics and society. A moderately sized fish in the small pond of Pembroke, he made little impression even in the immediate locality. This would change radically with the coming of war.

A final aspect of John Poyer's early life which we need to address, although it remains, like much else from this period of his life rather obscure, is his marriage. Poyer wed Elizabeth, the daughter of the vice admiral and arctic explorer Sir Thomas Button of Cottrell in Glamorgan.[75] This may seem an unusual match; the two south-Wales counties had little intercourse in the early seventeenth century, but the union opens up several illuminating connections and associations for better understanding Poyer and his milieu. While Button was a Glamorgan man, he married the daughter of a Carmarthenshire knight, Sir Walter Rice, giving him an interest in south-west Wales.[76] Moreover, probably through this marriage, Button became possessed of several Pembrokeshire estates including that at Lawrenny just across Milford Haven estuary from Pembroke, although before 1625 he took up residence a little further down the estuary at Sandy Haven.[77] Although Button married into the gentry of south-west Wales, he married his eldest son to the heiress of Cottrell, who was a scion of the Meyrick family. The connection with Pembrokeshire and the Meyricks probably brought Button into contact with John Poyer. Poyer must have seemed a sufficiently prosperous and ambitious individual for Button to have permitted his daughter to marry him. We do not know when this marriage occurred, but it was probably in the later 1630s. Also of note, and rarely discussed in the scholarship surrounding Poyer, Pembrokeshire or the civil wars, is the fact that Button married his other daughter, Ann, to another Pembrokeshire man, Rowland Laugharne of St Brides. Laugharne would become parliament's most important military commander in south-west Wales during the civil wars and was a close ally of John Poyer. Indeed, they would be sentenced to death together by court martial in 1649 for their joint rebellion against parliament. Few have given sufficient weight to the fact that the two men were brothers-in-law.

John and Elizabeth Poyer's marriage remains one largely of public record and basic facts rather than of private correspondence and testimonies of love and devotion. They lived through difficult and turbulent times, and their family was raised in the shadow of war and privation. They had four children together including the eldest son, John, who appears alongside his father in some records of their parliamentary service. In addition, there was another son, Thomas, and two daughters, Louisa and Elizabeth. We know they survived the horrors of war and even the difficulties of the interregnum. We will consider the fates of Poyer's wife and children again in Chapter 9.

So the early life of John Poyer is one of relative obscurity, but much of interest can be gleaned. He was a modest figure with a lowly background in a quiet and relatively isolated corner of the kingdom. A simple merchant with no pedigree or lineage to draw upon, he nonetheless managed to rise in the humble urban politics of Pembroke. This rise involved trade in leather, wool and other commodities, but was also connected to a powerful local family, the Meyricks, in whose household he seems to have found a trusted niche. South-west Wales was a sedate and quiet part of the realm, but Poyer was far from isolated from wider currents or interests. His trading concerns connected him with the local metropolis of Bristol. His marriage was to the daughter of a Glamorgan man who had sailed in search of the North West Passage. His ties with the Meyricks also brought him into a circle that was allied to one of the greatest nobles of the realm, Robert Devereux, third earl of Essex. Although Pembroke was a somewhat dilapidated and sleepy town, it was within all-too-easy reach of the restive and restless kingdom of Ireland. Pembroke was part of the wider polity that looked with worry and concern at some of King Charles I's policies and how they were affecting the kingdom as the 1630s wore on. As the new decade of the 1640s dawned, few could imagine the horrors and divisions which it would bring into this corner of the world. Yet these convulsions would thrust into the limelight the combative and aspirational merchant whose main claim to fame before this point was to have been elected Pembroke's bailiff and appointed a minor tax collector.

CHAPTER 2

The Irish Crisis and the Coming of Civil War, 1640–1642

The period between 1629 and 1640 is known to historians as the 'Personal Rule'.[1] This is because King Charles I did not call parliament into session for eleven years, but rather sought to rule through his own personal authority. This was the lengthiest intermission in memory, and it caused serious disquiet. Parliaments were considered vital in the counselling of the monarch, informing him about subjects' grievances which could then be addressed. The ongoing absence of any assembly suggested that Charles was reigning in a manner that was heedless, if not wilfully ignorant, of his subjects' concerns and anxieties. And many felt that there were pressing grievances to be addressed, chief among them being the direction of the nation's religious policy.

In 1633 King Charles had elevated to the archbishopric of Canterbury the controversial William Laud. Charles and Laud had a conception of the Church of England and worship within it, which placed a particular emphasis upon elements of decorum, order and beauty.[2] Charles and Laud therefore ordered a policy of beautifying churches and moving church furniture in a manner which they viewed as supporting ideals of decency, but which many considered to be hardly Protestant at all. There was a theological underpinning to the changes in church policy also, as the Calvinist Protestant orthodoxy, which emphasised the doctrine of predestination among believers, became less acceptable to those at the head of the regime. The worrying influence of Arminianism was felt to be creeping into the Church; a 'foreign' doctrine, it was seen by many as dangerous in emphasising that grace was available to all rather than simply to God's elect as was the case with mainstream Calvinism.[3] Although this might seem an abstruse point today, many contemporaries understood it to be essential to the saving of their immortal souls. For a significant proportion of the population, then, the 'Laudianism' of the 1630s seemed to be taking the kingdom back to the Catholic practices of the pre-Reformation Church. In concert with Charles's evident unwillingness to assemble a parliament to offer him counsel, it appeared that he had been captured by a cadre of advisers who were leading him, and the country, down a path which led towards damnation and destruction.

A critical moment came with the decision by Charles I and William Laud to impose a new prayer book upon the kingdom of Scotland.[4] The Scots were Presbyterians, a form of Protestantism which rejected bishops and was seen by many as purer than the Church of England. The promulgation of a new prayer book for the conduct of church services considered by the Scots to be tainted with 'Laudianism' caused a violent backlash in the summer of 1637 which quickly escalated into a national revolt. The Scottish revolters became known as the 'Covenanters' after the 'National Covenant', a subscription document of their loyalty to their vision of the church and state which gained widespread popularity and became something of a text of resistance against Charles's government.[5] Many puritans in England and Wales came to sympathise more with the position of the Covenanters than they did with that of their own king; a dangerous situation.

Scotland, like Ireland, and England and Wales, was one of Charles's three kingdoms over which, or so many contemporaries believed, he ruled divinely and supremely. He could not countenance such disobedience and disloyalty within his realms and so, in 1639–40, he attempted twice to mobilise a reluctant and often downright refractory population to defeat the Covenanters in battle.[6] These so-called 'Bishops' Wars' were disastrous for the king and his capacity to rule without parliament. The Covenanters defeated the king's forces at the Battle of Newburn in August 1640. The Covenanters had been reaching out to sympathetic figures within England who were critical of Charles's government for many months, and high-level contacts were mirrored by more popular expressions of sympathy and amity with the Covenanters in Charles's southern kingdom.[7] Evidence of the high-level sympathies with the Scots can be seen in the petition from twelve peers to the king after Newburn, imploring him to assemble a new parliament. Prominent among them was the earl of Essex.[8] Defeated and facing demands from the Scots which were impossible to meet from his own coffers, Charles was forced to call another assembly which convened at Westminster on 3 November 1640. This 'Long Parliament' was not dissolved until April 1653 and it was this body which would confront King Charles in the civil war that engulfed England and Wales in 1642, and which, ultimately, would inaugurate a decade of republican rule in 1649.

These developments electrified the political scene in all parts of the three kingdoms, and Pembrokeshire was no exception.[9] The county had not demonstrated any particular resistance to Charles's personal rule or the Laudian experiment in the Church, but this may have been because such policies were not carried out with any noticeable vigour in this distant part of the realm.[10] Nonetheless, this county was to be the only one in Wales which would show much in the way of parliamentary sympathy, and the actions of men like John Poyer and his sometime mayoral superior in Pembroke, Hugh Owen, were in the parliamentarian vanguard. The reasons why Pembrokeshire was notable in Wales for its parliamentarian sympathies are not entirely clear. Its parliamentarian sympathies may be related to the county's trading contacts with more advanced Protestant cultures such as that found in Bristol. Pembrokeshire's cultural distinctiveness may also have had a role to play: the English-speaking inhabitants of the county's southern region could access more readily than their monoglot Welsh neighbours English-language secular and religious discourses which were critical of Charles I's government. It is also the case, as we shall see in this chapter, that the county's experience of the unsettled politics of 1641–2 was influenced particularly by developments in the kingdom of Ireland which rose in a horrifying Catholic rebellion in October 1641. We should not, however, overemphasise the strength, pervasiveness and homogeneity of parliamentarian sympathy in the county. As we shall see in the following chapter particularly, political commitment for many of the county's leading figures was only skin deep, and side-changing was common. This was not to be the case with John Poyer and his associates, however, who were unusual in their steadfast adherence to the parliamentary cause. As the Irish crisis of 1641–2 brought questions of allegiance to king or parliament to the fore, so Poyer emerged as a prominent supporter of parliament. Such commitment brought him to parliamentary attention as his reports were discussed and scrutinised in a Westminster which was extremely worried about the possibility of invasion. This chapter considers Poyer's emergence during this time of crisis as parliament's most visible activist in south-west Wales.

The writs for a new parliament were issued in the autumn of 1640, and Hugh Owen of Orielton was returned for the borough of Pembroke. This was not unusual: he had represented Pembroke boroughs in the assemblies of 1626 and 1628, although in the parliament which sat briefly in April 1640 he had represented Haverfordwest, probably because he was again serving as mayor of Pembroke at that time, and so could not return himself as MP.[11] Hugh Owen's election return is in very bad condition, and although several townsmen are recorded as endorsing his election, it is unclear whether John Poyer was among them. We can discern that Owen's brother, Arthur, as well as the prominent townsman and captain of the trained band, Thomas Adams, added their signatures to his election. William Poyer, a tanner, was one of the town's bailiffs at this time and would have been involved in conducting the election, while another Poyer, Richard, also signed the return.[12] The relationship of these men to John Poyer is not known, but they are indicative of a wider Poyer affinity supporting Owen's election. It is uncertain whether John Poyer was merely absent at the time of the election, or whether the poor state of the return simply means that his endorsement has been obscured.

Hugh Owen was a powerful figure in south Pembrokeshire. He held a major landed estate centred on Orielton which lay only a short distance from Pembroke. He was well connected in the county; his fellow MP who sat for Pembrokeshire, John Wogan of Wiston, was his first cousin, for example. Moreover, Owen had associations with the Devereux circle and was distantly related to the third earl of Essex himself.[13] His authority and influence in the area generated friction, however, and an important dimension of the county's pre-civil-war political landscape was Owen's confrontation with another major family in the hundred of Castlemartin, the Lorts of Stackpole Court. We will discuss the Lorts and their allies in much more depth in future chapters; suffice it to say, at this point, that Henry Lort, and following his death in 1641, his son Roger, were Hugh Owen's enemies. Much of their discord seems to have revolved around disputes over land, but there were also allegations that Owen harassed and pestered Henry Lort over his enclosure policies; he may even have tried to get Lort thrown off the commission of the peace, which would have been a terrible blow to his local prestige and status.[14] These confrontations in the later 1630s engendered a feud which continued to fester throughout the turbulent years of the civil wars.

Hugh Owen and John Wogan, along with the MP for Haverfordwest, Sir John Stepney, went up to Westminster in November 1640 to participate in the most remarkable parliament ever to have been convened in this country. They heard debates and discussions about fundamental questions of religion, power, policy and authority as the members, effectively freed from the threat of royal dissolution by the Scottish occupation of northern England, explored remedial measures for grievances which had built up over the last decade and more. In its initial stages the Long Parliament was more united in its opposition to policies such as unparliamentary taxation and the influence of so-called 'evil counsellors' like William Laud, than it was in agreeing positive reforms in Church and state. Welsh MPs, for the most part, occupied the more conservative wing of opinion in the House of Commons, particularly over matters such as how to reform religion and the Church.[15] The urge to address the Laudian innovations of the 1630s, however, generated a feverish desire among the more puritan members for sweeping religious reforms.[16] These went far beyond merely rolling things back to the ways they had been under James I or Elizabeth I. Some now argued that the Church needed to be purged thoroughly of the corrupt Catholic elements which, they believed, had remained like a cancer at the heart of the partial and incomplete settlement achieved by Elizabeth in 1559.

Such calls for further reform worried many, including most of the Welsh MPs, but fired others with a giddy reforming zeal. One such reformist was a Pembrokeshire man, John White, a puritan lawyer who hailed originally from Henllan in the county, but who sat in the Commons for Southwark.[17] White's principal fame rests on a publication produced in 1643, *The First Century of Scandalous, Malignant Priests*, which detailed the corruptions and moral failings of a hundred clergymen who were held up as exemplars of all that was wrong with the allegedly unreformed Church of England. This was a best-seller in its day and earned him the appellation 'Century White'. John White was a close relation of the Lorts of Stackpole and, as we shall see, became an opponent of John Poyer and his associates during the civil wars.

Our records of the speeches and debates in this parliament are better than those for many previous assemblies, but they are still scanty and incomplete, often relying on personal diaries as well as the official record, the *Commons Journal*. As a result, it is difficult to know whether MPs spoke on particular subjects and their words were not recorded, or whether they were largely silent.[18] When it comes to Hugh Owen the record is thin and we do not know what his position was on questions of religious and secular reform. An exception, however, is very revealing for our purposes because it concerns John Poyer.

Soon after the opening of the Long Parliament, on 30 November 1640, the House ordered that Hugh Owen answer a petition which had been presented against him by one William Jenkins, a merchant. Jenkins claimed that Owen had abused his position by claiming parliamentary privilege to protect 'one John Poyer'. This related to members' privilege which gave their servants a degree of legal immunity while they attended on their masters' business.[19] Poyer, however, was 'none of his [Owen's] menial servants', or so Jenkins argued. While Owen prepared his response, the House ordered that Poyer, 'notwithstanding his claim of privilege, be kept still in safe custody, till the House shall take farther order in it'.[20] Owen soon replied, on 1 December answering emphatically that Poyer *was* 'his servant, necessarily employed in his service'. He concluded, however, 'as touching this matter, he would wave his privilege'.[21] The likely scenario behind this episode was that Jenkins, a Welsh merchant, had brought an action against his fellow trader John Poyer for some improper undertaking relating to a business deal. Poyer had then claimed privilege as Owen's servant, a claim of which Jenkins was sceptical, and so he petitioned the Commons for redress. Owen, despite acknowledging Poyer as his servant, did not wish to make a stand over a privilege question relating to a mundane business matter, and so allowed the action to proceed.

This episode thus provides crucial evidence of Poyer's close ties to Hugh Owen. While we have seen them operating alongside one another as Pembroke mayor and bailiff in 1633–4, here Poyer is identified as a member of Owen's entourage, a 'servant'. As Jenkins's objections made clear, however, Poyer was not simply a 'menial servant' or lackey. Rather, we might expect that he was operating in a trusted capacity in Owen's household, perhaps as something of a man-of-business. This is vital evidence which situates Poyer within the close circle of one of Pembrokeshire's most powerful landed gentlemen. It aligns him with Owen's interests which, as is discussed below, would see them acting in close concert over the crisis surrounding the Irish Rebellion a year later. It also lines up Poyer with

Owen's allies and against his enemies, which is another thread of the story that will continue through the 1640s.

The privilege case also makes it clear that Poyer had journeyed to London with his 'master', presumably to be on hand and to assist with the numerous businesses which would occupy a busy MP during this momentous first session of the Long Parliament. Poyer was thus at the centre of affairs in the febrile atmosphere of the metropolis as parliament began to address Charles's perceived abuses of power. This put him in the middle of the rich and creative, but also bitter and heated, debates which developed over the nature and extent of reform required in the Caroline state and Church. Poyer would also have witnessed at first hand the explosion of printed material in the capital which accompanied and became a crucial element of such debates.[22] The calling of the Long Parliament had effectively seen a collapse in royal censorship of the printed word, and cheap pamphlets, broadsides, ballads and other texts began pouring off the London presses in unprecedented profusion. Nothing like this had been seen before, as the number of printed titles surged to meet a seemingly insatiable demand for news, comment and discussion. Poyer would almost certainly have seen, read and digested some of this novel printed output. He may even have made the acquaintance of some booksellers or even printers. This expansion of print and debate was a formative element of the revolution which overtook England and Wales during the civil wars, and Poyer was to become part of it. As later chapters will show, he took to print on several occasions to make his case and to attack his enemies, while he himself was the subject of numerous printed diatribes in the next decade. He can have little suspected as he watched the deluge of printed paper running through London's streets in the winter of 1640 that he himself would soon be contributing to the flood.

Part of his experience in London, however, was another imprisonment; his second (at least) in the space of a year. The brief entries in the *Commons Journals* identify the name of his opponent, but further digging in the archives reveals his identity and the likely nature of the dispute which led to the discussion in the Commons. In the spring of 1639 William Jenkins, a mercer of Cowbridge in Glamorgan, brought a case in the Exchequer against a Pembrokeshire gentleman, Charles Bowen of Trefloyne.[23] The case concerned an agreement by Bowen to sell Jenkins timber, iron and other goods which had come from a ship wrecked near Bowen's house, which lay close to Tenby on Pembrokeshire's southern coast. Jenkins had purchased the goods but had yet to receive all which he had been promised. It is likely, then, that Poyer, whom we know was involved in the coastal trade along the Bristol Channel, was involved in this business deal. Charles Bowen died in early 1640, and seems to have been troubled by his unresolved dealings with Jenkins, noting in his will that 'if I have wronged or unduly or uniustly taken away or detained any thinge from anie man', his executor should 'make satisfaction and restitution thereof unto the persons wronged'.[24] In 1639 Charles's heir, Thomas Bowen, who would become Poyer's enemy during the civil wars, himself brought a suit at the Exchequer court against several individuals over the restitution of William Jenkins's goods.[25] Although Poyer was not among the defendants, the conjunction of Jenkins, Pembrokeshire and this legal dispute suggests that he was, in some as yet unidentified fashion, caught up in this business deal gone wrong, and that it pursued him to London.

Unfortunately, we do not know the outcome of any of these cases. It is very unlikely, however, that Poyer remained in gaol for long, and he was probably soon at liberty to attend upon Hugh Owen. His movements and activities between December 1640 and the autumn of 1641 are obscure, but it would appear that he returned home to Pembroke, perhaps during the summer of 1641 when many members drifted back to their constituencies after an unprecedentedly long session. What is evident is that Poyer was back at home by October 1641, when he stood as a candidate in the Pembroke mayoral election.[26] Significantly, he was successful in his candidacy, thereby obtaining the foremost position in town government which he would occupy, not necessarily legally, throughout the next few years, and in which he would become known not just in Pembrokeshire but throughout the nation.[27]

Poyer's successful candidacy for the mayoralty suggests that there was a substantial constituency among the town's governing body (to which the franchise was limited), and probably among the wider population too, which supported him. This may reflect his own energies as a successful local merchant with connections to the influential Meyrick family. However, as we saw in the last chapter, there had been damaging tensions between Poyer and the Meyricks, and it may well be that it was the influence of Sir Hugh Owen (who was knighted in August 1641) which helped to obtain the post for his 'servant'.

The auguries at the beginning of Poyer's mayoralty were inauspicious. In the same month as he took up office, a rebellion broke out in Ireland which was to transform Poyer's life and career and to help usher in the civil wars in England and Wales. The political situation in the latter part of 1641 in England and Wales was rather more settled than it had been for months. Many of the reforms demanded by parliament, such as the removal of unparliamentary taxation and the abolition of so-called 'prerogative courts' like Star Chamber and the Council in the Marches of Wales, had been agreed. Charles I's hated adviser and onetime leader of the king's government in Ireland, the earl of Strafford, had been executed after a controversial parliamentary trial in May 1641. Key reforms like the Triennial Act, which allowed for the reconvening of parliament every three years whether the king had called for it or not, had been passed. There were promising signs of a lasting agreement with the Scottish Covenanters too. Much remained unresolved of course, particularly in the sphere of religion and the Church, but a cautious drift towards rapprochement best characterises the politics of late 1641. Matters were still very delicate, however, with mutual suspicion the order of the day and an increasingly confident and strident minority in parts of England and Wales pushing for more radical reform. This fragile detente was shattered by horrifying news from Ireland of a mass rising of Catholics.

Ireland had long been a difficult and challenging place for monarchs who claimed the territory as one of the three kingdoms of the British Crown. The principal stumbling block to any easy integration of Ireland into the realm was its response to the Reformation.[28] Whereas England and Wales had slowly adopted the Church of England, while Scotland followed its own presbyterian but nonetheless Protestant path, for the majority of the king's Irish subjects, the Catholic faith was integral to their identity and a fundamental component of their sense of nationhood. Protestantism was associated with English (and Welsh) and Scottish subjection and colonisation: for most Irish men and women, it was the faith of the foreign oppressor. While Ireland had experienced frequent revolts and rebellions against English rule, the Stuart monarchy had overseen a largely quiescent kingdom. The Catholic Irish were, however, terrified by the possibility of Charles's peace with presbyterian Scotland, while the increased power of parliament was also deeply disturbing, as it seemed to be largely in the hands of English puritans who were sympathetic to the Covenanters. The puritans and the Covenanters, moreover, were widely understood to have designs on conquering Ireland and rooting out all vestiges of Catholicism there.

Thus it was that on 23 October 1641 a relatively small uprising by Gaelic Irish Catholics began. Their plan was to seize Dublin and several other key towns before negotiating with the king and parliament for the safeguarding of their faith, but the rising which began in Ulster soon touched off a much larger popular revolt.[29] In this complex society with its combustible mix of ethnic and religious resentments, matters quickly gathered a terrifying momentum of their own. Irish Catholics began to exact revenge against English and Scottish settlers with swift and often brutal violence. The scale and ferocity of the rebellion is difficult to ascertain accurately because much of the surviving evidence emerges from the English language milieu of survivors' reports and sensational pamphlets. These texts were often produced by individuals in London who were not eye-witnesses to events and who seized on the most shocking and salacious details to help sell their copy.[30] What is clear, however, is that this was a major revolt by the Irish Catholics, and that it discomposed and helped to polarise the political scene in England and Wales.[31] The Irish situation raised questions. How should the rebellion be addressed? Who should be in charge of the armed forces sent to suppress the rebels and protect the Protestants? What would the respective role of king and parliament be in this process? The fact that some of the rebels had risen in the king's name (although he had not, in fact, authorised any such action) helped convince many in England and Wales that they could no longer trust Charles I with the reins of government. Popular opinion, particularly in places like London, fed by the sensational reporting in the burgeoning printed media, looked to parliament as a bulwark and protector against a king who, many believed, could not be relied upon to control the militia without using it against his domestic enemies.

In the winter of 1641–2, then, King Charles and his parliament became increasingly estranged over questions of trust and control of the kingdom's armed forces. A critical moment came on 5 January 1642 when Charles I marched into parliament at the head of an armed body to arrest five of his principal parliamentary opponents. Having committed this gross breach of privilege, the king was forced to leave the House without his quarry, but his action intensified countermoves by parliament to raise and equip its own forces. The king left the hostile capital soon thereafter, and by October 1642 he had raised his own forces and the first major battle of the civil wars with his parliament was fought at Edgehill. The polarisation of politics was rapid and destructive. Questions of allegiance and loyalty to king or parliament needed to be answered not just by the great and the good, but by ordinary men and women as political division infiltrated towns, villages and hamlets the length and breadth of the kingdom. Responses to the Irish Rebellion were crucial in generating and giving momentum to this process of political breakdown and the recourse to military force.[32]

Shortly after John Poyer assumed the mayoralty of Pembroke, then, he was faced with a terrifying political crisis. The outbreak of the Irish Rebellion was shocking for people throughout the kingdom, but it was especially immediate and worrying in the western coastal communities of Pembrokeshire which lay only a few hours' sail from Ireland. Indeed, desperate Protestant refugees from Ireland soon began to appear in the county's harbours, presumably telling chilling stories about their experiences and heightening fears about supposed Catholic designs on England and the possibility of an Irish invasion. At Westminster, parliament fretted over the security of Milford Haven, and a report reached London on 3 December 1641 that a ship laden with arms and ammunition had been discovered in the Haven.[33] It soon became clear that John Poyer was acting as the key parliamentary informant for developments in and around Milford Haven, and also that he was responding positively to the Commons' directives. In this, he was rather different to many of his neighbours who wished to wait things out and declined to follow parliamentary orders while the assembly was estranged from the king.

On 28 January 1642 Sir Hugh Owen rose in the Commons to inform them that he had received a message from Poyer as mayor of Pembroke dated ten days earlier, informing him of 'divers poor English [who] come stark naked to Milford [Haven], and that the Irish report they will send 20,000 men to Milford forthwith, and that the rebels have taken all the sea towns in Ireland and may sail to Milford in a few hours'.[34] This gives us something of a sense of the desperate fear and anxiety which gripped the area in the wake of the Irish Rebellion. The influx of wretched Protestant refugees was frightening enough, but the additional force of rumour and the fear that Pembrokeshire was next in line for the kind of treatment meted out to these pitiable refugees encouraged an atmosphere of near panic in south-west Wales. Owen also related that Poyer had seized a Wexford ship in the Haven under suspicion that it might be supporting the rebels. In so doing, Poyer demonstrated that he was responding to parliament's order of 13 January which had directed mayors and other officials in the realm to secure local arms and ammunition and apprehend those whom they had 'just cause to suspect'.[35] Poyer was demonstrating his loyal parliamentarian credentials, in other words.

Poyer's letter was treated as an important piece of evidence in parliament. After Owen's presentation of Poyer's information to the Commons, the House directed that his letter along with some other documents be directed to a joint committee with the House of Lords. This powerful committee was considering a message from the king about how to deal with the Irish situation, but the Commons had also given it the additional power 'to take into consideration the quiet and safety of the kingdom'.[36] Poyer's missive, then, was feeding into discussion of the greatest importance in the highest circles of parliamentary power. This must have been a heady experience for a relatively humble merchant. His information was treated with respect and care and regarded as significant not because of Poyer's background, position or station, but because of its capacity to help parliament understand the impact of the Rebellion and the potential vulnerabilities in the kingdom's defences which such information might yield.

Poyer's communique, then, is significant in demonstrating that he saw the Irish Rebellion as a serious threat to the safety and security of his local community, but also that he was highly visible in responding positively to parliament's directives. The letter also provides further evidence of Poyer's close relationship with Sir Hugh Owen who demonstrated a similar deep concern with the Catholic threat. Poyer seems to be acting as something akin to Owen's agent in Pembrokeshire. The positive reception Poyer's letter received in the House must also have helped to convince him that parliament took his concerns about addressing the Irish threat seriously. This attention probably also flattered his ego and fed his sense of importance and perhaps encouraged him to show further initiative on parliament's behalf over the coming weeks and months.

On 12 February 1642, Poyer emerged again as a key local contact for parliament, this time as signatory to a letter which he sent along with the mayor of Haverfordwest, John David, to the Speaker of the House of Commons, William Lenthall.[37] The two Pembrokeshire mayors recounted that they had implemented parliament's orders for staying suspect ships in Milford Haven and accordingly had brought before them 'certaine Irishmen' who had landed at Pill in the Haven. These were Galway men who, being examined, 'did confesse themselves to be Romane Catholicks'.

Some of them refused the oaths of supremacy and allegiance, the litmus tests of religious and secular reliability. The mayors sent up the men's examinations, informing Speaker Lenthall that the suspects would remain in custody until the Commons directed their release. They followed this up four days later with another letter about 'more Irish papists [Catholics] come into the port of Millford', who had been apprehended and held in Haverfordwest gaol.[38]

The ongoing local unrest following the Irish Rebellion induced John Poyer to write another lengthy letter to his MP, associate and sometime 'master', Sir Hugh Owen, on 17 February 1642.[39] This was a rather more polemical and strident communication which revealed Poyer not just as a dutiful recipient of parliament's orders, but as a zealous agent willing to criticise local officials and lobby central authority about the dangers threatening Pembrokeshire. Poyer forwarded to Owen an examination of a ship's master which, he said, confirmed previous reports that the rebels were being aided by the French. He continued, however, that since his letter of 28 January, 'there have hundreds of poore English landed in Milford stript by the rebbels, who doe increase dayly'. He added that

> if aide be sente the rebbels, it is very likely some of them may be driven or willingly will come into the River of Milford where with 500 or 1000 men as I conceave [they] may possess themselves of the whole country and fortifie Pembrock towne with the Castle and other stronge places in the . . . county which will not soe lightly be regained.

Here, Poyer was repeating was the 'received wisdom' about the potential vulnerabilities – but also the worrying strength – of Milford Haven and Pembroke Castle if captured by rebels which had been articulated by George Owen several decades before. Just because it was a frequently repeated mantra, however, did not make it any less likely to be true. Indeed, this concern had taken on a frightening topicality, and Poyer was desperate that some measures be taken to shore up Pembrokeshire's defences and secure the position of loyal Protestants like himself. His letter continued by locating some of the problems closer to home, however. He requested Owen

> to move the honorable houses of Parliament that order may be taked that the trained bands and all other persons fitt to beare armes in the towne

& liberties of Pembrock may be putt in a posture of defence in these dangerous tymes and thatt course my be taken with all persons thatt are rated att armes & for providing of powder, lead and match in this towne and libertie, (for many are backward in the service).

This suggests that Poyer at this time was not in charge of the trained band as he would later claim, or at least that he did not have the authority and power to ready military volunteers as he desired. He also recognised the need to animate the near-moribund machinery for providing arms and ammunition which had fallen into decay during the long period of peace. Around the same time in nearby Haverfordwest, where his fellow correspondent with parliament John David was mayor, money was disbursed from mid-December 1641 in 'buying of armes, repayringe the ould, making upp the presse for powder, bulletts and match', while the corporation also bought muskets, swords and a 'head peece' from private individuals and repaired faulty firearms.[40] This was probably the kind of initiative that Poyer wished to pursue in Pembroke, but it seems he either did not possess the necessary authority, or was meeting with resistance from some vested interests in the corporation in gearing up for potential conflict.

Not content with his implicit criticism of members of Pembroke's corporation, Poyer then turned his fire on the trained bands of both the town *and* the county, who, he asserted

for wante of exercise are not fitt for sudden service yf they should be required; their armes are much defective, for punishment is not laide on the offenders . . . I lately viewed the armes of the store of the whole county of Pembrock kept in the towne of Haverford; I assure yow that upon a suddaine service these armes will nott arme 200 men (as I conceave) they are soe defective; I have divers tymes desired the deputy lieutennants of the county to deliver me armes for 40 or 50 musketeers with powder, match and lead out of the same store, for the safe guard of the towne of Pembrock yf occasion should bee offered, butt they have refused to deliver me any, notwithstanding this towne hath paied for the providing for the said armes, powder and lead; neither have they given any order of direccons for watch to be kept in this towne, either by nighte or day; we have nott in this brave River of Milford one peece of ordinance mounted, the trayned bands are not exercised, armes provided or power granted for punishing of persons refractory in this service. I

desire your worship thatt yow will spedily acquaint the honorable house
of parliament of these particulers.

This was a remarkably bold and forthright criticism of the county's military preparedness, which amounted, in effect, to an outright attack on
those who oversaw the local militia and its provisioning: the deputy lieutenants. This appears surprising as Pembrokeshire's deputy lieutenants
included Sir Hugh Owen, as well as the county MP, John Wogan, and a
future Poyer ally, John Laugharne of St Brides.[41] It may well be, however,
that his letter was a more targeted attack. Also numbered among the county's deputy lieutenants were Sir John Stepney, MP for Haverfordwest and
a future royalist, as well as two men who would not only become royalists
in the early civil war but would emerge as Poyer's sworn enemies: Roger
Lort of Stackpole and Thomas ap Rice of Scotsborough. It was, perhaps,
against these men that his letter was principally directed, for Lort and
ap Rice had remained at home while Owen, Wogan and Stepney were
in parliament, and it would be the former who would have to answer for
defects in the county militia. Poyer's letter also reveals that there were not
only problems with the arms and training of the county militia, but also
that his requests for support at Pembroke had been denied. This almost
certainly was an attempt to point the finger at Lort and ap Rice for their
recalcitrance, but also, perhaps, for their opposition to his activist parliamentary stance.

Poyer's letter is a remarkable text when one remembers that only a
year before he was a glover with hardly any experience in local office.
The letter's tone and nature display a striking confidence and assurance
from this inexperienced first-time mayor. One can see how this might be
seen as the insolence or abrasiveness for which Poyer would later gain an
unenviable reputation. Poyer was tackling the institutional weight of the
county gentry as well as powerful interests within his own borough, but
he seems to have been inspired by a sense of mission and purpose. He
was obviously animated by the anti-Catholic sentiments which, while not
the preserve of puritans, were nonetheless a particular trait of that group.
There is, however, very little religious language in his letter, and this would
be the case with his later writings too. In fact, Poyer was, as we shall see,
a committed supporter of the Church of England, although doubtless a
Church shorn of its Laudian accretions. Rather, Poyer seems activated
by parliament's call to safeguard against possible Irish incursions and to

root out and frustrate all Catholic enemies, both foreign and domestic. In this letter Poyer draws on parliament's authority to challenge and face-down local interests who were unwilling or unable to safeguard the region; indeed, he seems to present himself as the embodiment of that authority. Perhaps partly because of his close relationship with Sir Hugh Owen, and partly because of the positive responses his earlier letters had received at Westminster, it appears that Poyer felt empowered and emboldened in confronting the powerful gentry interest among the deputy lieutenancy. In addition, his letters also give us a sense of Poyer as a prominent and dedicated parliamentary servant in a locality which was otherwise com-paratively uncommitted.

Poyer's letter was clearly passed to the Commons Speaker, William Lenthall, as it survives among his papers at the Bodleian Library in Oxford. However, there is no indication that Owen or Lenthall took any concrete action in response to his communication. No directives were sent down to Pembrokeshire over and above requirements to stay merchant ships coming from Wexford. The refugee situation continued to cause deep local anxiety and concern, however, and on 22 April Poyer once more addressed the Speaker, again in concert with John David of Haverfordwest.[42] They expressed their thanks to the Commons 'in taking notice of our weake endeavours in performing theire comaundes touchinge the staye of such as were goeing into Ireland and coming from thence'. They had sent up to London the most dangerous and notorious of those they apprehended, including a Franciscan friar Hugh Molloy.[43] They further requested, however, 'in the behalfe of our poore countrey', that 'some care may be taken by the honourable house for the safty thereof, and enabling us to performe the service we desire, which cannot be donne unles some shipps be sent to this port'. There was evidently a sense that parliament was not holding up its end of the bargain when it came to securing the realm, and that its agents in Pembrokeshire had been left feeling dangerously exposed. Lenthall reported this communication to the Commons on 17 May, and, after a debate, they ordered the lieutenant of the Tower to 'look to the safekeeping' of Poyer's prisoners. However, on the other issues contained in the letter, described by the diarist Sir Simonds D'Ewes as 'matters of less moment', once more nothing was done.[44]

Perhaps as a result of this inaction and the lack of any moves to send a defensive force to guard Milford Haven, when one of the dangerous prisoners secured by Poyer and David, Colonel Christopher Bellings, came before the Commons on 4 June, Sir Hugh Owen 'declare[d] to the House what care had been taken in the county of Pembroke in Wales, and yet that they were so little regarded [by parliament] in respect of their safety as if they were no part of the kingdom, lying open to spoil and invasion from the west parts of Ireland'.[45] As a result of his entreaties – and perhaps because of the pressure being applied by Poyer and David, too – Owen was ordered to go to the earl of Warwick, admiral of parliament's navy, and request 'that a ship of some good force may be appointed to ride about Milford Haven and those coasts for the defence of those parts'.[46] Once more, however, the Commons' preoccupation with other matters seems to have resulted in little concrete assistance. On 21 July 1642 Owen once again rose to inform the Commons how Turkish pirates had taken ships near Milford Haven, and he once more begged for 'some course to be taken to secure those coasts'.[47]

Poyer's efforts in the spring and summer of 1642 thus consisted of keeping parliament informed of the local situation through Sir Hugh Owen; attempting to police the waters around Pembroke and Milford Haven; trying to apprehend Irish rebels and Catholic insurgents; and enjoining greater efforts in local military preparations.[48] He was an active limb of the emerging parliamentary state in the far west, and, along with John David of Haverfordwest, drew on its authority and power to bolster his own position. His efforts in this regard, however, also opened him up to accusations of wrongful imprisonment. In June 1642 Poyer was arrested at the suit of one Sidrach Pope, a mariner, for having stayed his ship while *en route* to Galway.[49] As a result Poyer was imprisoned, for the third time that we know of but not, alas, the last. He was incarcerated in Plymouth which suggests that he may have been travelling to London at the time of his arrest, perhaps accompanying some high-level prisoners to parliament, or possibly on a visit to Sir Hugh Owen. Be this as it may, on 27 June his case was raised in the Commons by Owen and the House directed Plymouth's mayor to examine Poyer and 'if he find the cause thereof to be for arresting or staying of some ships . . . by virtue of an order of this House and was a special service done to the kingdom . . . then he [to] be forthwith discharged of his imprisonment'.[50] Moreover, if this was indeed the case, then Pope was to be placed in custody and brought up to the Commons. The mayor of Plymouth received the order and evidently Poyer was set at liberty as having been discharging 'a special service to the kingdom' for parliament in apprehending Pope's vessel.[51]

Poyer returned to Pembroke by the summer of 1642 when formal demands for military action and demonstrations of local loyalty to one of the two emerging sides or the other arrived in the shape of King Charles I's commission of array and parliament's militia ordinance. These texts named prominent local gentlemen (who were often appointed to both bodies) who were enjoined to support the militia or the array, and to raise men, money, horses and weapons, ostensibly to safeguard and protect the kingdom, but in reality to prepare for armed conflict with the other side. In Pembrokeshire, parliament named local MPs Sir Hugh Owen and John Wogan as militia commissioners along with Hugh's brother, Arthur Owen, and John Laugharne of St Brides. These would be Poyer's supporters and associates in the coming weeks and months. However, parliament also nominated men who would support the king's party in the initial stages of the war and who would soon become Poyer's sworn opponents. These included Roger Lort of Stackpole, John Eliot of Amroth, Thomas ap Rice of Scotsborough and Griffith White of Henllan.[52] Interestingly, Poyer's name was nowhere to be found among those parliament included on the county's militia commission. Why was its most visible and vocal supporter entirely overlooked? The answer is probably a mundane one as it is noticeable that John David, Haverfordwest's activist mayor for parliament was also absent from this list. It would appear that parliament settled on the major landed gentlemen of the area and perhaps felt that the county's corporate boroughs such as Pembroke, Haverfordwest and Tenby were separate jurisdictions which would answer to the county gentry. It remains the case that, despite his prominence and vigour on parliament's behalf, Poyer was still a relatively lowly merchant figure who may not have been expected to command respect and allegiance in the wider county.

Despite his absence from the militia commission, it seems likely that Poyer was busy in the summer of 1642 repairing Pembroke's defences and trying to obtain as many men and weapons as he could manage. His own account of this period, as always, needs to be treated cautiously, but it indicates as much. Poyer stated that

> when the unhappy differences first began, they [the inhabitants of Pembroke] did unanimously joyn with me (by the encouragement of some noble gentlemen) to preserve and fortifie the town and castle of Pembroke to the use of the parliament (the castle being my right (long

before these troubles) as Captain Cowney [Walter Cuny] can justifie, when all other towns and counties in Wales were against the parliament.[53]

The claims of unanimity among the Pembroke inhabitants in supporting Poyer do not ring true, although he must have commanded a good deal of support in the town to remain in command for the next few years.

The identity of the 'noble gentlemen' Poyer mentioned as supporting him in his efforts at Pembroke is illuminated by a hitherto unknown pamphlet which casts much new light on developments in Pembrokeshire during the spring and summer of 1642.[54] The anonymous author of this tract was an eye-witness to events in the county, and described how a small group of men sought parliamentary support for their undertakings in the county. In the spring of 1642, having no commission from the parliament, John Laugharne, Rowland Laugharne and Arthur Owen sent a messenger, Captain Philip Bowen, to the earl of Essex, who had been appointed the leader of parliament's military forces, 'to acquaint his excellency of the true estate of their country'.[55] He returned with a commission for Rowland Laugharne as colonel of a foot regiment as well as commissions to Sir Richard Philipps, Sir Hugh and Arthur Owen, John Laugharne and Lewis Barlow, to assist Rowland Laugharne 'with a speciall charge to defend their townes and Milford Haven as a place of principall importance, to the uttermost of their power until some other ayds might be sent unto them from the parliament'. As a result, they raised some fifty or sixty horsemen and two or three foot companies, 'and fortified the townes of Tinby and Pembrook, Iohn Poyer, major [i.e. mayor] of the place being very active in the repaier of the walles, then much demolished'.[56] In February 1647, Poyer would submit an 'expenses claim' to parliament in which he described spending 'great summes of money . . . in the repairing, fortifying & building of gates, works and walles of [Pembroke] . . . towne, garrison and castle, and in armes, ordinance and amunicion, clothes, victuals & pay for the souldiers in the . . . towne'.[57] Some of this was work was done between 1643 and 1645 when Pembroke faced several sieges, but some of the expenditure related to his efforts in 1642.

In addition to the gentlemen identified in the anonymous pamphlet, it is also possible that the extremity of the times helped Poyer build bridges with the Meyricks of Monkton. This family were aligned with the earl of Essex. Indeed, one of their number, Sir John Meyrick, had been elected MP for Newcastle-under-Lyme on the Essex interest, and was appointed commander of artillery in Essex's army.[58] Among the captains of his regiment were John Poyer's brothers-in-law, Thomas and Miles Button, the latter of whom would be with Poyer in Pembroke when it was besieged by Cromwell in 1648.[59] It is likely, then, that a common parliamentarianism in the face of many local royalists helped broker a rapprochement between Poyer and his former master's family. The Meyricks's influence would undoubtedly count for much in the struggle to control Pembroke for parliament in the early stages of the war.

As political collapse translated into military confrontation, then, Poyer faced a tricky conundrum. His mayoral term ended in October 1642, but he must have asked the question whether he should continue in post as an emergency measure to ensure the Pembroke's parliamentary loyalty at such a delicate time and when he was directing the town's refortification. It appears, however, that he did step down but was soon forced to resume effective control over the corporation. One anti-Poyer publication related how, around May 1643, 'upon a disagreement between the mayor of the town of Pembrook and the townesmen, Poyer, with a loose rabble of the meaner sort of the town, got into the castle, [and] having some armes, kept the castle in opposition to the mayor and his party. The major part made choyce of Poyer to be their captain'.[60] Another pamphlet had it that he 'with a rabble of fellowes loose as himselfe, tooke the advantage of the unsetlednesse of the time [and] wrested the possession of the Castle of Pembrooke from Captaine Cuney, the owner thereof, and nominated Poyer their captaine . . . [who] fortified himself in the . . . castle'.[61] Sifting the truth from the propaganda here is problematic. However, a likely scenario appears to be that a mayor was elected in October 1642 who made friendly overtures to the royalists when they approached the county in 1643. As a result, Poyer and a group of loyal followers took a cache of arms and seized the castle, while the mayor and his supporters held the town beyond the castle walls. After a brief confrontation with the mayor, Poyer was nominated as 'captain', and 'deputy mayor', and the pro-parliament group regained control over the borough. He continued as deputy mayor, although this was probably a courtesy title as he was effectively in control of the town, until October 1643 when he once again assumed the mayoralty on his own. He would hold it down to at least 1645.[62]

It is a shame that we do not know the name of the mayor who attempted to face down Poyer on this occasion. It was not Captain Walter Cuny, a parliamentary loyalist in 1642 and a Poyer supporter in the first civil war.[63] It is likely that Cuny held the constableship of the castle which was thus nominally his 'property'. It is also the case that Cuny later fell out with Poyer and aligned himself with Poyer's enemies at a time when these pamphlets were written.[64] This episode is a fascinating glimpse into the divisions which must have existed within Pembroke at this time. We should not consider places like Pembroke or the county itself as entirely 'royalist' or 'parliamentarian'. There were shades of opinion which could change and mutate under pressure of events. Poyer's claims of unanimity in his support were illusory, then, but this episode suggests a powerful force of will and a personality which was capable of convincing a majority of the townspeople to support him.

It is the case that Poyer's parliamentarianism in 1642 was vigorous, strident, precocious and comparatively lonely. Wales was a country in which puritanism and the kinds of critical discourses that underwrote parliamentarianism elsewhere had made very little headway. It was, for the most part, a bastion of royalist fervour, 'the nursery of the king's infantry' as one royalist christened it.[65] Pembrokeshire was unique in possessing a significant parliamentarian impulse, although, as we shall see in the next chapter, this was far from universal. This impulse, however, was most significant and most visible in its corporate towns, particularly in Pembroke and Tenby, perhaps because these English-speaking communities had been exposed to the more advanced Protestantism which emerged from places such as Bristol and parts of south-west England. It was a source of considerable pride that Poyer could write 'it is well known unto the enemie and freinds with what faith and constancie the towne of Pembrocke have served king & parliament from the beginninge of this unnaturall warre to the uttermost of our abilities'.[66] And he was particularly proud of his early commitment to the parliamentarian cause, describing himself as 'one of the first that declared in armes for the parlyment in south Wales'.[67] On another occasion he wrote of his lonely defiance in Pembroke 'when all other towns and counties in Wales were against the parliament'.[68]

It is difficult to explain exactly why Poyer became a parliamentarian. He had connections with influential local parliamentary supporters like Sir Hugh Owen, but it is insufficient to read off his allegiance simply from that of his patron. It seems likely that the shock of the Irish Rebellion and his intense suspicion of Catholicism had a crucial role in forging 'Poyer the Parliamentarian Man'. There was probably a religious element in this, but Poyer was not a thoroughgoing puritan, and there is little sign of religious commitment in his writings. However, it is quite possible that his commercial interests had connected him with some puritan groups, while the rebellion in Ireland also demonstrated not only that Catholics were capable of inflicting brutal violence, but also their capacity for disrupting Poyer's commercial interests. He was also located within a family and kinship group that supported parliament and probably shared an outlook of vigorous Protestantism. His long-time association with the Meyricks and his connection by marriage with parliament's leading local military figure in Colonel Rowland Laugharne are suggestive of these relationships. We do not have the sources that allow us ready access to his motivations for supporting parliament's cause. What is clear, however, was that Poyer emerged from a very humble background to seize the initiative in 1642 and become one of the most important supporters of parliament's war effort in south Wales. His many difficulties in shoring up the fragile parliamentary cause in Pembrokeshire during the first civil war will be the focus of the next chapter.

CHAPTER 3

Allies and Enemies: Poyer and Pembroke during the First Civil War

This chapter considers Poyer's stout resistance in Pembroke during the first civil war. It is concerned principally with the manner in which Poyer, as parliamentarian governor of Pembroke, confronted the numerous threats which assailed him. It was not only royalist forces from outside Pembrokeshire which threatened him, however. Poyer also had to face down a closely connected group of local gentlemen whose initial royalism and subsequent shift to the parliamentarian party bred a visceral dislike of the steadfast Poyer. John Poyer's stubborn resistance in 'impregnable' Pembroke offered a refuge for local parliamentarian supporters. Sustaining the Pembroke garrison came at a considerable cost, though, and Poyer's sometimes violent efforts to provision the town and castle often led to friction and confrontation with the communities surrounding Pembroke. This helped to generate further criticism and animosity towards him.

Poyer busied himself with the reparation of Pembroke Castle and the town's walls in late 1642. He did so in the face of the threat not only from Ireland, but also from a hostile surrounding countryside. In a letter to parliament dated November 1642, Poyer's allies Sir Hugh Owen and John Wogan, who had come down to the county from parliament, wrote how 'this county wherein we live is only amongst those of Wales which standeth firm and faithful to the parliament's cause, whereby we are so much environed with ill neighbouring counties'. They begged for 'speedy aid . . . or otherwise our lives and goods will be made a sacrifice to those malignant spirits for our loyalty to the public good . . . If they plunder and reduce us, all Wales is theirs'.[1] Soon after this, in January 1643, Wogan once more wrote of 'the desperat condition of this countie', describing how 'the malignant parties of this kingdom are already come soe neare unto ower doores that they have alreddy plundred the estate of Captain Gunter in the verie hart of ower cuntrie'.[2] He added that 'it is not ower livelehood they aime att soe mutch as theyr surprise of ower Haven of Mylford . . . wherby a doore may be op[e]ned to receave forren forces to preiudice this troubled state more then themselves can'.[3] Poyer's resistance at Pembroke was thus key to securing the strategically vital harbour at Milford as well as representing something of a keystone which supported the parliamentarian interest in the county.

The sense of an encroaching enemy found in these letters was borne out on the ground. Pembrokeshire may have demonstrated a parliamentarian sympathy in Wales which was unusual, but the county was full of royalists too, and many of these looked to make common cause with the king's supporters in neighbouring Cardiganshire, and especially in Carmarthenshire.[4] Royalist designs in the area intensified in this period because of royal policy concerning Ireland. The king was negotiating to obtain a cessation of arms with the Catholic forces of Ireland by which he hoped to bring back to England soldiers who had been sent over the Irish Sea to suppress the rebels of 1641. Perhaps the easiest entry point would have been through Milford Haven, particularly if there were no parliamentarian outposts to annoy his troops. These returning soldiers would then be able to march through the friendly royalist terrain of south Wales and to enter the main theatres of war in southern England on the king's side.

The region's leading royalist commander was Richard Vaughan of Golden Grove, earl of Carbery.[5] King Charles appointed him general over the three counties of south-west Wales, and in July 1643 Carbery came to Whitland Abbey on the border between Carmarthenshire and Pembrokeshire and summoned the local gentry to meet with him and declare their allegiance. As one parliamentarian commentator put it, 'some of the more newtrall and tymorous of them punctually observed their time'.[6] Among these newly minted royalists were most of those whom parliament had named as the county's militia commissioners. They included powerful gentlemen such as Sir Richard Philipps of Picton Castle, Roger

Lort of Stackpole, his brother Sampson, John Eliot of Amroth, Griffith White of Henllan, Thomas ap Rice of Scotsborough and Thomas Bowen of Trefloyne.[7] These men were related closely by marriage and ties of kinship. The fact that they assisted the royalists in 1643 became a stick with which Poyer would later frequently beat them. As a result of this, they formed the core of a group which, when they turned later to parliament's fold, resolved to destroy Pembroke's governor.

At this time also, and damagingly for Poyer, his close associate Sir Hugh Owen was arrested by royalists at Haverfordwest on a charge of treason and conveyed as a prisoner to the king's headquarters at Oxford.[8] The defection of the major part of the county's gentry community to the king, along with the loss of his most important patron, left Poyer and his fellow parliamentarians desperately isolated. One Pembrokeshire correspondent wrote in August 1643 of the rump of parliamentary supporters in the county 'who are now in the way of colapsing [sic] since the [royalist] taking of unconstant Bristoll'.[9] However, their survival seemed a mark of God's favour, and another commentator described their holding out in providential terms:

> it is one of the wonders of the times, how they [the Pembroke parlia-
> mentarians] durst stand up as they did, but rather a peece of a mirackle,
> and to speake in tearmes of truth, the immediate hand of the Almighty,
> that from such small beginnings, so great, and so many actions should,
> in a nooke of a little county surrounded with powerfull enemies, be
> performed by a poore handfull of unarmed men.[10]

Poyer, Laugharne and their allies, this 'small party' as they were called, were not idle, this commentator tells us, 'for howsoever their strength were not much considerable, as being so forsaken by so great a party of the gentry, yet had they by this time well fortified their towns of Pembrook and Tinby and stood upon their defences, they being then of so inconsiderable a number'.[11] This commentary on events in Pembrokeshire was written in 1646 when the author knew parliament had triumphed, and he could interpret these small shoots of resistance to royalist rule as destined to grow into triumphant boughs of victorious parliamentarianism. At the time, however, Poyer and his allies must have felt friendless and vulnerable. Carbery's invitation produced a declaration in August 1643 from men like the Lorts and John Eliot that they would raise men and money to 'secure the townes of Pembrock and Tenby with what forces his lordship shall thinke expedient to be garrison'd in them'.[12] The borough garrisons of south Pembrokeshire were thus the focus of royalist designs, and if Pembroke fell, Poyer could expect to join Sir Hugh Owen in facing a charge of treason.

Carbery now marched into Pembrokeshire and established a garrison at Haverfordwest. The situation became even more desperate for Poyer and his local allies when Tenby was betrayed into the king's hands in late August 1643, after which, according to one account, 'the whole county stood amazed in great perplexity'.[13] The story of its loss is too complex to relate here, but the town was given up to the royalist Colonel Roger Lort by its mayor, Thomas Wyatt. A report of Tenby's defection was printed in the royalist newspaper *Mercurius Aulicus*, which christened Poyer's forces in the sole remaining parliamentarian stronghold in the county, 'Pembrokian Rebels'.[14] In order to further publicise this victory, the royalist press at Oxford also produced a broadside of the agreement reached between Carbery and the corporation, along with a list of signatories who undertook to be 'alwaies obedient to the kings . . . royall commands', adding that they would 'assist him against all rebels and rebellions'. Among the signatories we are surprised to find 'Iohn Poyer'.[15] This was, however, almost certainly John Poyer of Pembroke's eldest son who had been resident in Tenby at the time it was taken.

The loss of Tenby and the parading of his son's name in a royalist declaration must have shaken John Poyer, who was now alone in resisting the royalist forces that pressed in from all sides. The royalist *Mercurius Aulicus* gloated over the royalist strength in the area, writing that the local gentry had declared their loyalty to Carbery, adding

> let the world judge what true Brittaines this county of Pembrook hath at last shewed it self, to the silencing of those weekly printed boastings of the faction at London, who upon all occasions are ready to tell us what vast advantage they would make of Milford Haven, Tenby, and the rest of the haven townes in the county of Pembrook, which are now most happily reduced to their wonted loyalty and obedience.[16]

Poyer's own contribution to the war effort at this time was, then, necessarily limited. His lines of communication were cut and his support among the gentry of the surrounding countryside was negligible.

Nonetheless, Poyer did what he could to defend Milford Haven and worry the royalist forces. It was reported, for example, that in the summer of 1643 'there was then but one small ship of John Poyers . . . in all the Haven, which somewhat before he had surprized by a very bould and adventurous stratagem, and had taken out all her gunns into the towne and Castle, then utterly unprovided of ordinance'.[17] This 'small ship' was later described by Poyer as a vessel of some sixty tons and four guns, commissioned by Sir John Pennington as a man-of-war, which had been bound for Ireland to transport soldiers back to England for the royalist cause.[18] His vessel was crucial in securing the coast and, as he himself later put it, 'assisting and encouraging parliament's ships within the harbour of Milford'.[19] This incident became grist to the mill for Poyer's enemies in the later 1640s, however. In one version of events, they endeavoured to claim that Poyer's ship was not his but belonged to 'one Jenkins of Cowbridge'.[20] Evidently, they were dredging up his troubles with William Jenkins, the Glamorgan merchant, which had shadowed Poyer in the early days of the Long Parliament. Intriguingly, Eliot had stood surety for Jenkins in a Pembrokeshire lawsuit in 1636, so he likely had close knowledge of the case involving Poyer and the ways in which it might be manipulated.[21] In another tract, Poyer's opponents rendered his seizure of shipping in the Haven as an act of self-interested privateering. This pamphlet from 1648 related how, at the beginning of the war, Poyer 'seized upon two merchant ships of great value which came into Milford Haven, kept them by force, made sale of the ships and their goods & likewise seized the goods of divers merchants which came into Milford Haven'.[22] It was even suggested that these ships were full of tobacco and salt worth £6,000 which Poyer appropriated to his own use.[23] It was through such actions, Poyer's enemies alleged, that he managed to raise a company of foot and a troop of horse for parliament. Although there was doubtless a significant element of animus and distortion in these accounts, the claims that Poyer had acted in an arbitrary and high-handed fashion to support his forces were made on several other occasions and there may well be elements of truth folded into these narratives.

Another charge such pamphlets laid at Poyer's door, and which would be repeated elsewhere, was that he had 'no commission or power from the Parlia[ment] or any under them', and was thus acting in an illegal and arbitrary manner in seizing shipping or detaining goods.[24] There is some truth in this because, as we saw in the previous chapter, Poyer was never officially nominated under parliament's militia ordinance and he does not seem to have received a military commission. At his trial in 1649, Poyer denied that he was commissioned by parliament, but claimed rather that, as mayor, he was de facto captain of the town's trained band, and so had authority in his local capacity to raise independent forces.[25] Moreover, it is possible that the Commons' order of January 1642 empowering him to stay shipping from Ireland was considered to constitute sufficient license for his naval actions, while the 'speciall charge' in the commission the earl of Essex delivered to Rowland Laugharne in the summer of 1642 to 'defend their townes', may have been understood as authorisation for Poyer to act on parliament's behalf in his capacity as mayor. It is noticeable that when Poyer came to address the question of his commissioned status in his own publications before his trial, he rather fudged the matter and never established where his authority for raising troops and requisitioning provisions came from.[26] He called himself 'Captain', but this seems to have been as an adjunct of his mayoralty rather than any reflection of his official status within the parliamentarian military command structure.

As the summer of 1643 waned, parliamentarian Pembroke stood alone not just in the county but in the whole of Wales. It had a garrison of perhaps only 200 infantry and 50 cavalry to defend it. One pamphleteer described how Pembroke's 'security and support consisted meerly in their expectation [of relief] from [the] sea'.[27] The significance of Pembroke's resistance in the wider war effort should not be underestimated. Although Poyer's naval presence was meagre, as long as Pembroke continued to hold out for parliament, the royalists could not have full possession of Milford Haven. And in the military situation of mid- to late 1643, this was significant. Pembroke was an important impediment to the ready use of Milford Haven as a disembarkation point for royalist troops from Ireland.[28] Royalist successes at Bristol and in the South West in 1643 meant that the town was a crucial point of parliamentarian power in an otherwise royalist western seaboard facing a hostile Catholic Ireland. The Commons Speaker William Lenthall described the service around Pembroke and Milford Haven in late August 1643 as crucial 'not onley to the preservacion of those partes, but of both kingdomes of England and Ireland'.[29] As another contemporary put it, a royalist capture of Pembroke and Milford Haven would have 'proved exceeding pernitious to the state, in regard you have no harbour to finde between that [Pembroke and Milford] and Plimouth, and consequently the Irish . . . had been much advantaged at and about their own home'. Local supporters like Poyer thus requested protection of Milford Haven from parliament in early 1644 'as a matter more importing the common[wealth] than their own particular safeties'.[30] Poyer even risked his own small vessel at one point in an attempt to 'acquaint my Lord Admirall with the distress of those parts and to implore speedy ayd', but it was captured by royalist ships sailing out of Bristol.[31] Despite Milford Haven's strategic importance, however, parliament failed to send much in the way of support to the area. As a response to the incursion by Carbery's royalists and the fall of Tenby, in late August 1643, parliament did order that a squadron of ships be sent to call regularly at Milford Haven, but this fell short of a sustained relieving force.[32] It seems that parliament's resources were simply too tied up elsewhere to spare much for the far west.

It is no surprise, then, that the royalist gentry under Carbery turned their attention to pressuring Pembroke into capitulation. On 18 September 1643 a declaration was issued in the name of forty-seven of the county's leading royalist gentlemen.[33] The document is worth considering for the detail it provides on what Poyer was doing at this point, as well as for the efforts which were being made to bring him to heel. The subscribers undertook that they would not victual ships which supported parliament (probably referring to Poyer's vessel then riding in Milford Haven), nor would they 'contribute directly or indirectly to maintaine forces nowe in Pembroke towne and castle, and will oppose any leavy of money or other ayde in this countie to that purpose'. Moreover, the gentlemen undertook that they 'to the utmost of our power [will] endeavour spedily to reduce [Pembroke] . . . to his Majesties obedience. And will preserve this county from incursions of shipping and the rapines of the souldiers of that towne and castle'. Poyer had clearly been successful in raising forces and garrisoning them in the town and had evidently also levied monies and aid to support the soldiers. His capacity to control the shipping and access to Milford is also suggested here, while the soldiers' 'rapines' presumably refer to the kind of requisitioning from the nearby countryside which were necessary to support the embattled garrison. One of the subscribers to this 'protestation', John Eliot, would go on to compose the pamphlets against Poyer in the garb of a parliamentarian loyalist, and so we can perhaps see how the royalist reference to 'rapines' in this document would become transformed in his later pamphlets into references to Poyer's 'free booting' and 'plunder'. Such allegations were common enough during the war, but they were also often damaging and difficult to refute.[34]

The royalist newspaper *Mercurius Aulicus* reported on 24 October 1643 that, as a result of this declaration, Pembroke's inhabitants had sent 'an instrument' under the town seal to Carbery (and thence for the king) wherein they agreed to 'preserve the towne and castle for his majesties use and none other'. The newspaper described Pembroke as 'the last piece of the good worke unfinished' in the principality.[35] This 'instrument' was reproduced with relish by Poyer's opponents (now wearing parliamentarian rather than royalist clothing) in 1646.[36] Theirs was evidently the text from which *Mercurius Aulicus* was working, and the author claimed it had been presented in October 1643 with Poyer's subscription and the town seal attached. However, by mid-December at the latest, the town, under John Poyer as mayor, was once more opposing Carbery.[37] The north Walian MP Simon Thelwall described arriving at Pembroke shortly before Christmas 1643, to find the town 'invironed almost on every side with adverse garrisons under the command of the Lord Carbery'. This contradicted reports by *Mercurius Aulicus* in early January that Pembroke was under royalist rule, a mistake the newspaper was forced to acknowledge later that month. It explained that the town had 'made a tender to deliver up it selfe', but this was 'not performed according to promise'.[38]

What had happened? An important and hitherto unnoticed discussion of events can be found in one of the parliamentarian weekly news-sheets, *Mercurius Civicus*, published in February 1644.[39] Its report began,

> It hath been the common ostentation of the malignants and others of the Cavaliers party about London and in other places of the kingdome for above these foure moneths past, that the kings forces have possessed themselves of the whole Principality of Wales, and that Pembroke-castle was also surrendered unto them; but that we may see how fictious that report is.

Describing the mistaken *Mercurius Aulicus* as 'the common source and spring of all their fictions', the newspaper reported that it had intelligence 'that the . . . Castle by the meanes of the faithfull govenour thereof (notwithstanding all the frequent designes of the enemy to surprise it) doth still continue under the command of the parliament'.[40] In this account, then, Pembroke had never been delivered, and Poyer was the 'meanes' of its continued resistance. It is possible, of course, that the newspaper was seeking to gloss over any brief capitulation which may have occurred in October 1643, but in this version of events, Pembroke had *never* yielded and Poyer was instrumental in securing its continued fidelity to parliament.

It seems crucial that the tender of capitulation to the royalists was made in October, the month when the borough's mayoral term ended. It seems likely that, as had happened at the beginning of the mayor's term in October 1642, a pro-royalist body in the town, probably with the connivance of the mayor, sent the 'instrument' to Carbery with the town seal attached. However, the claims by Poyer's opponents that he subscribed the document are impossible to substantiate and no evidence is offered beyond their own narrative of events.[41] Certainly, this does not align with Simon Thelwall's account, describing 'Captain Poyers, our trusty and carefull major [mayor]' back in harness in December 1643, or with *Civicus*' description of Pembroke's 'faithfull govenour' a few months later.[42] It seems probable that Poyer's enemies sought to blur the chronology of events, and that, while there was indeed an approach made to Carbery under the town seal, this was likely done by Poyer's superior as mayor (although maddeningly we do not know who this was) rather than Poyer himself.[43] Indeed, it was probably this very offer of capitulation which encouraged Poyer to assume role of mayor once more in the autumn of 1643. It was because of this change of personnel and the heading off of an internal royalist coup that the earlier 'promise' was not kept.

Pembroke's recalcitrance produced another remonstrance from the local royalist gentry which emerged from a meeting at Carmarthen on 11 January 1644. This mentioned reports sent down to the country from the royal Court that parliament was putting 'great forces ... in readinesse to enter and invade' south-west Wales. These forces were 'especially incouraged by the present withstanding of his majesties authority now exercised by sundry persons who, having possessed themselves of the towne and castle of Pembroke, doe in a hostile manner keepe the same' and refuse to submit to the king.[44] To this end, the royalists endorsed moves to use the trained bands and raise a company of horse to reduce Pembroke 'to due obedience'. The author of *Mercurius Civicus* reproduced this protestation

for a more eminent testimony of the safety of the . . . Castle of Pembroke, and that if there be necessity or occasion, some course may be taken for the reliefe of those honest Britaines who so bravely stand up for

the defence of their ancient liberties and privileges when the rest of
their ignorant countrymen take up armes to enslave themselves and
their posterity.[45]

These pleas had, in fact, already been heeded and the planned assault on
Pembroke was never undertaken. The reports of parliament's sending
forces to support and assist Pembroke mentioned at the start of the royalist
declaration proved to be true. In fact, by the time the royalist remonstrance was printed by the London presses in late January, a parliamentary
naval force had already arrived at Milford Haven. Poyer, and indeed the
parliamentarian war effort in south-west Wales more generally, was saved
at the eleventh hour by the appearance of *The Leopard Regis*, the *Swallow*
and four other vessels with forces commanded by the parliamentarian vice
admiral of the Irish seas, Richard Swanley.

All commentators agreed that Swanley's arrival was vital in saving
Poyer's embattled position in the county. Indeed, it was probably crucial
in the wider theatre of war too, as it saved parliament's enclave in the
far west, secured a port of call for vessels in the Irish sea, and hindered
the ready landing of Irish troops along the western coast.[46] One account
mentioned how Poyer and Rowland Laugharne came aboard the *Leopard*
on 24 January 1644, the day after the fleet arrived, when they informed
Swanley of 'the feeble condition the well-affected party was in; as also of
the strength, power, and insolence of the adverse party'.[47] Poyer's future
antagonist, John Eliot, would later depose that Swanley's arrival 'was the
onelie meanes of the preservinge of the countrye and saveng the surrender
of the townes of Pembroke and Castle Marten hundred to the earle of
Carberrye whoe was then upp with an army in the countey consistenge
of about two or three thousand'.[48]

Swanley found a county held firm by the royalists, but in garrisons
which could not be readily mobilised to defeat an army in the field. The
royalists were also fired by their dislike of Pembroke's mayor. One parliamentarian account of Swanley's arrival wrote that Carbery had supposedly
voted that they would plunder the houses of Pembroke's parliamentarians,
and that several would be executed. Particular attention was to be paid
to Poyer who 'they sayd should be put in a barrell of nayles and brought
to Prickspill [a fort on Milford Haven] and from the top of a hill should
be rouled down into the sea'.[49] On another occasion, Poyer claimed that
a bounty of £500 had been put on his head by Carbery's forces.[50] Poyer

had clearly become a bugbear and particular focus of royalist resentment. He had escaped the anonymity of his early life but had swapped it for an unwelcome notoriety.

At his arrival, Swanley sent a letter to the gentry of Pembrokeshire which was full of the language of zealous Protestantism and a vision of the county's providential deliverance from the tyrannous yoke of the earl of Carbery. It is worth quoting at some length. Swanley asked the county's royalist worthies:

> what stand yee gazinge like the timerous Israelites over the host of the Philistines? Did not a little youth, David by name, slay their champion and overthrow that idolatrous hoast? And shall a Jesuiticall and a pop-ish armye, with a malignant party, as odious in the sight of God as that cursed Philisten, make you dismayd? Noe, be comforted; God and the state hath preserved you a more visible me[a]nes of deliverance in sendinge this fleete . . . And by God's assistance I am confident that if the gentry of this countye will joyne with me in our endeavours, we shall drayne that malignant route who seeke to ensnare this great nation under the yoake of the antichristian beast, not only out of this county but consequently out of the dominion of Wales.[51]

He requested that the royalists join with him, or otherwise look for no favour at his hands 'but what God's enemyes and destroyers of theire countrey deserve'. It was, perhaps, this kind of zealous puritan religiosity which would put Swanley and Poyer on a collision course in the coming months; for now, however, Poyer must have seen him as some kind of liberating angel out of the east.

The Pembrokeshire gentry's response was not what Swanley would have hoped. They sneered at his professed fidelity to the king and hoped for better testimony thereof 'than your spotted Leopard'. They rejected his notion that 'we could be deluded by that stale theme, or affrighted by that citty bugbeare, Popery. The disguise of religion is too longe worne and become transparent eaven unto mean intellectuals'.[52] The gentlemen rejected Swanley's characterisation of them as malignant or anti-Christian, and considered it abhorrent to 'see sedition varnisht with scripture'. His appearance, they said, had stiffened their resolve, and they concluded 'you may rest assured, that if you be soe far wanting in peace and loyalty as to invade our country, we will not be soe far wantinge in courage and duty as not to defend it agaynst all hostile attempts under what sacred maske whatsoever'.

Their bullish resolution on paper did not translate into obduracy in the field, however. With Swanley at their back, parliament's modest forces in the county rallied and took the fight to their onetime oppressors, who melted away like snow before a Pembrokeshire spring. This suggests that royalist commitment in the region was, like a good deal of its parliamentarianism, relatively superficial; much royalist activism, and, indeed, many troops, seems to have come from neighbouring Cardiganshire and particularly Carmarthenshire, where the earl of Carbery resided.[53] Prominent for the first time in the actions against the royalists was parliament's senior military commander in the region, and Poyer's brother-in-law, Major General Rowland Laugharne. He presumably had been holed up in Pembroke with Poyer, but now, with his own small force augmented by a company of Swanley's men, he cut a swathe through the royalist positions in a series of lightning actions that reversed the military situation and placed the county firmly in parliament's hands.[54] The strongholds of Stackpole, Trefloyne, Haverfordwest and Tenby were taken, while Carew Castle, 'a very strong place', which lay only a few miles outside Pembroke, was delivered into the hands of John Poyer himself. As Simon Thelwall, Poyer's fellow resident in Pembroke while it was surrounded by royalist forces, later observed, the delivery of Carew, the last parliamentarian stronghold, was done in 'cleansing week, the first week in Lent, the whole countie was cleer of the malignant party, that had long infested, and almost ruined it'.[55] Thelwall further enumerated Poyer among a short list of Pembrokeshire men who 'were industrious on all opportunities to advance the cause, and had so farre ingaged themselves in the service, that they were resolved either to stand or fall with it'.[56]

Poyer was now being referred to as 'Captain Poyer' with his own 'companie' of men. It seems that Laugharne made him governor of Pembroke Castle at this time. One account of the military action in the spring of 1644, however, gives a hint of the over-zealous nature of Poyer's command which may have helped alienate sometime supporters later on. The recovery of Tenby in March 1644 with relatively little bloodshed was accounted a remarkable deliverance, for the town was considered a very difficult prize to win because of its coastal position and stout defences. Rowland Laugharne supposedly offered his own forces £200 to leave the fallen garrison untouched, but, so one account runs,

such was the greedinesse of Captaine Swanleys sea men, with some
others of Capt. Poyers companie, that he could not pervaile [sic] but
the towne and many an honest man were, without mercy, and respect
of more than three or foure persons . . . generally plundered and
utterly undon.[57]

This account is given greater credence by the fact that it is found in a
sympathetic parliamentarian text rather than a piece of royalist propaganda. Moreover, a contemporary newsletter, albeit a royalist one, told
a similar story, that parliament's forces took the town 'plundring to the
utmost but gave quarter for life'.[58] This may have been the beginnings of
the unsavoury reputation of Poyer and his soldiery, who would later be
called his 'bullies' by John Eliot and the Lorts. Perhaps we might recognise in the soldiers' actions at Tenby a desire for revenge after months of
privation behind the walls of Pembroke. However, we perhaps can also
see here the germ of the notion that Poyer could not control his men,
and that the 'mere rabble' who had supported him taking the mayoralty
of Pembroke were the kind of wild soldiery who generated so much fear
and anxiety among the civilian populations of England and Wales during
the 1640s.

Pembrokeshire was now entirely in the hands of the parliamentarians
and Rowland Laugharne set about subduing the neighbouring county
of Carmarthenshire. This was a remarkable reversal of fortune and one
which, for the most part, redounded to Poyer's advantage. He embodied
the spirit of committed resistance among the embattled parliamentarians
of south-west Wales as Thelwall's pamphlet makes clear. However, his
special status as leading light of this group quickly dimmed, outshone
by others' military successes. It was Rowland Laugharne and Richard
Swanley who gained the plaudits for rolling back the royalist tide in
Pembrokeshire, while Poyer remained on the margins. That he was not
held up as one of parliament's notable worthies might be attributable to
his rather volatile and acerbic reputation, which had not been helped by
his men's conduct in taking Tenby. Poyer's low profile in the parliamentarian advances of early 1644 might also reflect his mean social origins. The
parliamentary party, like the royalists, respected rank and status, and it
may be that it was much easier to reward and celebrate a gentleman's son
with ties to the earl of Essex such as Laugharne, rather than a onetime
household servant like John Poyer.

We have already observed parliament's tendency to overlook Poyer in his omission from the militia ordinance in the summer of 1642, and this was to be repeated with parliament's nomination of a committee to run Pembrokeshire's affairs in the summer of 1644. Since the beginning of the war, parliament had established a system of local government centred on the county committee. In each county which parliament controlled or conquered, the committee was established as a powerful executive body which effectively oversaw matters of administration and justice. Such committees were thus enormously powerful in the localities. When the county committee for Pembrokeshire was appointed in June 1644, however, there were several surprises in store for faithful parliamentary servants like Poyer. Although his name had been included in the nominations made by the House of Lords – nominations perhaps by the earl of Essex at the suggestion of Sir John Meyrick or Simon Thelwall – he was ultimately excluded from the final committee.[59] Indeed, even devoted parliamentarians like Rowland Laugharne and Arthur Owen were omitted. In a still more surprising turn of events, a number of ex-royalists who, when the going got tough for the king's local supporters in early 1644, had declared a new-found enthusiasm for parliament, *were* appointed to this body. These included men such as Sampson and John Lort, Thomas Bowen of Trefloyne, John Eliot of Amroth and Herbert Perrot of Haroldston.

It seems that Westminster politics played a vital role in determining the committee's final composition. One pamphlet related that it was John White, the puritan lawyer sitting for Southwark who hailed originally from Henllan, who had engineered this turn of affairs.[60] He was the brother of Griffith White, a key local figure, who was closely related to the Lort family by ties of marriage and kinship. Through their political machinations, Poyer's opponents of only a few months previously had been rehabilitated and were now acting in the role of parliament's trusted agents in Pembrokeshire! One of the committee's first acts was to remove the stain of royalist 'delinquency' from the group's local leader, Roger Lort, who was shortly thereafter appointed to the committee himself. This stunning turn of events embittered Pembroke's mayor against his ex-royalist rivals for the remainder of his life. He would rarely miss an opportunity to rehearse how they had stood out against him when the parliamentary cause in south-west Wales was in its most desperate hours. The problem for Poyer was that these men now held the levers of power in the county and it was difficult to cross them or persuade parliament of their chequered pasts in distant Pembrokeshire.

It is clear that complaints about the committee's composition were indeed made at the time, for parliament did eventually add men like John Laugharne and Arthur Owen to the body.[61] Poyer's name, however, remained noticeably absent. As with the nominations of the militia ordinance in 1642, Poyer's conspicuous loyalty had managed to bring him very little substantive reward in terms of power or authority in the county. This might partly be explained by the loss of his principal ally and patron, Sir Hugh Owen, who was vilified in the parliamentarian press in April 1644 as 'having some affection to parliament, but more full of fear of the enemy, not daring to express it, [and] is slighted by both sides'.[62] After the royalist defeat it seems he retired to his ancestral lands in Anglesey.[63] Another local patron who might have assisted Poyer in forging useful contacts with London was the Pembrokeshire MP John Wogan, but he fell sick around this time and soon died, depriving the county of an important voice in parliament. Poyer had the backing of his brother-in-law Rowland Laugharne, but he was an active military man rather than a political player. There were few who were willing and able to make the case in London for Poyer's inclusion in the charmed circle of parliamentarian power in Pembrokeshire. This marginalisation would have fatal consequences, as it forced Poyer into the extremes of rebellion in 1648 as he felt helpless at the hands of enemies such as the Lort brothers and John Eliot.

These political considerations were soon overtaken by another startling reversal of military fortunes in south-west Wales. The king had removed the ineffectual Carbery as his commander in the region and replaced him with the much more dynamic Colonel Sir Charles Gerard. A Lancashire man, Gerard had been a brave and effective military leader for the king, serving at Edgehill, Litchfield, Bristol and Newbury, receiving several battle scars in the process. Gerard moved through south Wales in the summer of 1644 assembling a force of nearly 2,000 men, including some 700 horse and 200 dragoons. Parliamentarian resistance in the region was, for the most part, based on very thin foundations, and it evaporated in the face of this 'new and furious generall' and his determined fighting force.[64] Laugharne and his men retreated to Pembroke and Tenby, while Gerard's forces quickly overran the remaining parliamentarian positions and installed their own garrisons to surround these fortified towns. Gerard, meanwhile, embarked on a brief but devastating reign of terror, 'wasting, spoyling and firing all the chiefe seates and houses of the gentry and . . . driving away all the inhabitants cattell, sheep, horses, swyne and whatsoever else of valew'.[65] One parliamentarian naval commander wrote in June that the royalist 'destroyes the country'.[66] Another opponent estimated that Gerard burned 1,000 residences in Pembrokeshire alone, and was bent on the 'depopulation and utter destruction of the whole county'.[67] Some reports of these outrages were reminiscent of the claims made in 1641–2 against the rebels in Ireland, and it may be significant that Gerard's forces had a significant Irish contingent.[68] Such depredations by a force 'infected' with Irish troops probably helped stiffen Poyer's resolve against them, for one of the touchstones of his parliamentary allegiance seems to have been anti-Irishness and anti-Catholicism. Although Gerard and his forces did considerable damage throughout the county, they did not attempt to take Pembroke or Tenby, perhaps reasoning that they would take the towns, weakened of provisions and supplies by his troop's attentions in the countryside, the following spring. In the event, Gerard was called back to England following the king's defeat at Marston Moor, though his forces remained in place.

It was around the time of Gerard's invasion, according to Poyer's later account, that his enemies tried to tempt him into switching sides to save his skin. He averred that the three Lort brothers, Roger, Sampson and John, invited Poyer to a feast 'where great shew of kindness was offered'. Their discussions, however, turned into a sinister kind of palace intrigue. Poyer wrote that they looked 'to engage me to joyn with them against Major Generall Laughorne and his party, and they would procure me the king's commission to command the towns of Pembrook and Tenby, with the country thereabouts'.[69] There is no independent corroboration of his claims and he was making them in a highly partisan pamphlet at a point when he was awaiting a court martial on a charge of treason. While this allegation cannot be taken as fact, then, neither can it be dismissed out of hand. Other commentators accused the Lorts of swapping sides on several occasions in this period, particularly when the royalists threatened, with Roger Lort being given the delicious title of a 'subtill ambodexter' by one opponent.[70] Moreover, side-changing was rife at this time, as Captain Robert Moulton wrote in June 1644, 'all the jentry of the country desert us. Here is not above 3 or 4 left'.[71] Poyer's command of Pembroke, perhaps the key which would unlock the whole of south-west Wales and the Irish Sea, made him an attractive target for 'turning'. Although Poyer's story might be a fabrication, then, it is plausible. And if such an approach was made, Poyer rejected it, which may help explain the poisoning of relations between himself and the Lorts for the remainder of the 1640s.

After Gerard's departure, the parliamentarian forces rallied behind Rowland Laugharne who concentrated his offensives initially in Carmarthenshire and Cardiganshire. In this he was joined by an able commander who was newly come out of Ireland, Colonel Rice Powell of Greenhill, whose father had been a prominent Pembroke merchant and was doubtless well known to Poyer.[72] Between the autumn of 1644 and early 1645, Laugharne managed to recapture much of the royalist territory which had been lost in the spring. In accounts of these actions Poyer is a shadowy presence. He does not seem to have been involved any of the field actions, but rather occupied himself with his (not inconsiderable) duties as 'governor' of Pembroke. His enemies would use his lack of visibility in the field against him, recalling that he never 'had . . . so much gallantry as to charge an enemy'.[73] It is worth noting too that there is no record of any new election for mayor of Pembroke being held in October 1644. Presumably, because of the extraordinary nature of the times, elections were suspended and Poyer continued in post.

Although in March 1645 much of the county had been cleared of royalist garrisons, many threats remained, and Poyer was becoming concerned. On 27 March 1645 he therefore wrote to Speaker William Lenthall in his capacity as Pembroke's mayor and governor, requesting support and assistance.[74] He began by emphasising the town's loyalty from the war's beginning, which, of course, was a way of highlighting his own record of fidelity to the cause. He requested supplies for the 'preservacion' of Pembroke garrison. His request had been prompted by reports that Irish forces were 'prepared to be landed in Pembrock shire', and, indeed, he was taking depositions from Irish traders who might have provided him with such information.[75] Moreover, one pamphlet referring to this period described how the royalists were understood to have designs on securing Pembrokeshire 'to shake hands with the Irish army, so long expected and noysed then to be in readiness for transport'.[76] Poyer concluded his letter to the Speaker with an unusual parting shot:

> I would to God the honourabll howses of parliament were truly informed
> of the present state of this countrey, for should the enemie gaine the

townes of Pembrocke & Temby [sic], they will soone beate the ship-
pes foorth [of] Milford Haven, and then from Waxford [Wexford] and
other places of Ireland land their forces, which may prove dangerous
to the kingdome.[77]

Here we have Poyer's deep anxiety about the threat from Ireland which,
as we have seen, had been crucial in shaping his pro-parliamentarian
responses since 1641. It is interesting, however, that he also expressed
his desire that parliament was 'truly informed' of Pembrokeshire's current predicament. This was a not-so-coded reference to the fact that the
Pembroke county committee – stuffed with members of the Lort family
who, so Poyer would later allege, had recently induced him to betray the
county to the king – was not doing its job of providing parliament with
accurate information about the county's (and in particular Pembroke's)
defensive needs and vulnerabilities. And these needs were significant.
The schedule of Pembroke garrison's deficiencies which Poyer sent up
to parliament with his letter was extensive and troubling. He maintained
that they required: one month's pay for 250 soldiers and their officers;
20 barrels of gunpowder; 50 cases of pistols; 100 muskets; 200 firelocks;
300 swords; shot for small canon; moulds to cast bullets; two tons of iron
to make portcullises and chains; and cloth for soldiers' shirts.[78]

In an accompanying petition, Pembroke's inhabitants described how
they had stood alone against much of the surrounding countryside, which
had left the town 'greatly distrest, wanting victuals, armes, amounicions
and monies of the maintenance of the souldiers'. Because of a lack of
support, they were 'forced to mainteyne the garrison to our great chardge
to this present strayning our selves to the uttermost, and not able longer
to undergoe the charge without speedie reliefe'.[79] This reinforced the
message that parliament's executive body, the county committee, was not
doing its job in providing the basics for Pembroke's defence. The town
was clearly short of firearms and powder, but also lacked fundamental
supplies such as adequate clothing and basic pay for the soldiers. It seems
that Poyer was opening up a front against his enemies on the county committee while also trying to ensure the garrison's security. Later in 1645,
Poyer would complain that he wrote 'many letters' to Richard Swanley
'desiring him to furnishe the garrison of Pembroke', but that he had been
consistently denied.[80] As we shall see, Poyer and Swanley were to become
estranged, but this statement again suggests a genuine sense of neglect on

the part of the parliamentarian authorities in the area, as well as a sense of grievance on Poyer's part.

This sense of more general discontent is suggested by the petition which accompanied Poyer's letter. This is a fascinating document which was drawn up on 29 March 1645. As mentioned above, it emphasised Pembroke's record of loyalty and steadfastness but also its desperate under-provisioning. Perhaps the most interesting element of the document, however, is the 121 signatures which accompany it. The sheer number of signatures suggests that Poyer enjoyed the support of a good proportion of Pembroke's leading householders and that his grievances were shared widely in the town. Poyer himself signs first as 'maior', and he is accompanied by Captain Walter Cuny, the man who seems to have held title to Pembroke Castle. The other names are a rare snapshot of the town's (male) population and provides our best approximation of a 'census' in this period, although some of the signatories would presumably have been outsiders but members of the garrison. The list would repay further research, but such an analysis is beyond the scope of this book. However, we might note here the presence among the signatories of Poyer's son, John, jr, and his brother David. Also present were probable relations like George and William Poyer. Pembroke's parliamentary resistance was, then, something of a family affair. In addition, there were several future mayors of the town as well as numerous bailiffs, which suggests that the core of the borough's governing oligarchy were behind Poyer's representation. We should be careful of characterising these as simply Poyer's 'party', however. Although prominent townsmen like William Hinton and Matthew Bowen were willing to support Poyer in 1645, in 1648 they would be found opposing their former governor.[81] A good deal of water was clearly to flow under the bridge between 1645 and 1648.

It is unclear whether Poyer's letter and Pembroke's petition were brought to the attention of the Commons; no record survives in the journals. What Poyer's representation did achieve, however, was to outrage the county committee, which now mobilised to challenge his allegations of inadequate command and insufficiency of supply. The committeemen wrote their own letter to Speaker Lenthall on 1 April 1645, only three days after Pembroke's petition was drafted, and their excoriating response represents the opening of public hostilities between Pembroke's mayor and his antagonists on the committee, many of whom were also once his military opponents.[82] This breach would constitute a fundamental reference point in local politics for the next three years. The committee members informed the Speaker that it was their duty to 'make itt knowen to you that the publique service entrusted to our care in these parts hath suffered manifold interruptions by the insolent opposicions and insatiable oppressions of Captain John Poyer, Mayor of Pembroke'. They promised a full enumeration of his misdeeds at a future date, but for now seized on his activities with respect to Carew Castle, the stronghold which had been surrendered to Poyer in the spring of 1644. They maintained that Carew was the possession of Sir Richard Philipps of Picton Castle, himself a member of the Pembroke committee, but that Poyer, 'by his owne usurped power' had 'converted to his own private comodity' the castle's crops, as well as appropriating the building's lead and timber.[83] Their letter claimed that Poyer held Carew 'by strong hand', which indicated the use of illegitimate force. They requested that Philipps be allowed to garrison Carew by 'removing the obstacle' of Poyer's possession, as 'our endeavours cannot effect itt'. Poyer's continued occupation of Carew, they claimed, 'produceth a general discontent among the contry, disableth the raising of means for advance of the publique service and opinionateth the enemy wee are ruining upon divisions'. The committee also asserted that Rowland Laugharne had shown his disapproval by 'openly disallowing and abhorring his [Poyer's] actions'.

This was a stinging accusation which sought to tar Poyer with the brush of misappropriation and embezzlement of public funds. We know that he was indeed maintaining a garrison there, as on 4 January 1645 he signed a receipt for £13 7s 0d of corn and malt which he had received 'for provission of the garrisson of Carew Castell'.[84] Another receipt signed by Thomas Beede from 9 December 1644 recorded supplies from Carew 'receaved into the storehowse at Pembrock'.[85] Evidently, then, some of Carew's produce was being sent to Poyer's garrison, and it would have been easy enough to allege that Poyer was profiting from the arrangement. The Lorts were also involved with accounting for issues from Carew, however, with John Lort signing for the receipt of thirteen bushels of wheat in November 1644 as part payment of the 'bishop's rents'.[86] Another intriguing scrap of evidence among a bundle of receipts from Carew in this period shows these sums being signed off by an auditor (who is not named). Lort's receipt was passed without comment, but the auditor noted that 'for Mr maior [i.e. Poyer] he cannott allow untill itt be ordered by the comittee'.[87] Meanwhile Beede's accounts were not to be agreed 'untill he be spoken with'. Evidently the Pembroke committee members had refused to pass Poyer's accounts for Carew because they saw his involvement as illegitimate. Moreover, there is the suggestion that they wished to interview Beede to gather damaging information on the Pembroke end of the case they were hoping to build against Poyer.

As the committee was the public body responsible for wartime accounting of parliamentary funds in the county, it was in an enormously powerful position to make these allegations against Poyer. It also seems to be the case that Poyer had put many noses out of joint in the county and that there was a degree of resentment against him which they could draw on. For example, one pamphlet which supported the parliamentarian war effort in Pembrokeshire was highly critical of Poyer's conduct and that of his forces. It described Poyer's own regiment as 'the very skum of the county of Pembrooke' and 'none of the honestest men', and castigated them for being 'suffered to robbe and plunder as the have done'.[88] Poyer himself was characterised as a quarrelsome man who refused to respect rank and decorum, especially 'when on the humour and his drinking mood'. The author suggested he needed 'a Parliament mus-rowle [muzzle] to put on his nose'.

The committee's claim that Laugharne was endorsing its position against his brother-in-law seems unlikely, but there is indeed some evidence of strained relations between the two. A few weeks after the committee's letter was written, and when war had returned to the shire, there were reports in the parliamentary press of some 'differences' between Poyer and Laugharne which the author hoped would soon be composed. These concerned 'some private points of commaund', particularly the fact that Poyer had 'a regiment of his own'.[89] This suggests that Poyer was bridling at Laugharne's authority over his men (they were both in Pembroke, Poyer with his own regiment and Laugharne with 500 foot and three troops of horse).[90] In a later publication, it was suggested that Laugharne, via the county committee, had questioned Poyer as to what authority he had to raise forces in Pembroke. Poyer later claimed that he could do this as mayor and captain of the local trained band, and apparently answered that the committee had no authority to examine him. Upon hearing this, Laugharne, 'collecting [Poyer's] . . . ayme to be independent to his commission', made another man captain of Poyer's troops.[91] Another publication which was critical of Poyer, sets up a clear contrast between the unimpeachable conduct of Laugharne and his forces on the one hand, and the plundering, turbulent and unruly nature of Poyer and his troops. One can easily imagine how friction between such characters turned readily to confrontation when they were holed up together in Pembroke surrounded by a superior military force.

It must be said that the committee's allegations of Poyer's despoiling Carew have the ring of truth. As we have seen in Lucy Meyrick's accusations over the Upton fulling mill, Poyer had 'form' when it came to stripping buildings of lead and timber for his own use. It may be, however, that such provisions were taken from Carew to help equip the more important defensive position of Pembroke. However, such actions readily shaded into accusations of plunder, and we have seen that Poyer and his men were accused in other contexts of such excesses during this period.

Whatever the truth of the committee's charges, what is clear is that allegations of corruption and misappropriation, in the murky but money-saturated world of wartime provisioning, was to prove a profitable avenue of attack for Poyer's enemies. They resurface, for example, in partisan assaults on Poyer in the later 1640s mobilised by John Eliot of Amroth, a signatory to the committee's letter.[92] Pembrokeshire was a long way from the organs of central parliamentary financial oversight, and such allegations had a tendency to stick, and to cause serious damage.

The Pembrokeshire committee followed up this attack with a further letter to Lenthall on 23 April.[93] This was another full-throated denunciation of the mayor, which underlines just how serious the breach had become amongst the parliamentary party in Pembrokeshire. They described the 'great disturbance of the publique service of the state in these partes . . . by the turbulent opposicions and oppressions of Capteine John Poyer'. The committee members claimed to have held their silence over Poyer's enormities in an effort to support the service of the state in a common cause, but 'our constreyned connivency hath increased his licentious contempt & opposicion'. They sent up a series of articles against Poyer and demanded not only that he receive the Commons' immediate censure but that he be arrested and detained. Their evident desire for speed seems to have been occasioned by the fact that Poyer 'is sett out for London'. Evidently their earlier letter had prompted Poyer to try and clear his name. Perhaps mindful of the committee's power and reach in Pembrokeshire, he seems to have resolved to go over their heads and argue his own case in London.

Whether he made it to the capital or not is unclear, for the shadow of armed conflict once again fell across the county even as the committee's letter was en route to the capital. Charles Gerard had been operating in north-west England but the royalist command had ordered him back into Wales to shore up its royalist defences and roll back parliament's recent advances. He recruited forces in Montgomeryshire and then struck westward with a lightning advance that surprised the local parliamentarian forces. On 23 April 1645, Gerard defeated Rowland Laugharne at Newcastle Emlyn in Carmarthenshire.[94] He then turned his attention to Pembrokeshire and swept through the county in a devastating series of attacks with perhaps as many as 5,000 men, taking Haverfordwest, Picton Castle and Carew Castle in a matter of days.[95] Once again, Laugharne, Rice Powell and the bulk of parliament's forces retreated behind Pembroke's stout walls. This time, the royalist commander decided to try and take the key parliamentary stronghold, and in May 1645 began a siege of the town. Poyer was present in the town during the siege. This was a serious challenge to parliament's position, and, once again, Pembroke's strategic importance was emphasised in contemporary publications. In May 1645, one pamphlet described the significance of Pembroke and Milford as 'the onely harbour to friend between Plymouth and Leverpool; bloody Irelands greatest curb and terrour; the marriners security; if preserved, nay, they are verily perswaded, and so are all that know it, that there is not one place in England more considerable, *consideratis considerandis*, than that'.[96] Similarly, a report of Gerard's victory at Haverfordwest in the royalist press described how his forces now had possession of one side of Milford Haven and 'six parts of seven in Pembrokeshire, which is the onely county of south Wales wherein are any rebels', who were driven back to their 'last stake' in Pembroke and Tenby.[97] As one pamphlet later put it, the 'Pembroke-men [were] . . . reduced almost to their first handfull'.[98]

Painfully aware of their isolation and their importance to the wider parliamentarian war effort, Poyer and Laugharne sent letters to London imploring aid. They were read in the Commons on 26 May which then recommended that 'some special care [be taken] of sending forces and assistance speedily for the preservation of Milford Haven and the town of Pembroke'.[99] Simon Thelwall, Poyer's associate in Pembroke in 1643, was appointed to oversee this initiative. Intriguingly, the Commons also ordered on this occasion that Poyer 'be added to all the committees of Pembrokeshire to all intents and purposes'. This was a belated recognition of Poyer's omission from the county committee the previous spring. It was also something of a coup for Poyer and his supporters in the county and a blow to the Lort political interest. The order clearly indicates that Poyer had friends in the Commons who were arguing for his inclusion. They may have included Thelwall himself or perhaps Sir John Meyrick. It is unclear what practical difference Poyer's nomination to the committee made, however, for he does not seem to have taken up this post; he was unable to serve while besieged in Pembroke, and the fact that this order needed to be re-issued in August 1645 argues that he remained effectively 'frozen out' of the county's main decision-making body.[100]

Additional men and resources were indeed committed to securing Pembroke from Gerard's forces over the next few months, although parliament was well aware of its own shortcomings in this regard.[101] The Committee of Both Kingdoms, the executive body which oversaw the running of the war effort for parliament, sent a letter in July to Sir Thomas Fairfax, the leader of parliament's newly reorganised army, acknowledging that:

> our affaires hitherto hath beene such (togeither with the scituation of the place [Pembrokeshire] distant from all our forces and capable of releife onely by sea by reason of the enemies forces & quarters interposing) that we could not give them [Pembroke and Tenby] the reliefe they desired & which both their necessitie & the consequence of the place call for.[102]

This sense of urgency may have been sharpened by Gerard's depredations in the county the previous autumn, and reports that similar plundering of the countryside was happening once again.[103]

Supplies of men and provisions trickled into the county in the summer, but the key development was Gerard's recall to England after the king's devastating defeat at the Battle of Naseby. Although Gerard left a large detachment of troops behind him, the royalist forces were weakened while their opponents' strength, and consequently their confidence, grew. In late July, Laugharne drew his forces out from Pembroke and joined with those of Rice Powell at Tenby and, on 1 August 1645, they met the assembled royalist army at the decisive engagement of Colby Moor near Haverfordwest. Laugharne was victorious, with the enemy, in his own words, 'totally routed'.[104] The king, his cause dwindling in England, did not have the resources to throw into saving the county, and Laugharne mopped up Pembrokeshire's remaining royalist outposts over the following weeks. Parliament appointed 2 October as a day of thanksgiving and public fasting in London 'for the successe in Pembrokeshire', among other victories, while on 9 October those parts of the kingdom under parliamentarian control were directed to celebrate Laugharne's victory.[105] The first civil war in Pembrokeshire was over, and the end of hostilities elsewhere in the kingdom came the following summer with the king's surrender.

Reports of the parliamentarian actions against Gerard's forces in the summer and autumn of 1645 did not mention John Poyer. The limelight was once again taken by Rowland Laugharne who proceeded to subdue the remainder of the region and became parliament's leading military commander in south Wales, receiving the sequestered estate of the Catholic John Barlow of Slebech as a reward. In many ways the civil war had been the making of John Poyer – but it also contained the seeds of his ruin. This obscure glover had become parliament's first and most conspicuous supporter in the region. His tenacious defence of Pembroke was vital in securing the area and had a wider significance for protecting parliament's naval lanes in the west and guarding against the threat from Ireland. He was clearly a dedicated, but also an unyielding, parliamentary servant who alienated friends and foes alike in his governorship of Pembroke. It seems telling that one of the only occasions on which he surfaces in the press during the summer of 1645 is in a report of a division over military command with his brother-in-law. It was a parliamentary commentator rather than a royalist one who described how he 'affronted . . . his betters' and 'would find any occasion to pick a quarrel'.[106] Poyer and Laugharne would soon be reconciled but there were many others who were sharpening their knives for Pembroke's governor. Although parliament's military victory should have seen the loyal Poyer lauded and rewarded with plaudits, offices and power by grateful MPs, he was now plunged instead into a world of political strife and factional backbiting. His struggle with local enemies and the desperate straits to which it brought him, is the focus of the next chapter.

CHAPTER 4

The Struggle for Supremacy: Poyer and Post-War Politics, 1646-1647

The civil war was won, but the conflict had opened up profound divisions within Pembrokeshire society, although these did not always, or even primarily, follow our simple image of 'royalists' versus 'parliamentarians'. Part of the county's post-war narrative, as elsewhere in the kingdom, is the fragmentation of the parliamentarian coalition, although, as we have seen in the last chapter, in Pembrokeshire this was a coalition already under severe stress even before the fighting concluded. The county thus witnessed a factional struggle between 1645 and 1648 which pitted John Poyer against a cadre of county gentlemen led by Roger Lort and John Eliot. This chapter examines this political breakdown and considers the difficulties Poyer faced, not just in reaping the rewards of his loyal service, but in receiving basic compensation for his civil war expenditures. The post-war period was one of shifting political and religious landscapes, and Poyer struggled to adapt his convictions and behaviour to the new terrain. He retained vital allies and sought to bolster the position of political and religious moderates in Pembrokeshire but was confronted by a set of opponents who were implacably bent on his downfall. Poyer struggled to convince parliament of his case for reparations and his continued service as Pembroke's governor. This was partly because his enemies were able to pour their poison into the ears of powerful interests in London. This chapter explores Poyer's struggle with his local enemies, and how it pushed him, ultimately, into open rebellion against parliament. First, however, we need to consider the nature of the political and religious divisions which bedevilled the victorious parliament and its supporters in the provinces during the mid-1640s.

From the earliest days of the conflict, the parliamentarian party contained within it a spectrum of opinion on questions of religious settlement and political authority.[1] All parliamentarians wished for change in these areas, but there were significant divisions over the nature and scope of the reform required. In the early stages of the conflict such divisions were largely subordinated to the need to mobilise a war effort against the king. However, the severe stresses of war increasingly exposed a damaging rift between radical reforming elements and more moderate groups in both parliament and the army. During 1644–5 these groups acquired names which were religious in origin, but which came to embody political positions that comprehended ideas about the prosecution of the war and the role of the king in the body politic. These groups also had divergent ideas about the nature and extent of religious reform which would accompany any peace settlement.[2] The more moderate elements came to be called 'Presbyterians' while their antagonists were characterised as 'Independents'.

One of the key developments in the struggle between these groups concerned the army and the prosecution of the war. The earl of Essex, leader of parliament's forces from 1642, was seen by many Independents as excessively cautious and timorous in his military strategy; critics from within the parliamentary ranks openly wondered whether he was committed to the king's defeat at all. Partly because of concerns about such timid aristocratic military leadership, in 1644–5 parliament's army was fundamentally reorganised in a victory for the Independents. Presbyterians like the earls of Essex and Manchester were ejected from their commands and politically marginalised. The result was the formation of the New Model Army led by Sir Thomas Fairfax, but in which Oliver Cromwell was a leading light. The New Model had close ties with the Independent interest in parliament and the provinces.

These developments shifted the nature of parliamentary politics and transformed its military fortunes. The Scottish Covenanters, who had been key parliamentary allies in the early 1640s, were horrified by the rise of Independent power. They had sympathetic supporters among those parliamentary moderates who envisaged some changes to England and Wales's political and religious landscapes but who were deeply concerned by the growing calls for more far-reaching reform in these areas. Conversely, more radical political and religious figures in the English and Welsh provinces were emboldened by the zealous messages of change emanating from the Independents. Although the division between royalist and parliamentarian remained a fundamental fault-line, then, differences *between* parliamentarians in London and the provinces became an increasingly important feature of the political and military terrain from the mid-1640s.

As we have seen, Poyer was a resolute and consistent supporter of a moderate parliamentarian cause. His political connections had been with elements of the Essex faction within Pembrokeshire which were Presbyterian in character. Figures such as Rowland Laugharne, Arthur Owen and the Meyricks, for example, were supporters of Essex and his brand of politics. Poyer too seems to have been a political Presbyterian, but his religious position was rather more complex. The touchstone of Poyer's political creed in 1641–2 seems to have been anti-popery and fear of invasion from Ireland.[3] This did not, however, shade into any kind of Presbyterianism in religion. Although Poyer was certainly a dedicated parliamentarian, he remained committed to the Church of England and its liturgy throughout the 1640s.[4]

While we might talk of 'Presbyterians' and 'Independents' as coherent groups, we should realise that such a model obscures a messier and more complex reality. Many fought on the parliamentarian side who were supporters of the Church of England, although most of these men and women wished to see church services stripped of their lingering Catholic elements. It seems that Poyer was one such parliamentarian: a political Presbyterian but in religion a supporter of the Established Church; he was what might be described as an 'episcopalian'.[5] There are several pieces of evidence which direct us towards such a conclusion. Perhaps the clearest cut are his own statements in 1648–9. In his *Declaration* which he published in April 1648, Poyer was at pains to defend the Book of Common Prayer, a key text in Church of England worship and something which was anathema to reforming puritans (including most religious Presbyterians) who saw it as a deeply suspect, even near-Catholic, text.[6] In this publication Poyer expressed his desire to 'maintaine the Protestant religion and the common-prayer as it is established by the law in this land', a construction which suggests a moderate vision of a Jacobean-style Church.[7] This was perhaps the kind of thing one might expect from a text in which Poyer sought to support his rebellion for the king (who was head of the Church, of course); as a result, its sincerity might be considered suspect. However, in his *Vindication*, published in 1649 after the establishment of the republic, and when such sentiments could probably only harm him, Poyer nonetheless continued to assert that, 'it is well known, my religion to be such as is professed by the Church of England'.[8] This statement seems unequivocal and argues that Poyer was indeed a convinced episcopalian. Moreover, in his last speech as he faced the firing squad in April 1649, Poyer maintained that he died 'a true Protestant according to the discipline of the Church of England'.[9] His opponents also portrayed Poyer as an unreconstructed episcopalian. John Eliot, for example, jeered that Poyer was a 'stiffe maintainer of the Booke of Common-prayer'.[10]

Perhaps as revealing of Poyer's religious sympathies was his decision in 1645 to donate new silver gilt chalices to both of Pembroke's parish churches, St Mary's and St Michael's. The St Mary's cup remains in use and carries the inscription, 'The Guift of Captayne John Poyer Governor of the towne and castle of Pembroke to the parish church of St Marye in Pembroke Anno dom[in]i 1645'. At St Michael's, a communion chalice from 1717 survives, but it too carries an inscription which informs us that it was made from the melting down of two earlier chalices, 'the larger one given by Capt[ain] John Poyer governour of the towne and castle of Pembrook . . . in 1645'.[11] These fascinating pieces of material culture are revealing. Such a donation in 1645 was far from a neutral act. This was after a point when the parliamentarian cause had officially adopted a Presbyterian religious goal following its conclusion of a treaty with the Covenanters in 1643. Poyer was thus declaring himself very visibly as a supporter of the embattled Church of England and the rites and ceremonies enshrined in the Book of Common Prayer.[12] In the midst of war, when religious politics was undergoing a rapid transformation, Poyer bullishly offered up to the world a very visible symbol of his connection to an older politics of moderate Reformation. It may not be coincidental that he had recently chased a Presbyterian minister, intruded by his enemies, out of Pembroke.[13] His declarations of loyalty to the Established Church in 1648–9, then, seem to have been sincerely held and of long duration rather than simply the products of expediency during a royalist revolt.

His religious sympathies might seem to put Poyer on a collision course with political associates such as Rowland Laugharne who were more thoroughly Presbyterian. However, this was not necessarily the case. Although religious differences were an important component of intra-parliamentary strife, from the mid-1640s, accommodations between 'prayer book Protestants' and Presbyterians were not unusual. Indeed, the common enemy of religious radicalism, often referred to derogatively as the 'sects' or 'sectarians', did much to ameliorate tensions between religious moderates.

A further complication of this already complicated picture is that we cannot easily model Poyer's opponents in the post-war world simply as religious 'Independents'. Many of them, in fact, seem to have held Presbyterian sympathies in religion, while Roger Lort was later described as someone 'of any principle or religion to acquire wealth'.[14] There was a more vigorous form of radical religion among some of the Lort associates, particularly in the case of Roger's brother, Sampson Lort, who was later described as a man who supported 'schismatickes' and 'phanatickes'.[15] It is also the case that the man who helped Lort and his associates in parliament down to his death in January 1645, John White, was a committed puritan and religious reformer.[16] Although there was a strain of religious zeal which ran through the Lort group, then, it does not seem to have been its defining characteristic. We should remember, moreover, that most of the Lort associates had supported the earl of Carbery in 1643–4, something difficult to accommodate with a zealous commitment to further reformation. Although not thoroughgoing religious radicals, then, this group nonetheless made fruitful contacts with the New Model Army and the Independents. These Pembrokeshire factions can thus be understood as broadly representing local iterations of the Presbyterian and Independent groups.

As we have seen, Poyer had crossed swords with members of the Pembrokeshire county committee in his letter to Speaker Lenthall of March 1645. The signatories to the committee's bitter denunciation of Poyer by way of answer provides us with a roll call of his political opponents. Here we find the three Lort brothers, Roger, Sampson and John, along with their close associate John Eliot of Amroth. Also present were Griffith White of Henllan, John White's brother, and Thomas Warren of Trewern. The first and most prominent signatories, however, were Admiral Richard Swanley, the man who had been Poyer's saviour in January 1644, and his deputy, Captain William Smith. Some discussion of Swanley's subscription to this document and of his developing feud with Poyer is necessary.

Upon his arrival in Pembrokeshire in January 1644, Richard Swanley had been welcomed as a providential deliverer, saving the embattled parliamentarians in Pembroke from their encircling royalist oppressors. On that occasion William Smith described how Poyer, along with Rowland Laugharne, came aboard Swanley's *Leopard* the day after his arrival to discuss Pembroke's perilous situation and how to meet the royalist challenge together.[17] Relations were clearly cordial at this early stage with Smith describing how Laugharne and Poyer were, 'like gallant men', resolved 'rather [to] die than outlive the honor of their country or see the ruine thereof by a Jesuiticall and popish faction'. As a result, they 'resolved to put themselves under the providence of the Almighty and with the help of our sea-men to affront the enemy, the which was without delay put in execution'.[18] Thereafter there was indeed a good working relationship between Poyer, Laugharne and Swanley as they combined to root Carbery and his forces out of the county.[19]

However, at some point in the next few months a breach opened up between the admiral on the one hand and the mayor and Rowland Laugharne on the other.[20] This seems to have partly been caused by Swanley's growing affinity with the Lort group who had foresworn their earlier royalism and been welcomed into the parliamentary fold. The royalist colonel Roger Lort was described as coming in 'voluntarily to Captain Swanley, and was received by the Admirall and Committee . . . in February 1644', which is to say very soon after Swanley's first appearance in the county.[21] The fact that he turned himself over to Swanley rather than Laugharne may be an important detail. Religious sympathies may also have had something to do with the breakdown between Poyer and Swanley. Richard Swanley was clearly a puritan enthusiast, as is suggested by his summons to the Pembrokeshire royalists in February 1644. Poyer's religious conservatism may have helped sour relations between the two.

There were also, perhaps, more mundane reasons for their estrangement as Swanley reaped all the praise for defeating the royalists in early 1644, receiving gold chains from parliament for his service in June, while Poyer received little thanks and remained excluded from the inner circles of local parliamentary administration and authority.[22] At one point, for example, Poyer was said to be 'enviously jeering at their [Swanley and Smith's] gold-chains, falsely and arrogantly terming himself the actor, and them but assistants to the service of those parts'.[23] One hostile commentator even claimed that relations were so poor between the two that at one point Poyer struck Swanley 'to the effusion of his blood'.[24] Simple jealousy and rivalry over who was responsible for saving parliament's cause was mentioned in other sources too, with Poyer's thin skin and volatile temper doubtless adding fuel to the fire.[25] Perhaps as a result of this disagreement, by the time of Gerard's campaigns in the county in 1645, the fractious relationship between Poyer and Swanley was even said to have affected the war effort, as Swanley apparently withheld supplies and munitions from the garrison partly to spite Poyer.[26]

This breach burst into public view with the committee's letters to Speaker Lenthall in April 1645, but the end of military hostilities in the county signalled a new phase in the feud between Swanley and the committee on the one hand, and John Poyer on the other. In the summer of 1645, complaints were sent to parliament's admiralty committee about Swanley's conduct and he was recalled to London.[27] Hearings against Swanley began in the Admiralty Court in October, and the allegations against him seem to have emerged from Poyer and his fellow critics of Swanley in the far west.[28] Several of the accusations against Swanley were salacious in nature. It was alleged that the admiral's ship, as it rode in Milford Haven, was employed as 'a water baudie house' and a 'wyne tavern'.[29] Swanley was said to entertain royalist gentlemen and, more damagingly, royalist women on his vessel, often in his private cabin. James Lewis, one of the prominent family of Tregibby in Cardiganshire, even claimed that he saw the daughter of one of Swanley's captains in the admiral's cabin, who 'stood betwixt his leggs & his hatt was off'; Swanley responded that she was merely 'lousing his head'.[30] Another deponent observed that there 'was a scandalous & ill report raised in the country about Milford of Captain Swanley & those woemen & songs made of him & them & comonly sunge upp & downe the country'.[31] This man even claimed that Swanley showed him a copy of one of these songs! In addition, Swanley was charged with having clandestine contacts with and offering support to local royalists; allowing illicit trade with Dublin; and causing a rift between the Pembroke committee, of which he was a member, and the 'well affected' of the county.

Interestingly for our purposes, one of Swanley's most stalwart defenders was John Eliot of Amroth, an intimate of the Lorts who was made the 'agent' or local representative of the Pembrokeshire committee in London around May 1645. Eliot made a vigorous defence of Swanley before the

Admiralty Court, noting that he had frequently been aboard the *Leopard* and had seen no evidence of any wrongdoing. Moreover, he claimed to be unaware of any correspondence between Swanley and the enemy, or any attempt to divide the committee from the gentry. He deposed, to the contrary, that Swanley's 'carriage was sweete and deservinge the love of the well affected of the countrye'.[32] He also stressed that Swanley had been Pembrokeshire's saviour in January 1644, averring that Pembroke itself would have soon been lost for Poyer and others had subscribed to the royalist 'instrument' to support the king shortly before. Eliot concluded his testimony by stating that Swanley's prosecution was 'done out of malice and scandoll to soile the proceedings of the said Captaine Swanlye and for some other . . . sinister ends'.[33]

In December 1645, Poyer himself appeared before the court to give evidence.[34] Unsurprisingly, his testimony was far more critical of Swanley. He asserted that he had examined several seamen in his capacity as Pembroke's mayor, who had confessed that they came out of the enemy's quarters to buy commodities from Swanley.[35] He also maintained that Swanley allowed frequent traffic of ships laden with corn to Dublin; that 'the comon report in the country' was that Swanley was 'too familiar' with the daughter of one of his captains who had been a royalist; and that he had allowed a royalist prisoner to go ashore when Rowland Laugharne had forbidden it. His most damaging accusations, however, concerned Swanley's denial of support during the recent battles with Gerard. Poyer claimed that he wrote Swanley 'many letters' asking him to furnish the Pembroke garrison with casks for storing water and making barricades, but that he had answered he would spare none. Moreover, he said that during the recent siege of Pembroke, Laugharne, Poyer and their council of war 'did often sende & wrote to Captain Swanley for convenient supply of amunition . . . being then in great want thereof & the enemy giveing then continuall alarums & sometime assaulting', yet once more Swanley replied that 'hee would not spare any more'. These were potentially damaging allegations of misconduct. Although there is no clear evidence that Poyer was the animating force behind Swanley's prosecution, he was certainly eager to support it, and he seems to have been gathering damaging evidence against Swanley to produce in court.

Swanley was cleared of wrongdoing in March 1646 and was returned to his former command. His successful defence prompted an impassioned editorial in one parliamentarian newsbook which lamented that too many of the parliaments best servants have been thus traduced and aspersed . . . endeavours have been set on foot to blast the reputation of that unblemished, vigilant, valiant and faithfull sea commander, Capt. Swanley, whose sea services in this present war have merited a lasting fame to future ages and a vindication to the present generation.[36]

The edition then proceeded to recount Swanley's many services and dwelled on his Pembrokeshire successes in detail. This suggests that John Eliot may have been behind this very public vindication of his friend and ally.

These hearings took place in London, and, as we have seen, Poyer journeyed to the capital in December 1645, and remained there for a few months, although not as long as many have suggested.[37] Initially he said that he was sent to the capital by Laugharne 'for the special service of the Parliament & his countrey'.[38] This may have been an euphemism for testifying against Swanley, but his intentions were wider than this. Poyer wished to obtain reparations for the monies he had expended in Pembroke's defence, but also wanted to present his case personally before his parliamentary masters and to undermine the position of the committee members and their London agent, John Eliot. These two ambitions were inextricably linked. Poyer would never easily recoup his monies while his enemies retained control of Pembrokeshire's administration. Poyer had complained the previous winter that the county committee was stopping his servant and his letters reaching parliament. As communication with London was effectively closed down, he clearly felt his presence in the capital was required if he was to vindicate his conduct, claim his arrears and inform Westminster about the dubious political backgrounds of their local agents.[39] A hostile pamphlet confirms this interpretation, describing how Poyer had 'arrive[d] in London where, no sooner come, but he presently boggles at the committee of Pembrookesheire'.[40]

On 3 December 1645, probably shortly after his arrival in the capital, Poyer presented a petition to parliament. Interestingly, he seems to have petitioned the House of Lords rather than the House of Commons, which suggests he believed he might receive a more sympathetic hearing there. Perhaps significantly, this was a day when the earl of Essex sat in the Lords, and it may be that Poyer was hoping to mobilise some of his connections and to persuade the earl to promote his cause. In his petition Poyer rehearsed his loyal service against Carbery and Gerard and

his efforts to keep Pembroke in parliament's hands. He claimed to have
borrowed £2,000 'besides all the money your petitioner had of his own',
which he had spent in fortifying the town and providing food, ammunition
and clothing for the soldiers he had raised. In addition, he related how
Gerard had burned the houses, barns and crops of individuals from whom
he had borrowed money. As a result, Poyer requested that he be allowed to
recoup his losses out of delinquents' estates in Pembrokeshire. The Lords
recommended the petition to the Lower House.[41] This was a potentially
worrying development for the Lort–Eliot interest as allowing Poyer to take
money from royalists' estates would cut across their authority to manage
local delinquents' property. It also potentially created an avenue for Poyer
to bring actions against some of them for their royalist pasts, or to try and
recoup monies from their estates or those of their friends.

Perhaps because of the potentially damaging nature of Poyer's request,
his petition was not adopted by the Commons. Roger Lort or John Eliot,
likely through the agency of the ailing MP John White, probably prevented
it from even being considered. In any event, Poyer's initiative was soon
stopped by Swanley, who had Poyer arrested. Swanley may have been
acting as the committee's cat's-paw in this action, but he certainly had
enough justification for wanting revenge on Poyer for the evidence he had
given to the Admiralty Court a month before. Poyer himself attributed
his apprehension to Eliot and Roger and Sampson Lort whom he saw as
standing behind Swanley's action.[42]

On 8 January 1646, Poyer once more petitioned the Lords but also sent
a representation to the Commons' Speaker, William Lenthall. He wrote
from his confinement in the Bailiff's House, Westminster, complaining
that, 'after many affronts by some gentlemen whome he had formerly
forced in to the obedyence of the parlyament, he was yesterday arrested at
Westminster by Capteine Swanley without any ground at all'.[43] Upon his
discharge that morning, Swanley had then charged him with a new action
for £2,000 'at his owne suite . . . only to hinder him [Poyer] from doing
the service he came for'. The wording of the petition is interesting. Poyer
linked the 'turncoat' Lorts and Eliot with Swanley's action at law without
publicly making the claim that they were behind the suit. Accusing committeemen in this fashion without hard proof might have got him into hot
water with the Commons. It is also clear that Poyer interpreted his arrest
as an attempt to stop the 'service' for which he had come to London:
namely to recoup his war losses and obtain official confirmation of his

appointment as Pembroke's governor.[44] Yet he was also keen to inform parliament that they were employing ex-royalists as committeemen who were trying to manufacture the ruin of loyal parliamentary servants such as himself and Rowland Laugharne.[45] Poyer would later describe how he was 'cast in prison' by this suit 'to hinder my lawful proceedings against them [Eliot and the Lorts]'.[46] The £2,000 action almost certainly concerned claims that Poyer had misappropriated public funds during the war.

Upon reading his petition, the Lords (with Essex once again present) ordered that Swanley appear before them to show cause why Poyer had been arrested; Poyer was also to be present.[47] Unfortunately, we do not know the nature of any further proceedings before parliament or the outcome of this case. One surprising aspect of Poyer's defence, however, is that he retained as his legal counsel John Cook: the man who would present the case of treason against Charles I at his trial in January 1649.[48] It is something of an irony that Poyer, who would rise in the name of the king in 1648 and ultimately hasten his monarch's journey to the scaffold, should once have retained the king's prosecutor as lawyer. Poyer and Cook must have made rather uncomfortable bedfellows. A short month after Poyer's case, Cook was appointed counsel for the celebrated Leveller John Lilburne in a review of the latter's Star Chamber conviction from the 1630s. Lilburne was a political and religious radical of a completely different stripe to Poyer, so it is intriguing that they shared a lawyer. We cannot map political convictions from the selection of legal counsel, of course, but Cook's acting for Poyer might suggest the latter's connections to radical circles which are now lost to us. However, it may simply have been Cook's commitment to parliament's capacity to 'utterly breake the necke and cut the very hearts-strings of all fraud, deceit, oppression, cruelty and injustice', which drew him to Poyer or vice versa.[49] It is easy to see how Poyer might make his case emblematic of a wider assault on the corruption of parliamentary justice by those who acted in its name. In this sense, although in little else, there was something of a connection between the causes espoused by Poyer and by Lilburne.[50]

As Poyer languished in his Westminster prison, his case was picked up back in Pembrokeshire by his brother-in-law and the hero (with Swanley) of the parliamentarian victory in south-west Wales, Rowland Laugharne. Writing from Haverfordwest to Speaker Lenthall on 16 January 1646, Laugharne pulled no punches in his assessment of the situation.[51] He described how Roger Lort and John Eliot 'are so whollie taken with the prosecution of private malice they cane spare noe thoughts for the pub-lique good'. He continued, 'I perceive Captain Poyer is molested by some gentlemen [who] in our distresse were our greatest enemies and [whom] successe onlie induced to profess our frindshippe'. He maintained that these quarrels were 'meerelie private', adding that if the charge related to 'publique defecte', then he offered himself 'to iustifie his [Poyer's] vigi-lancie, activitie, constancy, resolution, judgement and fidelitie against all the malignant detractors on earth'. This is a useful perspective, seeing Poyer's troubles as wholly a product of local faction. His assessment of Poyer's qualities is also important as they echo those elements which Poyer would repeatedly emphasise in his own service, particularly constancy and fidelity. Laugharne then offered his own take on Poyer and the situation in Pembrokeshire, which offers a rare balanced view from someone who knew him well. Laugharne wrote that

> the man maie have his infirmities and slipes as other men, and in pri-vate considerations maie bee blame worthie, yett, I am confident, not in soe high nature as ought to obscure those eminent good parts well approved in him. His virulent traducers malice terminates not in his person or fortunes, but designe the infamie of my selfe and all they know are faithfull with mee in the states service as the sole antidote for their own malignancie.[52]

Like all who spoke of Poyer's character, then, Laugharne clearly recognised his brother-in-law's personal weaknesses, those 'infirmities', which seem to have frustrated his allies and deepened the hostility of his detractors. Moreover, Laugharne's comments are revealing in what they show about the Lort–Eliot group's attempts to attack the Major General through Poyer's sides. Poyer was a target, then, but also something of a stalking horse for a wider attack on the Presbyterian interest in the county. It is also noticeable that Laugharne, like Poyer, locates the fount of the Lorts's opposition as stemming from their early royalism, their 'malignancie', which must have been a serious point of political weakness as the fighting ceased. After offering this assessment, the Major General then requested that Poyer be returned to his command of Pembroke and volunteered himself to be 'accoumptable for his miscarriages in his trust', effectively offering to act as guarantor for Poyer's quiet return to parliamentary ser-vice. Laugharne finished by asking that 'distressed' Pembrokeshire be spared the excise, concluding, 'no county in the kingdom, I am assured, is become such an object of pity'.

This letter shows that the tensions of the spring of 1645 between Laugharne and Poyer over the latter's independent military command had been put to rest. It also endorses the view that while the suit brought against Poyer may have been brought in Swanley's name, it was Eliot and Roger Lort who were ultimately behind the action. It reveals too that Poyer and Laugharne were close political as well as military allies, and that the split in Pembrokeshire's local politics was now essentially defined as a confrontation between the Lort–Eliot and Laugharne–Poyer factions. Also praised in Laugharne's letter was Arthur Owen of Orielton, brother of Poyer's sometime patron, Sir Hugh. It is clear, too, that Laugharne shared Poyer's contempt for the Lorts and John Eliot as malignants, turncoats and opportunists.

It is uncertain whether Laugharne's letter received a sympathetic hearing or if Poyer was immediately released. Our next glimpse of him comes in February 1646 from a hostile petition which refers to the fact that Poyer was about to petition parliament once again.[53] This would indicate that he had indeed been liberated, as does the fact that he received £400 by order of parliament the same month.[54] In his own account of his travails with Eliot, Poyer referred to having been released from the £2,000 suit without costs, 'which so wrought with [John] Elliot that he procured another writ to be delivered to the Bailiff of Westminster, immediately on the discharge of my former troubles, he conceiving me not out of custody, thought thereby to have continued his enterprise'.[55] This is a slightly confusing chronology but the next event mentioned in this account is Poyer's return to Wales following a rising in Glamorgan. This probably refers to the revolt of February 1646 led by the county's sheriff, Edward Carne, which took the form of a conservative royalist reaction against parliamentarian 'schismatiques' who had taken power there.[56] Poyer was certainly back in Pembroke by August 1646.[57]

In early February 1646, John Eliot petitioned parliament. He discussed an anticipated petition from Poyer which would request payment of £4,000 for his services to the state.[58] Eliot maintained that he would show that Poyer had 'money and other goods of the states to a great vallew unaccounted for, soe that . . . Poyer wilbe found more indebted to the state than can be by him justly demaunded'. He requested that Poyer be brought before parliament's Committee of Accounts to answer Eliot's charges 'in behalfe of the state for mony and goods by him receaved'. Eliot thus presented himself as an upholder of financial probity and the guardian of parliament's ('the state's') interests against a corrupt official who would fleece them of money and resources. In a publication he brought out later that year, Eliot returned to these issues, maintaining that Poyer captured ships and converted their cargo to his own use 'yet he hath the face now to petition the Parliament for no lesse than foure thousand pound disbursments, which is desired may appear in particulars, that the state be not cozened'.[59] It was in this guise of rigorous accountant for the state's interests that Eliot would attack Poyer again and again, particularly in print.

In the face of these attacks by Swanley and Eliot, Poyer took the decision to make his case publicly through his first foray into the world of print. One aspect of the British civil wars which has received increasing scholarly attention in recent years is the way in which the world of print and political publicity was transformed during the 1640s.[60] The calling of the Long Parliament had effectively seen the machinery of royal censorship of print collapse. Although a new apparatus for controlling what issued from the press was erected by parliament from 1643, this period nonetheless witnessed a remarkable expansion in the volume and nature of available print as well as its democratisation and increased geographical and social spread. In addition, the civil war witnessed important innovations in genres of printing too, perhaps the most important being the emergence of a vibrant topical news media with the production of a plethora of partisan weekly newsbooks.[61] This enormous expansion of the printed sphere constituted something of a transformation in communication, and John Poyer now became caught up in what has been well-termed a 'print revolution'.

In early 1646, probably in mid- to late February soon after his release from incarceration, John Poyer published a text publicising his plight and attacking his enemies.[62] Historians have been unaware of this text, which is unsurprising as no copies have survived. However, we can reconstruct much of it from a publication designed to answer the work. This was produced by John Eliot, and this text too has never been discussed by historians.[63] It is a tricky job trying to recreate a lost text from a work designed explicitly to undermine and impugn it, but a good deal can be gleaned from a careful reading of Eliot's responses. Poyer's text seems to have been called the *Relation*, although the title was probably much longer (as was the way of civil war publications), and that is how it will be referred to here. It was almost certainly a small quarto pamphlet of perhaps eight pages. It appears to have been published anonymously. We also know that, while Poyer may have printed this work to publicise his parliamentary service and sufferings at his enemies' hands, he did not necessarily publish it to reach a wide audience, but rather produced the text for a targeted group of influential readers. Poyer was described as 'dispersing the books with his owne hand to his acquaintance in London'.[64] This, then, was a form of 'coterie' publication, with a small print run which was distributed personally (and probably *gratis*), probably to members of the House of Lords and the Commons, individuals who had the power and authority to confirm Poyer as Pembroke's governor, assist with his search for financial compensation, and protect him from his enemies.[65]

Poyer's *Relation* included a brief history of the civil wars in Pembrokeshire which redounded to his glory and the discredit of Roger Lort and his allies. He offered a narrative which emphasised his early and vigorous support for parliament, his fortification of Pembroke's defences and his seizure of enemy ships in Milford Haven. Poyer's stead-fast resistance against encroaching royalist forces in 1644 was combined with accounts of his involvement in retaking royalist garrisons such as Stackpole and Trefloyne, the houses of his enemies Roger Lort and Thomas Bowen. Notably, Poyer presented these military actions as joint ventures alongside the parliamentary favourite Rowland Laugharne. The narrative then moved on to Gerard's appearance in the county during the spring of 1645, when Poyer complained about having to purchase arms for Pembroke's defence at unreasonable prices from Richard Swanley. Poyer also emphasised his efforts in raising, equipping and providing for troops of horse and dragoons which, he said, had left him desperately out of pocket. The *Relation* then offered an account of Gerard's siege of Pembroke, which Eliot claimed 'assum[ed] all to himself'; Poyer even placed himself among Laugharne's victorious forces at Colby Moor.

In addition to celebrating Poyer's civil and military service, the *Relation* also focused on disparaging and denigrating his enemies, concentrating particularly on Roger Lort, John Eliot and Thomas Bowen of Trefloyne. Poyer highlighted their early royalism and support for the earl of Carbery and made much of their role in the betrayal of Tenby and a journey made in late 1643 to the king's headquarters at Oxford. He attacked Lort and Bowen for garrisoning their houses for the king, charging them with 'the chiefest delinquency in that county', adding 'that they were sworn to the kings party'. He also accused them of cowardice by abandoning the county and running to London upon Gerard's second invasion in 1645. Unsurprisingly, given the fact that the text was produced around the time Poyer was arrested at Swanley's suit, the *Relation* criticised the Admiral's conduct in charging Poyer excessive amounts for purchasing arms and munitions. Moreover, it is clear that this text relegated Swanley to a supporting role in the parliamentary offensives of 1644–5 and emphasised instead Laugharne's contribution. Swanley was also upbraided for 'feasting and entertaining Mr [Roger] Lort a shipboard after his voluntarie coming in [to parliament's service]' in early 1644. Poyer's criticism culminated in an attack on the partiality of the Pembrokeshire county committee. For a 'farewell', Poyer 'bids defiance to his accusers in proving any disservice to the publick' on his part.

The *Relation* was evidently a mixture of exculpatory biography and incriminatory hatchet job. Its very existence demonstrates Poyer's need to get his version of recent events before the eyes of some powerful individuals in London while he was facing down attacks from Swanley and the Pembrokeshire committee. That he turned to print also suggests that Poyer wanted to lobby a wider audience than personal letters and briefs would allow. Further, it indicates his need to bypass John Eliot, the principal connection between Pembrokeshire and parliament, who controlled the flow of information from the far west into the political centre as county agent. Poyer's case thus has parallels with several other figures during the civil war such as the Devonshire colonel John Weare, who published an exculpatory tract in 1644 after having been accused of betraying the earl of Essex and assisting the royalists in the South West.[66] Like Poyer, Weare complained that he needed to 'vindicate my reputation' through print because of the 'aspertions cast upon me by the subtile enemy whose interest is the discord of friends'.[67] Along with evidence such as Laugharne's letter to Lenthall of 16 January 1646, publication of the *Relation* suggests a concerted effort by the 'Presbyterian' interest in Pembrokeshire to appeal to, and gain the support of, sympathetic elements within the parliamentary caucus. The *Relation* was likely an attempt to animate potential Presbyterian allies in parliament to support Poyer's claims for office and compensation, and also to begin investigating the war record of those who now controlled Pembrokeshire's county committee.

In this it evidently had some success, for at least one parliamentary newspaper seems to have picked up on the *Relation*. Ruminating on the revolt led by the former royalist Edward Carne in Glamorgan in late February 1646, the *Moderate Intelligencer* lamented how ex-royalists in south Wales (such as Roger Lort) had sought parliament's favour and been indulged and rewarded with office 'for reason of state'. But such indulgence, the newsbook went on, had simply produced results like the Glamorgan rising. It further argued that

> had all the true-hearted to the parliament, such as the major [i.e. mayor] of Pembroke, and others who had adventured all, and been constant from the first to last, been also encouraged, and the supreme authority in several places put into such mens hands, the revolt in all likelihood had not been.[68]

The argument about service and loyalty not being rewarded, as well as the problems of giving ex-royalists office, were clear echoes of Poyer's *Relation*. The newsbook went on to report how Laugharne had suppressed the Glamorgan rebels, concluding, 'thus are the poor-despised-constant-true-hearted again masters of their implacable enemies; our prayer is that now they may be incouraged, and not made up into a piece of Linsey Wolsey [i.e. a confused mixture of royalists and parliamentarians]'. These words would have been music to Poyer's ears and suggest the kind of response he was trying to generate: that parliament reward the few in Wales who had supported it from the beginning rather than relying on suspect gentlemen like Roger Lort whose loyalty to the cause was questionable at best.

Poyer's move into print may have been encouraged by the fact that, around this time, his associate Arthur Owen of Orielton was elected as Pembrokeshire MP in the place of John Wogan who had died in 1644.[69] Owen defeated the Lort candidate, Herbert Perrot, at the county hustings and Poyer may have seen this as the beginnings of a fightback by his 'side' in Pembrokeshire's intra-parliamentary feud. It is also the case that in early 1646 Rowland Laugharne was at the height of his influence and authority as he cleared south Wales of its royalist remnants and was lauded by parliament. The prominence of his ally must have encouraged Poyer's lobbying campaign.

Stung by Poyer's pamphlet and the response it received in at least some sections of the parliamentary press, John Eliot now went on the offensive by publishing a vituperative pamphlet of his own. The agent's text was entitled *An Answer in Just Vindication of Some Religious and Worthy*

Gentlemen of Pembrokeshire Against a Scandalous Pamphlet Published . . .
by one John Poyer, Late Mayor of Pembroke. Eliot did not announce his
authorship anywhere on the pamphlet, but his style and choice of subjects make it clear that he penned the work. In an address to the reader,
Eliot remarked how the text had been composed just three days after
sight of Poyer's *Relation*, but rumours that a second part was intended 'by
another hand', caused Eliot to pause publication. This projected sequel
never appeared, so Eliot thought it 'requisite no longer to defer the dis-
abusing of them that have seen and read the Relation'.[70] No clues are given
as to who this other 'hand' might have been, but one possibility is Arthur
Owen, the recently elected MP for Pembrokeshire.

Eliot's reply, as one might expect, challenged directly Poyer's claims
and essentially presented the *Relation* as a tissue of lies, a 'fardle of
untruths'. He attacked Poyer's low social rank as undermining the weight
and gravity of his testimony, before striking at each detail of his opponent's narrative. At every turn a different gloss was placed on events. Far
from Eliot having been one of the agents of Tenby's betrayal in 1643, for
example, here it was Poyer who had caused its fall. The mayor's insolence
and vaulting ambition, it was alleged, saw him rob the town of its ordnance
which he moved to Pembroke, thus leaving it easy prey for the earl of
Carbery who was able to take the town without resistance. Eliot described
this episode as 'the source and fountaine of that counties calamity and of
Poyers rising'. Thereafter, Eliot attempted to tar Poyer with the brush of
royalism, reproducing Pembroke's 'instrument' of October 1643, which
undertook to hold the town for the king, and which, Eliot maintained,
Poyer had signed. He sneered at Poyer's efforts to place himself at every
notable parliamentarian victory in the county, suggesting instead that
he was a coward who had remained safe behind Pembroke's walls while
others did the fighting. Eliot sought to exculpate himself, Roger Lort and
Thomas Bowen from Poyer's accusations of royalism. For example, while
he acknowledged that they did go to Oxford, it was only as prisoners, and
they were reviled and abused as 'Roundheads' in the royalist capital. He
was also keen, as he had been in his testimony before the Admiralty Court,
to restore Swanley to his rightful place as Pembrokeshire's liberator and
principal defender. Eliot bullishly maintained that 'Admirall Swanleys
arrival (whom the Relator [Poyer] slightly mentions here and disgracefully
elsewhere) was the prime instrumentall cause of the parliaments successes
in those parts'.

Eliot's pamphlet consistently emphasised Poyer's alleged moral and personal weaknesses; his supposed financial corruption; and his 'irreligion'. Throughout the piece Poyer was portrayed as a violent boor and a drunkard. Eliot, in an argument clearly designed to exonerate himself, alleged that few gentlemen took up residence in parliamentarian Pembroke because none 'could indure his [Poyer's] insolency'. Poyer was said to have eaten with Cavaliers on a fast day (the suspicion of his irreligion was never far below the surface) and to have drink 'himself and them drunk in a beastly manner'. Adjectives like 'arrogant', 'insolent' and 'tyrannous' were used to build up a picture of an unreliable man whom parliament should not trust with power or authority. Even more pervasive, however, were accusations of Poyer's corruption. This connected with the social critique of a low-born individual possessing no pedigree or estate, and thus bereft of the qualities needed to rule. Eliot wondered at the nature of Poyer's 'rise' and found it in the way he had fleeced the parliamentary state. He detailed myriad ways in which Poyer's 'indeavour . . . hath alwayes been to ingrosse plunder in all places to the advance of his private interest'. Here was a man 'who before these wars began had neither lands nor goods of value, [but who] now hath neer 400 head of cattell and is grown rich'. The terms used to describe Poyer were those employed in parliamentary discourse to describe royalists, such as 'plunderer' and 'freebooter'. Eliot revelled in details such as Poyer's selling corn destined for the garrison at Carew then billeting the soldiers on neighbouring inhabitants upon free quarter; his using his forces to carry off the resources of sequestered royalists; and his imprisonment and ransoming of locals who could afford to pay.

The pamphlet concluded with something of a flourish by including first-hand testimony from what looked like 'impartial' observers about Poyer's savage demeanour and impiety. Eliot reproduced damning testimony from two clergymen. One was Evan Roberts, 'a godly minister', who was probably the man appointed to preach at Llanbadarn Fawr near Aberystwyth in Cardiganshire by parliament's committee for plundered ministers in 1642.[71] In 1647 he would sign a petition alongside John Eliot and Richard Philipps as 'well affected' individuals plundered by the royalists, who requested monies from parliament to repair a damaged bridge across the River Teifi.[72] Roberts's story was, in fact, rather small beer, relating how he had been in a ferryboat coming to Pembroke during the war when Poyer had struck the boatman with his cane. When Roberts

attempted to upbraid him, Poyer had hit him also. The other clergyman
was Nathaniel Cradock. The pamphlet reproduces the order of November
1644 from the committee for plundered ministers appointing Cradock to
preach twice every Sunday in Pembroke and providing him with an £80
annual stipend. The order was signed by Roger Lort's associate in the
Commons, John White. We should note, too, that Craddock had, since
1622, been minister of Eglwys Cymmin in Carmarthenshire, which was
the possession of Sir Francis Annesley, Roger Lort's brother-in-law.[73] It
seems, then, that the Lort faction had intruded a 'godly and orthodox'
puritan divine into Poyer's backyard.[74] Knowing Poyer's attachment to
the Book of Common Prayer, they likely hoped that such a move would
challenge Poyer's religious message and his authority in the town more
generally. There was certainly friction between the cleric and the mayor.
Eliot reproduced Cradock's petition to the committee for plundered ministers which informed them that he had repaired to Pembroke just before
Gerard's invasion in April 1645. Cradock alleged that he had been met
with hostility on Pembroke's streets before Poyer reviled him as 'stinking rascall and stinking scab', pulling him off his horse and trampling
Cradock's hat under his horse's hooves. He detailed other abuses at Poyer's
hands which caused him to flee to London where he continued 'very
greatly disabled in body and mind'.

We must treat such tendentious evidence very carefully. In this narrative Poyer simply attacks Cradock for no reason. However, there was
probably some difference over religious worship in the town, or the status
of the committee which sponsored Cradock, that ignited the confrontation. Nonetheless, the image of Poyer beating a 'godly' cleric, holding him
at sword point and chasing him from the town was striking. Eliot would
recycle it whenever possible as a wonderful example of Poyer's arbitrary
rule, violent temper and contempt for godly religion.[75] Cradock's narrative
played into Eliot's broader thesis about Poyer's unfitness for office and also
the unreliability of his *Relation*. Indeed, Eliot's *Answer* formed the tem-
plate and provided the material for many of his subsequent publications
against Poyer, which were essentially variations upon claims he made here.
Drawing on testimony such as Cradock's as well as the litany of misdemeanours and excesses detailed in his text, Eliot rounded off his *Answer* by
declaring, '[N]ow let the world judge whether in these times of professed
and Covenanted reformation, this relator [Poyer] . . . be a man fit to have
any trust, power or authority over any who desire to be called Christians'.

The upshot of these paper skirmishes was inconclusive. Swanley's case against Poyer does not seem to have stuck. By his own account, Poyer 'was commanded to my charge' around the time of the Glamorgan rising in February 1646, which presumably meant he returned to act as governor of Pembroke.[76] For the most part the war between Poyer and his enemies seems to have turned cold for the next few months. We catch a glimpse of Poyer in a newsbook from August 1646 which described a report that 'the major [i.e. mayor] and governor of Pembroke is taking great care in fortifying that towne; he doth well in a fayre day to bestirre himselfe and to provide against a storme before it comes'.[77] The possible 'storme' referred to was probably the perceived threat from Ireland which remained a very real worry despite the fact that the civil war in England and Wales had ended. In the event, the 'storme' turned out to be Poyer's defence of the town and castle against his former parliamentary masters in 1648, and part of the reason for his rebelling was parliament's undermining the military authority of his ally Rowland Laugharne.

After the first civil war was over, the exhausted population expressed resentment against the continued existence of the parliamentary armies. They were expensive and associated in many minds with free quarter and arbitrary government. Parliament planned to reduce some of its forces to address these concerns, although the attempts to demobilise the New Model Army was fraught with difficulties because of soldiers' worries about arrears of pay and indemnity for their actions in the war. The reduction of the New Model was also problematic for the Independents, as a good deal of their power and influence came from their connections with the army. The Independents were, however, keen to reduce and remove smaller, so-called 'supernumerary', forces which did not come under the New Model's control.[78] One such force was that led by Laugharne. Dismantling this army would clearly strike a blow at Laugharne and Poyer's power base in south west Wales. The Lort–Eliot group had already attacked Laugharne's military authority through their associate, the Pembrokeshire sheriff William Phillips. In March 1646, Phillips had claimed in a letter to Speaker Lenthall that his authority was being undermined by Laugharne's troops, describing a 'great usurpation of the martiall power on the civill'.[79] There were growing signs, too, of the Lorts reaching out to the New Model and the Independents. In late 1646, for example, Roger Lort composed a book of Latin epigrams in which he lavished praise on the leader of the New Model Army, Sir Thomas Fairfax, while denigrating John Poyer as a rapacious lout.[80]

Lort and his associates, then, would have welcomed parliament's move to reduce Laugharne's forces in August 1646. This review concluded that most of Laugharne's troops should be sent to Ireland, while a small rump would be maintained to guard against any local royalist recalcitrants such as those who had troubled Glamorgan earlier in the year. If this plan was implemented, Laugharne (and Poyer) would be robbed of much of their authority in the area. As deliberations about reducing these forces continued, John Eliot in London made a submission to the Commons committee considering the issue. His paper noted that Laugharne had 600 horse and 1,400 foot, 'parte of them Englishe Irishe', in addition to the county trained bands. He maintained that this force should be slashed to a mere 200 horse. A final passage demonstrated the determinedly partisan nature of his proposal, arguing that if it was concluded that Pembroke and Tenby should continue as garrisons, then 'It's much desired that two comaunders with theire companies maie be sent downe to the said garrisons out of the armie of Sir Thomas Fairefax, that the county of Pembrock maie nott suffer as now it doth by the oppression and tirany of the governor'.[81] Eliot thus counselled that the New Model take control in Pembrokeshire, which would effectively emasculate and neutralise Laugharne as a political and military force. His submission clearly locates the Lort–Eliot group firmly within the Independent camp, and against the Presbyterians Laugharne and Poyer. The parting shot against 'the governor' was also revealing of the deep mistrust and resentment against Poyer which continued to colour the politics of post-war Pembrokeshire.

These proposals were not implemented at this time, but the question of reducing parliament's forces would return in the new year. Poyer, meanwhile stepped down as Pembroke's mayor in October 1646 after an unprecedented marathon term. He was succeeded by William Cozens, a prominent townsman of Pembroke whose political affiliations are unknown, but who was evidently an ally as he remained part of Pembroke's ruling council when Poyer ousted the duly elected incumbent in late 1648.[82] Laugharne and Poyer suffered a political blow in the latter part of 1646 with the earl of Essex's death. This almost certainly robbed the pair of an important ally in parliament and someone who might have helped them in their confrontation with the growing power of political Independency and the rise of the New Model Army in south Wales.[83]

Despite such setbacks, Poyer appears to have journeyed to London again in early 1647 in another effort to obtain his arrears. On 13 February he petitioned the House of Lords once more, describing himself as 'governor of the towne, garrison and castles of Pembrocke'.[84] In this detailed submission, Poyer described the 'many violent attempts' by Carbery and Gerard against Pembroke which had been met by Poyer's 'zeale to the publiq'. He now claimed to have raised, borrowed and spent £5,000 in parliament's service defending the town. He also maintained, and would later reiterate, that he also raised a troop of horse, two of dragoons and three foot companies for Laugharne's forces.[85] In an attempt to amplify his parliamentary service he conflated his military successes with those of Rowland Laugharne, as he seems to have done in his *Relation*, claiming to have been involved in the taking of Carmarthen, Cardigan and Laugharne.[86]

Poyer's persistence in petitioning demonstrates that he clearly felt he was owed significant compensation by parliament, and the tone of his petition does convey a sense of desperation and need. He maintained that he was 'utterly unable . . . to support himselfe, his wife and family', and described his and his family's 'distressed & lamentable estate'. Poyer had creditors to satisfy as well as his own empty pockets, and a sense of urgency and deprivation pervades his petition. He claimed to have 'never received any pay yet' from the parliament (this was because he had never received a commission) and asked, as he had in February 1645, that he might satisfy his arrears from delinquents' estates. Poyer evidently made a compelling case to the Lords, as his petition was 'specially recommended to the House of Comons'.[87] Despite having supporters in the Commons such as Arthur Owen, however, Poyer's claim for arrears fared no better than his request two years previously. The petition sank without trace, probably stymied by Poyer's Independent opponents in the Lower House.

Despite this setback, Poyer evidently had some support within the Commons, which still had a Presbyterian majority in early 1647, for he and Rice Powell were confirmed in March 1647 as governors of Pembroke and Tenby, respectively, despite Eliot's best efforts to have them removed.[88] Later, John Eliot would note that Poyer was never put out of his offices as he 'still had a party in the House [of Commons which] kept him in command'.[89] Much less encouraging, however, was a vote in parliament of April 1647 regarding Rowland Laugharne's military leadership. Although parliament confirmed Laugharne as commander of its forces in south Wales, the motion only passed by three votes. Moreover, it was decided to install a radical New Model officer, John Okey, as his effective second-in-command.[90] Evidently there were serious concerns among some in the Commons about Laugharne's authority, and it is telling that in the vote confirming him, those who acted as tellers for the 'yeas' were staunch Presbyterians (Sir William Lewis and Sir Philip Stapleton), while those for the 'noes' were Independents (Sir John Danvers and Henry Herbert). The split in parliament ramified into the provinces, and Laugharne's authority was becoming increasingly shaky as Independency and the New Model gained increasing political traction.

The threat to Laugharne's military autonomy must have caused Poyer considerable disquiet. His enemies in Pembrokeshire were lining up behind the Independent faction which supported punitive measures against the king, a radical overhaul of the Church and forms of religious worship, and the authority and rights of the New Model. This alliance threatened Poyer's liberty and livelihood. His opponents had shown few scruples about prosecuting him for his conduct during the war, and, despite the hysterical tone of some of Eliot's allegations, it was clear that Poyer had enough skeletons in the closet to make any investigation very uncomfortable indeed. It was thus deeply worrying for Poyer when the Lorts, operating through John Eliot in London, secured control of the Pembrokeshire sub-committee of accounts by mid-1647.[91] This effectively placed the apparatus of investigation and prosecution for wartime accounting in the hands of Poyer's sworn opponents. He, Laugharne, Powell and their Presbyterian allies, were losing ground rapidly to the Independents.

Poyer must have felt increasingly isolated and vulnerable in the face of the growing threat from those whom he had once faced down as royalist enemies. At some point in 1647, Poyer was brought before the central parliamentary committee of accounts, almost certainly upon a charge brought up from Pembrokeshire. He faced a demand for £6,000 of wartime receipts which, it was alleged, he had not accounted for.[92] Obviously he was unable to meet any such obligations and left the capital hastily. Such demands illustrate why Poyer became so keen to obtain indemnity for his actions during the war as an insurance policy against harassment by the Lorts. There was little sign that such indemnity could be obtained from either a local or central administration run by the Independents. Indeed, Poyer later wrote that the Lorts, along with John Eliot, 'combine[d] together that no indempnity should be granted me, as by their letters may appear'.[93] In September 1647, charges against Poyer regarding his wartime finances were presented at the army headquarters at Putney.[94]

Isolated, surrounded by enemies on all sides, implicated in massive financial wrongdoing and open to a multiplicity of actions which would ruin him and his family, while at the same time lacking the authority or power to fight back effectively, Poyer contemplated desperate measures. As we shall see in the next chapter, he eventually rebelled against the parliament he had once been so prominent in defending. This was obviously a drastic move, yet we can surely understand why he was driven to such extremes. A parliamentarianism of radical religion and political Independency adhered to by ex-royalists like Roger Lort and John Eliot was not the cause for which he had declared in 1642 and for which he had fought down to 1645. As the country grew increasingly restive about the direction in which parliamentary politics was heading, so Poyer found his local troubles meshing with wider concerns. As we shall see, his defiance of the Lorts snowballed into disobedience against the New Model Army, and Poyer quickly found himself at the centre of a nationwide resistance to parliamentary rule which has become known as the Second Civil War.

CHAPTER 5

The Road to Rebellion, August 1647–March 1648

The ascendancy of Poyer's enemies left him bitter, frustrated and vulnerable. He had been parliament's most steadfast supporter in south Wales but was now facing marginalisation and ruin because of his opponents' capacity to make fruitful links with the Independents and the New Model. Although Poyer's particular circumstances were unique, he was far from alone in his frustrations. Widespread disappointment about the lack of settlement with the king and the absence of any visible peace dividend combined with disillusionment about the growing power of the Independents in many parts of the kingdom.[1] Poyer's case was thus emblematic of a much larger constituency, among both defeated royalists and frustrated parliamentary moderates, who looked with baffled alarm at the direction of politics in the latter half of 1647.

There were many causes of resentment between 1646 and 1648, which produced a society full of simmering resentment and hostility. Important among these was the sense that all the bloodshed and hardship of the war years had achieved no concrete gains; no viable settlement of the kingdom was in prospect, and many grew concerned that no such settlement would be possible with intransigent Independents in control of the process. People also grew increasingly resentful at the heavy taxes which were still being levied upon them to support the New Model Army.[2] Indeed, many asked why there needed to be an army at all given that there was no longer any war to fight. There was a widespread desire to return to established ways in government and the Church. Many were also concerned about the king's treatment: kept under house arrest by parliament, it seemed that he was being treated as a pawn in a game of factional politics. A large constituency wished instead to see him restored to his rightful role at the top of the social and political pyramid, but there was little evidence that this was an immediate prospect. The settlement of the Church also seemed an insoluble problem. While parliament had been active in removing clergymen who were seen as insufficiently godly, it was much less successful in building up the New Jerusalem which had been envisaged in the early 1640s. Although parliament was in theory committed to instituting a Presbyterian settlement along Scottish lines under the terms of the Solemn League and Covenant of 1643, in fact this project was stillborn and failed to take off outside a few enclaves. A sense of spiritual desolation and abandonment thus accompanied concerns about ongoing political instability. There was, moreover, a deep disquiet in many quarters about the rise of radical religious sects which appeared to embrace devotional anarchy rather than offering spiritual consolation.[3] Such concerns about 'sectarians' were closely connected to anxieties regarding the growing power and confidence of the New Model Army, which was seen as a breeding ground for disturbing new religious opinions. As a reaction against these trends, the year 1647 saw something of a revival of 'Anglicanism' or outlawed prayer book worship, as many religious moderates attempted to resuscitate pre-war forms of piety.[4]

The continued rule of parliament's county committees, such as that dominated by the Lorts in Pembrokeshire, was also resented in many quarters.[5] Such bodies were intrusions of (an often hated) central government into the provinces, and were frequently seen as instruments of a radical political and religious clique populated by upstarts from outside the traditional circles of the ruling elite. Attacks on the county committees, on radical religious elements, on the New Model, and on the Independents in parliament and the provinces, all promoted a volatile political atmosphere.

All of these problems and resentments can be seen in Pembrokeshire, of course, and many of them can be traced through John Poyer's own experiences. His, however, was an unusual case of a committed parliamentary servant being frozen out and harried by opponents who, in outward show at least, had made the remarkable transition from royalists to Independents.[6] As we saw in the last chapter, Poyer's position by mid-1647 had become increasingly precarious. He was facing a determined set of antagonists who held significant advantages in their control of local government. Poyer remained governor of Pembroke, however, while his colleague Rowland Laugharne was still head of the local military, although his autonomy was shrinking in the face of New Model encroachment. The Pembrokeshire committee of accounts' investigation into the £6,000 which Poyer supposedly owed the state appears to have been a critical development. Not only this, after he returned to Pembrokeshire from a hearing before the central committee in mid-1647, Poyer seems to have become genuinely afraid that the Lorts intended not just to ruin him, but to take his life. In his *Vindication* published in 1649, Poyer wrote that at his coming to Pembrokeshire, 'the Lorts did set upon me severall times in the high-way, [and] likewise attempted to have murthered me in the Church'.[7] He repeated these claims elsewhere, alleging 'severall plots . . . to murder him in the Church at sermon time', and also described his life as 'thristed [thirsted] after, by men of bloude'.[8] While he likely exaggerated these threats, their repetition in several different contexts argues that Poyer truly feared for his safety. He decided to get his retaliation in first.

In August 1647, a parliamentarian tax collector in Hereford wrote to a correspondent about the political situation in and around south Wales. He had received a report from Pembrokeshire, and described how 'the Lortes are ymprisonde by the maior of Pembroke upon pretence of some plotte against him, but declares not the particulars as farre as I could learne when I was upon my iourney thither a fortnight since'.[9] All three of the Lort brothers had been arrested and imprisoned by Poyer. The letter also references a 'plotte' against Poyer, which supports his later claims that the Lorts had conspired to do him harm. It is noteworthy, however, that the writer suspected that the plot might have been a pretext for Poyer to move against the Lorts, and the possibility that he was manufacturing a crisis to justify a pre-emptive strike cannot be discounted.

An editorial in a newsbook from January 1648, which was composed by John Eliot, described how the Lort brothers were kept for '44 hours without as much as bread or water [and] were compelled to ly on the wet ground in an open place; and not suffered as much as straw to ly upon'.[10] The veracity of this report, of course, is difficult to establish, particularly as it was made long after the events and during the initial stages of Poyer's revolt against parliamentary authority. However, it does confirm the substance of the tax collector's letter from August 1647, and it seems likely that the editorial's additional claim that Poyer held the Lorts as prisoners, presumably in Pembroke Castle, for nearly a month, is true. Moreover, it is telling that a pamphlet published by Eliot after Poyer's rising had been defeated, dated the beginning of 'the late insurrection' to August 1647. The Lorts's arrest was the beginning of his road to rebellion.[11]

The Lorts's detention was an act borne of desperation rather than of strength. The plan may have been to neutralise them while Poyer launched his own attack on their nefarious dealings when they were effectively silenced. If this was the case, however, no trace of such an effort has survived. Eliot suggested that Poyer was hoping to squeeze money out of the Lorts, which seems unlikely, but, given the parlous state of his finances, it may be that he was trying to have his huge alleged debts to the state written off. Rather than receiving any financial or political benefit from this manoeuvre, however, Poyer instead obtained further evidence of his opponents' connections to the New Model Army. No less a figure than Sir Thomas Fairfax, commander-in-chief of the New Model, sent a messenger to Pembroke demanding that Poyer deliver up the brothers. Poyer refused to obey this direct order, which was a momentous move.[12] This action placed him in open opposition to his military superior, although Poyer probably saw his military authority as autonomous and separate from the New Model. Nevertheless, rejecting Fairfax's order identified Poyer as a rebel and set him on a path of stark choices: either he triumphed over his enemies or he faced his undoing. According to Eliot, the judges who sat on the local assize circuit enticed Poyer to Haverfordwest with assurances of protection, but then detained him until he agreed to release the Lorts, which, ultimately, he did.

As the troubled year of 1647 came to a close, so the storm clouds darkened for Poyer and also for his military and political confrères Rowland Laugharne and Rice Powell. In late December 1647, parliament made a final resolution to disband Laugharne's forces. Laugharne was a prominent Presbyterian sympathiser who had even been talked of as a leader of London's militia committee when, in the summer of 1647, it had contemplated a possible face-off with the army which was then considering a march on London.[13] He was clearly viewed with suspicion by the New Model hierarchy.[14] Disbandment was a troubling development for moderates like Poyer, but perhaps even more distressing was the fact that the commissioners parliament appointed in December 1647 to oversee parliamentary finance in Pembrokeshire, and who would clearly audit Laugharne and Poyer, were drawn entirely from Roger Lort's circle.[15] This put a devastating weapon into the hands of Poyer's enemies and they were hardly inclined to generosity. Yet even as these appointments were being passed in the Commons, it became apparent that Poyer was making preparations for armed resistance; whether he considered this to be primarily resistance against his local enemies or against the New Model is unclear.

In a letter sent to the senior New Model officer in south Wales, Colonel Thomas Horton, dated 24 December 1647, Roger Lort described how Poyer had already 'got many of his own and other captains companyes to be retainers to him in . . . [Pembroke] castle; by which meanes (though some of his bullyes have rellinquished him) his numbar is increased to forty'.[16] Clearly Poyer was making preparations to resist any attempt to force him to resign his command. Most accounts only see Poyer moving into open resistance in mid-January 1648, but matters were evidently in train before then. The letter also indicates that the decision to place the process of disbandment essentially in the hands of the Lorts and their allies had been the final straw. Lort's letter described how Poyer was stock-piling arms in Pembroke Castle and buying provisions for his men and was supposedly invoking Fairfax's orders for doing so. Lort wished to have Horton's authority to use force for stopping supporters joining him, thus 'preventing his further rebellion'. Lort also intimated that the plan was to bring Poyer to obedience 'in a more privat way', but that if this failed, 'we humbly desire he may be . . . proclaimed [a] rebell, that it may be lawfull for the country to resist him and his, and defend themselves'. In addition to his entertaining his troops with food and drink, Poyer was also said to be 'feeding himself and them with hopes of a new warr, or (if peace happen) with an act of oblivion'. Because of the general dissatisfaction with the direction of parliamentary policy and the king's negotiating an alliance with the Scots, many were predicting that a new war would shortly begin. Given his confrontation with the Lorts and opposition to religious and political Independency, it is unsurprising that Poyer would line up against the New Model. Yet, as we have seen, he also had important reasons for wishing the slate to be wiped clean, for his own and his men's indemnity. Lort's mention of 'oblivion' reminds us of Poyer's desire to be freed from the spectre of prosecution for his activities as mayor and governor of Pembroke between 1643 and 1646. Although war was in the air in December 1647, Poyer's desperate course in securing Pembroke Castle was also partly about trying to escape the shadow of the first civil war which hung darkly over himself, his family and his followers.

Poyer was not only preparing a military defence of Pembroke but had also executed something of a *coup d'état* in the town's government. The mayor elected in October 1647 was Matthew Bowen, a supporter of Poyer's petition to parliament for assistance in March 1645.[17] However, he evidently opposed Poyer's increasingly desperate actions in late 1647, and Eliot recounts that Poyer had 'deposed him'.[18] This is confirmed by the stray survival of a minute from the town's council meeting of 15 December 1647 which was signed by 'John Poyer, maior'.[19] Moreover, at this meeting it was resolved that Bowen should be 'excluded and putt forth of the counsel . . . for divers contempts'. Evidently Bowen had been removed by Poyer, who had seized control of the mayoralty so that he could resist the Lorts and disbandment.

It was probably at around this time, perhaps shortly before Roger Lort's letter to Thomas Horton, that John Eliot and Sir Richard Philipps of Picton Castle, as members of the Pembrokeshire committee, submitted a set of grievances against John Poyer to General Thomas Fairfax.[20] These offered a comprehensive attack on Poyer's current and historical actions as Pembroke's governor, and were likely designed to help convince Fairfax to send forces down to west Wales and curb his excesses. Eliot and Philipps described how Poyer, without any authority, had deployed a troop of horse to seize enemies and ransom them (a possible reference to the Lorts); that he took sequestered land from the committee and 'converted itt to his owne use'; and that he refused to appear before the Committee of Accounts. More troublingly, they confirmed Roger Lort's reports of Poyer's military preparations. He had returned from London, they said, and 'fortified himselfe in Pembrock towne & castle and manie of the well affected suspect him to have some dandgerous [sic] designe in hande'. He was also said to be issuing warrants for provisioning the castle and, if former experience held, he would extract it by violence if any refused. Eliot threw in further points about Poyer's drunkenness and his beating Nathaniel Cradock and Evan Roberts for good measure. This was certainly a disturbing submission in the nervous political climate of late 1647. It confirmed that Poyer was making unauthorised military preparations after returning to Pembrokeshire and suggested that his detention of the Lorts presaged something much more sinister.

Through such representations, then, the New Model high command were informed of Poyer's recalcitrance and Fairfax sent down Adjutant General Christopher Fleming to replace him as governor of Pembroke and to disband his forces. Fleming arrived at Pembroke in early January but, despite summoning the castle, Poyer refused to render it up or to appear at army headquarters in Windsor. He later claimed that he had granted Fleming possession of the town, but evidently had refused to surrender the castle; a tactic which he had probably used before in his battle with royalist insurgents in 1644.[21] According to his own narrative, however, Poyer offered to surrender if he received satisfaction for his 'disbursements, arreares and indempnity'.[22] Presumably Fleming had no authority to negotiate terms, but such an offer of immediate surrender if he could secure assurances of indemnity and compensation chimes with Poyer's public statements since 1645. His account should also give us pause in seeing Poyer as having resolved on a course of royalist resistance at this stage. He was, it seems, focused rather on the same grievances which had been animating him for nearly two years. Poyer's 'rebellion' had its origins in an army mutiny.

Fleming's summons was Poyer's Rubicon, and, despite his later protestations that he had no desire to offend parliament or the army, he crossed it without a backward glance. Poyer's recalcitrance was reported in the London press, which included an editorial intervention, from army headquarters at Windsor. This was an adapted version of the 'Grievances' against Poyer which Eliot and Philipps had submitted to Fairfax shortly before.[23] The edition of a title called *Heads of Chiefe Passages in Parliament* for the week ending 19 January 1648, described Poyer's opposition in Pembroke, but also dilated on his detaining of the Lort brothers the previous August; his beating of Nathaniel Cradock and Evan Roberts (although there was no mention of the fact that these incidents had occurred in 1645); and the fact that he 'is seldom or never sober, but continually drunk in the afternoon, and a great swearer and a stiffe maintainer of the Booke of Common-prayer'.[24] Eliot also related that Poyer had recently imprisoned the rightful mayor, Matthew Bowen, as well as Bowen's predecessor, William Hinton, and was plundering the people of Pembroke and the surrounding countryside to support his renegade soldiers. Interestingly, Eliot's piece also indicates that Poyer's cause had generated a good deal of sympathy since Roger Lort's letter of 24 December. The newsbook editorial observed that recently Poyer had only had thirty-six supporters in the Castle (a figure Eliot probably obtained from Roger Lort) but that he was now 'about 200' men strong.[25] This media intervention was something akin to 'black propaganda', designed to besmirch Poyer's name, highlight the Lorts's sufferings, and generally align the Lorts with the army's cause.

In his newspaper piece, Eliot also provides some insight into why Poyer undertook these desperate measures, noting that New Model forces would shortly be sent to take possession of Pembroke and adding that 'its hoped that he [Poyer] shall have no quarter upon articles, but . . . be left to the law, to receive a condigne punishment, the gallows'.[26] Poyer's claims that the Lorts and their allies were seeking his blood were perhaps not so paranoid after all. If this was the kind of 'justice' Poyer could expect locally, it was little wonder he was driven to such extremes. Indeed, Poyer would later claim that he was prepared to obey Fairfax's order, and was about to leave for the army headquarters, but the Lorts, fearing that he would appeal directly to Fairfax, sent out warrants to have him apprehended. They then proclaimed him traitor, which caused Poyer to retreat to the castle for his own protection.[27] This self-serving narrative is deeply suspect and there is little sign that Poyer seriously considered journeying to London. Nonetheless, the view that it was dangerous for Poyer to leave the castle and enter essentially hostile terrain controlled by the Lorts seems credible.

On the last day of January 1648, the Derby House Committee, the body which provided parliamentary oversight and coordination in military matters, sent a letter to Fairfax. They passed on a petition which discussed the 'state of Pembrooke Castle', which, 'besides the mischiefe to the well affected of the towne . . . may give beginning to a greate inconvenience'.[28] The petition Fairfax received was unlikely to have been a dispassionate account of the current situation, however: it was written by John Eliot.[29] Eliot's role in providing parliament and the army with intelligence about the situation in Pembrokeshire, as seen in this petition and his presence at Windsor in January 1648, provides clear evidence of the Lort faction's success in assimilating themselves within the structures of the Independent state. It also indicates the difficulties Poyer must have faced in communicating his version of events in Pembrokeshire to his parliamentary masters. Poyer later complained that Eliot's 'active solicitacion and false informacon' ensured that parliament either never saw, or that they ignored, his 'just requests', and were instead persuaded that he was a dangerous rebel.[30] Eliot was a formidable political operator and the evidence suggests that his activities in London helped poison parliament against Poyer. In its letter of 31 January, the Derby House Committee asked that Fairfax provide forces 'to the assistance of the besieging of Pembrooke Castle'.[31]

So Poyer was already facing down a siege which was evidently being maintained by the Lort brothers and by elements of the local militia who had refused to join Poyer.[32] Fairfax authorised the dispatch of 200 men from the Gloucester garrison.

It was perhaps around this point, then, that Roger Lort wrote another letter to a senior New Model officer, once more probably Colonel Thomas Horton.[33] The letter is undated and is difficult accurately to place in the chronology of events, but it seems to have been written prior to the appearance of a significant New Model force in Pembroke and while a new summons from Fairfax was anticipated. In the letter, Lort reported how 'the chiefe officers of the soldier[s] here are very reall in the buisness of reducing Poyer'. He continued that he and his allies had reported in the country that a new summons for Poyer's appearance at army headquarters was forthcoming 'to take off any suspicion of any warrant for his apprehension'. Fascinatingly, Lort requested that if any new summons for Poyer came then he and his allies should be allowed to publicise it 'to the end Poyers soldiers may be undeceived of the opinion they have that what he does is by order from his excellency [Fairfax]'. He further claimed that Poyer had forged letters as being sent to him from the Lord General and then 'read them to his bullyes as if they were really soe'. It is difficult to know how truthful such claims were, but the suggestion that Poyer's troops were wholly duped in this manner seems far-fetched. Nonetheless, the fact that he might not have been telling the whole truth is very plausible. This is not enough, however, to claim that Poyer's rebellion was built on deception and a group of gullible locals. Lort's letter does, nonetheless, cause problems for our easy understanding of Poyer's revolt as unproblematically royalist. Indeed, there is very little indication in these early stages of his defiance of any obvious royalist strain at all. While many in the kingdom were eager to see the king restored and were aware of his intrigues with the Scottish Covenanters to regain his throne, there is a sense that, at its inception, Poyer's disobedience was largely directed against his local enemies. While this had an ideological edge, its royalist character remained submerged beneath an accumulation of personal grievance and anti-army sentiment.

On 3 February, the Commons resolved to once again demand that Poyer give up his command. The letter was composed by Robert Scawen, a key architect of the new modelling of the army and chair of the influential Army Committee, and signed by Speaker Lenthall.[34] In addition to demanding Poyer's compliance, this letter apparently also contained an assurance of safe passage to army headquarters 'with promise of mediation for his arrears'. However, it was also made clear to Poyer that 'if he refuseth this order . . . he [Fairfax] will proceed against him [Poyer] as an enemy'.[35] Poyer's resistance was beginning to catch the eye of the national press in London. One newsbook of early February noted the need for 'honest men' to act as sheriffs, especially in Wales where Poyer's opposition to Fairfax and parliament demonstrated the problems godly rule faced in that country. The author added, ominously, 'some will be made examples and pay deere for their mischievous practices'.[36] A later issue reported that 'Poyers men are all Levellers and the governours voyce but one . . . where the poorest souldiers joyns interest'.[37] This was more satire and scaremongering than reportage, although it does suggest a recognition that Poyer and his men were operating together closely. The newsbook continued, however, that they would yield to the besiegers 'and never dispute the matter whether they be malignants or Roundheads'. Although there was no substance to this report, nevertheless it does suggest the fluid political categories at this early point in Poyer's resistance, with the Pembrokeshire men supposedly undecided on their royalist or parliamentarian status. Poyer was recognised, probably nationally, as a trusted parliamentary servant, so had he now become a royalist? Such questions demonstrate the problems contemporaries (and later historians) have had with labelling and identifying Poyer's political motives at this point.

At the same time, and offering a sign of things to come for Poyer and his followers, a resurgent stable of royalist publications had also begun to take an interest in Poyer's resistance and looked to recruit him to the king's standard.[38] In mid-February 1648, for example, one royalist publication described how the parliament

> care not a pinne for those that heretofore have done them the best service, shaking them off with a fine policy, not only without their pay, but also with scorne and contempt . . . But Captain Poyer is resolved not to loose all, and to make them and their Generall Tom [Fairfax] know that he will not loose all, and hangeth out a bloody flag of defiance, and is revolved none shall open to him but he that beareth a golden key.[39]

This fascinating report shows an awareness of Poyer's loyal service to the parliamentary cause as well as some of the grievances over pay which were causing him (and others in the kingdom) to defy his former masters. His 'bloody flag of defiance' was certainly not set out in vivid royalist colours at this point, but it was highly tempting for royalist supporters to suggest that it was; an enemy's enemy travelled a short distance in 1648 to become a friend. The implication seems perhaps to have been that Poyer would only allow those who compensated him for his arrears to gain entry to Pembroke. Such sympathetic noises from royalist supporters perhaps helped Poyer to decide in the spring of 1648, when his bridges with parliament had been burned, that he would find a sympathetic home among royalist supporters; indeed, that his political credo was perhaps best represented by their interests.

While his defiance was clearly not unproblematically 'royalist', Poyer nonetheless continued his policy of non-compliance. After receiving parliament's second summons to surrender Pembroke, on 22 February Poyer sent a letter to governor-elect Fleming.[40] This was apparently after a period in which Poyer had claimed 'illiteracy' after receiving the summons and had then delayed his response for several days, a tactic which was interpreted by some as 'little better than an absolute denyall'.[41] Poyer did, however, eventually draft a reply, albeit one which justified his defiance while trying to suggest that he was, in fact, willing to comply; in other words, it was paradoxical and unconvincing. Poyer maintained that he and the 'sowldiers' in the garrison would 'lay downe their armes and march forth presently' if their arrears were paid in full. However, they also demanded assurances of indemnity which had not been received.[42] Poyer himself suggested that he would obey Fairfax's commands and travel to Windsor or the capital, but the offer of his personal arrears was 'to[o] little to fitt me for my iourney', and that he did not know how long any stay in London would be. Poyer was raising the ongoing grievance of his crippling arrears, but he was also prevaricating by introducing questions of the cost of travel and the length of his stay in London (although he was surely sensible to be concerned about his own possible detention there). He finished with a passage that is worth quoting in full as it provides something of an insight into Poyer's mind and motivations at this time when he must have been under enormous personal strain:

> For my owne parte . . . I covet noe mans goods, his howse or castle much les[s] any mans life, as mine is thristed [thirsted] after by men of bloude. My desire is to live quietly, my owne shall give me content, and hee that

gapeth after the sweate of my labours and to take the bread foorth of my
wife & childrens mouthes in opinion is but a verie collerick complection.

This passage needs to be read in the light of Poyer's conviction that the
Lorts and John Eliot were bent on his destruction and coveted his money
and property. The disjointed and somewhat confused prose indicates a
degree of mental stress, and Poyer's fears, not just for his own life but for
those of his wife and children, suggest the profound threats he perceived
in his enemies' designs.

A significant problem for Poyer, however, was that Fleming was being
hosted and probably fed information by the Lorts. The day following
Poyer's letter, Fleming appeared alongside the Lorts as signatory to a letter from the Pembrokeshire committee to Speaker Lenthall.[43] The letter
described 'Collonel Poyers endeavours to begin a new warr' by fortifying and victualling his troops in Pembroke, and also his summoning the
country 'who are ever readye to obey him'. The committee requested
'speedy orders for his reducement' and military assistance to secure
Milford Haven, which 'lyes too open to forreigne forces whoe may give
him [Poyer] encouragment'. The 'foreign' force referred to was surely
anticipated royalist support from Ireland. It is noteworthy that the committeemen believed that the country was sympathetic to Poyer. This argues
that his stance was perceived in Pembrokeshire not simply as one of personal grievance but that it had a wider resonance. It seems reasonable to
suggest that Poyer's defiance acted as a focus for resentments about the
rise of political and religious radicals in a region where parliamentarianism
had always been a minority sport.

In addition to its content, the letter's signatories are also worth comment. The three Lort brothers affixed their names, as did Fleming. Also
present, however, were three Pembroke men. One was Richard Browne,
a mercer, who had formerly supported Poyer.[44] A second was Matthew
Bowen, the man whom Poyer had recently ousted as Pembroke's mayor.[45]
The third Pembroke man was Captain Walter Cuny, another prominent
townsman who had supported Poyer during the first civil war, but who
had evidently found his disobedience to parliament too much to stomach
(although he would soon fall out with his fellow signatory Roger Lort).[46]
These men's presence on the letter indicates that Poyer had alienated an
important section of the town's oligarchy which had supported him in his
struggles against Carbery and Gerard. His resistance had split Pembroke's

governing body as men like Cuny and Bowen balked at the treacherous waters Poyer now sought to navigate.

The committee's letter reached parliament on 2 March. The Commons responded by drawing up an ordinance.[47] The ordinance mentioned Poyer's 'contempts and disobedience' in continuing to hold Pembroke Castle by force, 'to the prejudice of the public peace and the endangering of a new war'. As a result, parliament gave Poyer a final warning. If he had not surrendered the castle within twelve hours of receiving the ordinance, 'then Col. Poyer and all that shall adhere to him are hereby declared traitors and rebels', and Fairfax was required to reduce the castle by force and bring Poyer 'and his adherents to justice'.[48]

The Pembrokeshire committee's letter occasioned some discussion in the press. One newspaper which had carried items by John Eliot before, discussed the character of Pembroke's governor in terms that once again carried Eliot's fingerprints. It described Poyer as having been mayor for the town 'since the beginning of these wars', and a man 'famous for enduring no rivall and contending with those that were for parliament in those parts, as well as having held the Castle of Pembroke for the King, Parliament, or for himself'. It dilated on the great importance of Milford Haven for the kingdom's security and, ruminating on Poyer's rejection of Fairfax's summons, argued that Poyer, 'having so long ruled . . . hath forgot to obey'.[49] Another report noted how Poyer expected 'assistance from the disbanded souldiers belonging lately to Major General Langhorn, with which souldiers, it is said that he daily holds intelligence'.[50] Another noted that Laugharne's recently disbanded 'supernumerary forces' had 'expressed some discontent', and that there had been a meeting of some 800 soldiers about the current situation. Although this meeting dispersed, 'it is thought that they hold correspondency with Col. Poyer'.[51] This was a troubling development for parliament as Poyer's opposition threatened to spread beyond Pembroke and sweep up discontented and disgruntled soldiers drawn from across south-west Wales.[52]

The soldiers' sympathy for Poyer is perhaps unsurprising. Poyer and Laugharne's forces had operated together throughout the war, while the two leaders were connected by marriage, had been long-time allies in adversity, were disgruntled at their treatment by parliament, and were identified with the 'Presbyterian' interest. It also seems that Arthur Owen, Pembrokeshire's MP and Poyer and Laugharne's ally, had endeavoured to keep Laugharne's supernumerary forces together, most probably as a bulwark against the New Model, but had been crossed by John Eliot who 'indeavoured what in him lay' to have the men demobilised.[53] Clearly, then, the disbanding of Laugharne's army had become a deeply partisan affair, and it is evident, given their shared history, that the soldiers' sympathies would lie with those opposing Eliot and the Lorts. As Laugharne himself later wrote, apparently to the commissioners for disbandment who were entirely composed of the Lorts and their allies, his soldiers could not 'expect much favour in our disbanding, knowing some of you have constantly designed our ruine from the begining & rather affected to their owne ends in promoting a faction then any way reflecting uppon the publique good'.[54] It seems that parliament attempted to head off problems with Laugharne's forces when news of Poyer's disobedience became widely known. On 6 January 1648, Fairfax wrote to Speaker Lenthall supporting a petition Laugharne had submitted to the Commons and praising the Major General's 'deportment . . . in obedience unto your commands' and 'faithfull service'.[55] This was probably the petition which survives among Lenthall's papers in which Laugharne requested £5,000 'to redeeme his engaged credit & supply of his present necessities', and which also discussed his soldiers' 'very great arreares & extreme want'.[56] This was the second time Fairfax had written to the Speaker, so his earlier entreaty had evidently been ignored. Although Laugharne's own case does not seem to have received much attention, the petition and Fairfax's letter may have motivated the Army Committee on 12 January 1648 to authorise the substantial payment of £2,500 for disbanding the south Wales forces.[57] This only represented two months' pay, however, and the soldiers claimed they were thirty months in arrears.[58] Such a small sum, then, probably inflamed their resentments rather than assuaged them.

There had evidently already been a significant rendezvous of soldiers in the county, although it is impossible to know how accurate the reported figure of 800 men was. This nonetheless represented a serious threat and a possible escalation of Poyer's resistance. Indeed, there were even reports that the governor and garrison at Conway Castle in distant Caernarvonshire were refusing to disband unless they were satisfied with full arrears 'as Pembrocke Castle does & as Laughornes regiment in Wales'.[59] As reports circulated against them in the press, Laugharne's ex-officers sent a petition to Fairfax on 1 March, which he forwarded to parliament three days later.[60] Among the signatories was Colonel Rice Powell, governor of Tenby, who would shortly join Poyer as one of the leaders of the south Wales revolt. The officers declared that they were 'iustly agreived at a malitious aspersion lately published in print uniustly tainting the honor of the Maior Generall and all his forces as ready to ioyne with Poyer'. By contrast, they maintained that Laugharne had sent them express orders to submit quietly to their disbandment. Although they stressed their loyalty, their petition nonetheless stressed their discontent about 'receiveinge lesse satisfaction by way of pay than any army in the kingdome'. Moreover, they focused their anger on the apparent author of the publication which had so offended them: John Eliot. They demanded that Eliot justify his accusations about their correspondence with Poyer or make reparation. They then attacked him as having been a royalist and a man who sought to 'defame all those who have ever truly & faithfully served the parliament'. The petitioners also criticised Eliot's 'usurped agency' in London. Such comments could have come from Poyer's own pen and are suggestive of the common enemies and common grievances which obtained among both Poyer's and Laugharne's forces.

Eliot rushed a defence against the petitioners into print under the title *A Just Vindication on the Behalf of Iohn Eliot, Esq.* He began by lamenting that nothing 'more saddens the hearts of honest men than to be unworthily traduced with false suggestions presented with a colour of truth'.[61] Eliot defended the publication (as yet unidentified) which occasioned the officers' response. He stood by its claims that Rice Powell had been requested by Thomas Horton to assist those besieging Pembroke (probably the Lorts), but that he 'did absolutely refuse it'.[62] Furthermore, Eliot claimed to have seen a letter from Fleming to Fairfax in which the Adjutant General had written, 'I finde that some of Major Generall Laughornes forces are of Poyers councell, and great hopes he hath of making his party good against any power'. Eliot also maintained that these officers had not quietly disbanded as had other companies in south Wales, but rather had drawn their forces to Tenby and begun to fortify the town where they 'mutter that they will declare for the king'.[63] Clearly, Pembrokeshire contained many restive ex-soldiers whose sympathies were with Laugharne and perhaps also with Poyer. It was also clear that Eliot was aware of serious trouble brewing because of the common grievances among and affinities between the demobilised soldiers and those holding out in Pembroke's garrison.

The ultimatum in the shape of the parliamentary ordinance arrived at Pembroke on 13 March 1648. Poyer's resolve to resist the party of Eliot and the Lorts remained unshaken, however, and he returned a defiant answer to this final summons.[64] He claimed to have read the ordinance to the soldiers of the Pembroke garrison who responded by demanding their arrears and assurances of indemnity. He himself requested 'my disbursements paid and my arrears, as other officers, according to my place and time of my service'. If such recompense was not forthcoming, however, Poyer assured them that he and his men were resolved 'to hold the castle for the king and parliament, according to the Covenant by us taken, untill such time that our arrears, disbursments and indemnity be assured us'. The construction he used here requires further analysis. Poyer was invoking the Solemn League and Covenant taken by parliament's adherents as a test of their loyalty following the conclusion of a treaty with the Scots in 1643. Thus, this was still not a declaration of red-blooded royalism which some have read into Poyer's resistance to parliament as early as January 1648. Declaring 'for king and parliament' would become something of a royalist badge in 1648, but it was also, of course, the form used in the earliest defences of parliamentarianism, although it had fallen from favour.[65] Poyer's language which combined 'king and parliament' with 'Covenant' thus looked back to the kind of moderate parliamentarian position he had held when facing down the earl of Carbery in 1643. Poyer seems to be mixing political formulations, ones which can best be rendered as politically Presbyterian rather than thoroughly royalist.

Also interwoven within his response was a set of personal grievances and concerns which have confused later commentators who see Poyer as essentially motivated by self-interest.[66] This is a mistake. His resistance was not simply about money (although it was partly about money); it was, more profoundly, about justice and safety for himself, his men and his family. Elsewhere, Poyer observed that justice against royalist enemies, adequate remuneration for long and dangerous service and indemnity against malicious prosecution for actions undertaken during the war had been at the core of the New Model's demands in 1647.[67] He wanted nothing more than they did. In this response to parliament's ordinance, he assured them that he and his men placed their trust in the Lord, and that, if blood were spilled, God would judge between he who 'seeks another mans life to enjoy what is his right, or that man that stands in defence to save what is his'. As in his earlier statements, we see Poyer's concern about the Lorts's interest in seizing his estate and ruining his life *despite* his own faithful adherence to the cause which contrasted so sharply with their political vacillation and apostasy. Poyer's language thus echoed that of the Levellers and the New Model agitators in demanding rights for himself and his men after their loyal service, and also in its mixing of scripture with more earthly demands.

The key difference between Poyer and the New Model, of course, was that their visions of the political and religious cause they were defending were radically dissimilar. Poyer lamented that he and his men had 'bestowed our times to good purpose at last to be proclaimed traytors and rebels for demanding our own; and no more but what your self and those mercenaries desire that you have brought to murder us, and to take bread forth of the mouthes of our wives and children'. He highlighted the similarity of his cause with the New Model's in that they both demanded merely what was due to them. However, the New Model was being corrupted by the Lorts and Eliot who, in a recurring theme in Poyer's writings which deserve to be taken more seriously than they have been, he was convinced wished to murder him and ruin his family.

Poyer concluded his response by invoking the Book of Samuel: 'As David spake to Saul when he hungered after his life, "The Lord be judge between us", whose heavenly protection I am assured'. This was an apposite text and helps reveal Poyer's thinking. It is taken from a passage in which Saul, who has unjustly sought David's death, is confronted by his enemy. David asks why Saul listens to those who try to convince him that David wishes him harm. David had confronted Saul in the hope that he would reveal the truth and engender a change of heart. David also maintains 'there is neither evil nor rebellion in my hand' and adds that if Saul wishes to take his life then he should, but that the Lord will judge between them and will ultimately avenge the wronged party. Poyer was obviously presenting himself up as David, and the themes of unjust persecution, misinterpretation of intentions, evil advice by wicked counsellors poisoning the minds of those who sought his life, and the lack of rebellion in the pursuit of reconciliation, were consistent with Poyer's other petitions and declarations. There was also, of course, a kind of providential fatalism here, a sense that the die was cast and that Poyer was rendering himself up to God for the ultimate judgment of right between the two parties. We generally see Poyer through the eyes of his enemies, and past assessments of him have consequently often been negative. Attending to his own words, however, suggests that in this difficult period between August 1647 and March 1648 he maintained a consistent focus on his rights and arrears as well as on the safety of himself, his men and his family. That such convictions would ultimately lead to his ruin does not mean that he was not sincere or justified in holding them. Discussing Poyer as acting out of mere 'self-interest' thus rather misses the wider picture.

Fleming answered that he was willing to proceed with 'gentlenesse', and, 'upon the advice and desires of the gentlemen of that county', he promised Poyer £200 and the same recompense as other disbanded supernumeraries. For his arrears, he promised Poyer would be 'audited' and given security for payment.[68] While this might have looked conciliatory, the fact that the Lorts were advising on Poyer's terms alongside the fact that he would be audited, likely by his enemies, offered cold comfort. This was no improvement on his situation in early January, and there must have been little surprise when Poyer refused to submit. Indeed, one wonders whether Roger Lort and his associates deliberately helped to engineer an unpalatable offer in order to ensure a rejection which would undoubtedly then be met with force of arms.

As Poyer's response was being reported in London, so the Lort–Eliot propaganda machine once more rolled into action. This took the form of a letter, supposedly sent from Pembroke at the same time as Poyer's response to Fleming, but it bore the indelible hallmark of Pembrokeshire's London agent, and may well have been a report from Roger Lort embellished and edited by Eliot in London.[69] This letter was published in a popular newsbook as context for its reproduction of Poyer's reply to Fleming. It was thus designed to help the public understand the 'deportment of Col. Poyer'.[70] In other words, it was a skilfully timed piece of disinformation which undercut the governor's message. Eliot's favourite theme of drunkenness was rolled out, and Poyer was said to be 'in two dispositions every day, in the morning sober and penitent, but in the afternoon drunk and full of plots'. The portraitist then painted Poyer as a highly erratic, even mentally unsound, leader who dressed some of his soldiers in fine clothing, sent them out then welcomed them back into the town and claimed they were emissaries from the Prince of Wales in France. This inconstant and unpredictable behaviour was also rendered in the following vignette: 'When he heares news that pleaseth him he puts forth bloudy colours, and then he is for the King and the Book of Common Prayer; but if that winde turn, then he is for the Oath and Covenant, and then puts forth blew and white [the colours of the Scottish Covenanters]'. This was designed to show Poyer as inconstant, unprincipled and a gadfly turncoat who would follow any political cause that caught his eye. It undercut any idea that his actions were animated by conviction and helped to reduce his political positions to ones based solely on personality and advantage. Historians have been rather too attracted to these easy characterisations, but the image presented in the letter does capture the medley of positions which Poyer articulated in early 1648. He was for 'King and Parliament', and for the prayer book as well as 'the Covenant'. As discussed above, this represented a somewhat unusual but nonetheless internally consistent set of positions which Poyer had probably held throughout the 1640s. It was relatively easy, however, to portray such loyalties as an inconsistent hotch-potch, and to suggest that, consequently, the man who held them was confused, capricious and unstable.

Poyer's 'Declaration' along with Fleming's letters and another from the Pembrokeshire committee were discussed in parliament on 21 March. The Venetian ambassador reported that Poyer had declared 'for the royal side', and that parliament was 'extremely moved by this news'.[71] An army correspondent described his 'very premptorie answer' to parliament's ultimatum and that 'some disturbance is feared in those parts from the cavaleers & that partie'.[72] It was resolved to confer with Fairfax and the Derby House Committee about sending sufficient forces to south Wales to reduce Poyer (the parliamentary press had it as 'this rebell') but also to disband Rowland Laugharne's remaining forces in the region. Arthur Annesley, Roger Lort's brother-in-law and an MP, was directed to prepare an ordinance for 'removing Colonel Poyer from being mayor of Pembroke, and for placing some other well-affected person'.[73]

The discussion in parliament touched off a whole series of orders.[74] Fairfax wrote to Colonel Thomas Horton, ordering him to assist the Army Committee in getting payment to the soldiers in south Wales 'so that they will have no colour of refusing to disband'.[75] If they still did not disband he was to 'compell' them and ensure that there were no further gatherings of troops. Fairfax also ordered Lieutenant Colonel Read at Bristol to send two companies from Colonel Overton's regiment to reduce Pembroke. Sir William Constable had been ordered to send ordnance and ammunition from Gloucester to Pembroke. Fleming, meanwhile, was ordered to use 'all strictnesse' in trying to reduce Poyer whom parliament now declared 'a traytor'. He was told not to agree any conditions with Poyer without consulting parliament first, but, if the soldiers 'being weary of such a master' would submit, it was left to his discretion as to how to proceed.

Importantly, Fairfax also directed letters to Rice Powell at Tenby and Rowland Laugharne in London. These figures were clearly seen as suspect and potential supporters of the gathering revolt at Pembroke. Fairfax referred to 'some dispute among the officers' about their arrears of pay and desire to be disbanded together. Fairfax assured them that payment had been agreed by the Army Committee, while collective disbandment was contrary to the form undertaken in all other cases and would not be allowed. Any hesitation in implementing these orders, he continued, 'cannot be out of a good meaning', but he hoped they would 'understand their duty to the state, and quit themselves of all blame by their ready obedience . . . being the last in the kingdome that are to be disbanded'.

The parliamentary newsbook that carried reports of these directives wrote that they looked forward to the messenger's return when they would hear Poyer and Laugharne's resolutions, whereof the author anticipated 'a good agreement in all'. He would be sorely disappointed. Indeed, his information was out of date. By the time this text was published blood had already been spilled in Pembroke. Poyer fired numerous shots from the Castle and discharged several pieces of ordnance at Fleming and his soldiers shortly after refusing parliament's ordinance. Correspondents claimed that between eleven and sixteen men were wounded and many houses 'defaced'.[76] This was seized on by the London press, which released an account of the skirmish under the sensational title *A Bloody Slaughter at Pembrooke-Castle*. This hostile narrative was produced by Robert Ibbitson, a radical printer of Smithfield who published numerous texts for the New Model Army.[77] Poyer's inconclusive volleys against the besieging forces were followed by a much more serious assault, supported by Laugharne's forces, on 23 March. The first shots of the Second Civil War had been fired, and Poyer's die was irrevocably cast.

CHAPTER 6

Poyer, Powell and the Prince, March–April 1648

The 'Second Civil War' is something of a term of convenience for a series of local revolts which broke out in many parts of England and Wales during the spring and summer of 1648.[1] Particular flash points were in Kent and Essex, while sympathetic risings also occurred in Norwich, Yorkshire and north Wales. The picture is complicated by the involvement of the Scots.[2] The Presbyterian Covenanters had fought on parliament's side between 1643 and 1646, but they looked with horror on the rise of Independency and the New Model, groups which were deeply suspicious of and hostile towards the Scots. The defeated King Charles, however, saw in the Scots the possibility of regaining his authority. It was an open secret as he languished under house arrest in 1647 that he and his advisers were negotiating with the Covenanters for a treaty which would see the Scots invade England, to defeat the New Model and restore him to his throne. The treaty, known as the Engagement, was agreed in late 1647, but it struggled to win hearts and minds north of the border because Charles I, mindful of his status as head of the Church of England, refused to take the National Covenant.[3] In England and Wales discontented ex-royalists and Presbyterians were sympathetic to the king's cause, but many were mistrustful of the Scots and even worried about the king's own reliability and trustworthiness. There were also a wide variety of reasons for communities to be discontented with parliamentary rule in this period: these included the suppression of the prayer book, high levels of taxation, the growth of religious radicalism and the continuing presence of the New Model Army.[4] This all made for a rather disjointed and uncoordinated opposition movement in 1648 which would ultimately crumble under the weight of its own contradictions.

Poyer's own position reflects aspects of this picture well. His grievances in 1647–8, for example, were largely local and personal in nature, although they certainly had a wider ideological dimension. As we saw in the previous chapter, his defiance of parliamentary and army authority from late 1647 rested upon grounds which were not especially 'royalist'. Nevertheless, resurgent royalist publications were keen to enrol him in their cause. One newsbook of early March 1648, for example, discussing Poyer's rejection of parliament's order for him to surrender, praised him as an example of 'true loyalty and resolution' and of the 'gallantry of Brittish spirits'. The text finished with a poetic flourish, describing 'Their credit in old chronicles and tales,/That England never wholly conquerd Wales'.[5] Such reports underline how Poyer was garnering national attention for his stand at Pembroke, and how the royalists welcomed him with open arms as a kind of noble resistance fighter. His national profile and rebel outlaw status thus received a significant boost when his defiance spilled over into violent resistance.

The commissioners sent down to south-west Wales to disband Laugharne's forces in early March 1648 encountered an ill-humoured body of men who were resolved to assist Poyer in his stand rather than follow parliament's directives to go home without their full arrears of pay. As we saw at the end of the previous chapter, Poyer's defiance had gone beyond words; he had already turned Pembroke Castle's guns on its parliamentary besiegers in a series of minor skirmishes which had left several wounded. Frustrated by his refusal to yield, on 23 March 1648, Fleming moved in to attack. Poyer, however, had been in contact with several leaders of Laugharne's infantry regiments who had agreed to assist him. One correspondent thought the forces these officers brought with them numbered 2,000 men. Poyer sallied out of the castle while Laugharne's troops 'being gotten together againe, came upon his [Fleming's] reare and kild & tooke most of them prisoner'.[6] The engagement lasted around half an hour and Fleming himself was injured.

One report described twenty or thirty men as having been taken prisoner, while another noted that many of Fleming's company were 'content' to be taken, 'fearing the country people would otherwise have cut their throats'.[7] This is telling evidence about the simmering resentment directed against the army officials in the Pembrokeshire countryside, and suggests the kinds of sympathies Poyer was able to mobilise to his advantage. Among the prisoners taken were Roger Lort, John Lort, Thomas Barlow, William Phillips, 'Mr Sedgwick', a minister, and Captain Walter Cuny.[8] Poyer, however, released them all after a short period. A correspondent in Gloucester wrote that Poyer was now in control of Pembroke town, which he had previously ceded to Fleming, as well as the castle, and that he was using the town to provision his forces. He was also sending out into the country for sustenance and support. The Gloucester correspondent also noted that Laugharne's troops had revolted and taken possession of Tenby, adding 'here is great talk in these parts of the raising of a new army for the king, the royal party giving out very high speeches'.[9]

The limited resistance against Fleming and the commissioners for disbandment had moved beyond simple grievances about pay and indemnity and was transforming into a more recognisably *royalist* revolt. This was not immediately obvious in Poyer's attack, although he too would soon declare for the king's cause. One nuanced report of the incident observed that Poyer 'is one who hath formerly done good service for the Parliament, and none engaged more against the Cavaliers'. It continued, however, that despite persuasion he would not disband and 'it is probable that some malignant flames from some inhabitants about him have kindled him into this fire'.[10] It seems that the flames were of Poyer's own making, but they certainly kindled a fire in south Wales and beyond. The conflagration, however, would ultimately consume him.

The fear and panic Poyer's actions aroused within the parliamentarian state were palpable. Correspondents wrote of 'the insolent deportment of the governor' having 'awakened again a discontented party in this kingdome which began to fall asleep of themselves, and by degrees to acquiesce in the orders of the parliament'.[11] A letter from Bristol reported, 'we now have advice of that spark at Pembroke to be grown into a flame which, if not timely prevented, may set the whole kingdom on a fire'.[12] A royalist correspondent observed that Poyer's actions 'much concernes them [the parliament], the ill example these give to other places to doe the like'.[13] Sampson Lort, the brother who had escaped Poyer's clutches at Pembroke, lamented in a letter to the Commons of 24 March that 'if great care be not speedily taken to suppresse this cockatrice in the egge, he will be able to raise a new warre, all men in those parts generally fearing him'.[14] Poyer's assault represented not just a challenge to parliament's authority in a remote corner of Wales but an existential threat to the parliamentary state itself. The combustible accumulation of grievances and discontentments were not just found in south Wales but throughout the kingdom. The imagery of Poyer's revolt as a spark which could easily touch off a wider conflagration was apt; indeed, it was prescient.

Fleming's defeat was seized on by the royalist press, which gleefully reported how parliament's commissioners were put into such a fright by Poyer's assault, that they had run back to Westminster to inform them that 'loyalty runs so in a bloud among the Welsh that it will be in vaine to attempt this last refuge of monarchy, which Providence seemes to have given in earnest for the restitution of the whole'.[15] Clearly, many saw Poyer's attack on Fleming as firing a starting gun for a wider national mobilisation to restore Charles I to his rightful authority, destroy the Independents and the New Model, and reduce parliament to its proper role in the state. One royalist newspaper asked exasperatedly of its English readers, 'Shall tyrants still reigne over you? . . . Shall Scots or Welchmen have the honor of setting your king on his throne whil'st you stand like cowards with your hands in your pockets?'[16] In the same vein, another publication played on Pembrokeshire's epithet as 'Little England Beyond Wales' by noting that 'Great Englands honour lies in the dust, and Little England lends a hand to raise her up'.[17] It is unsurprising that contemporaries should have thought of Wales as a royalist refuge given its solid support for the king during the first civil war.[18] It would have been confounding to most who knew of his record, however, that it was John Poyer who stood in the vanguard of this royalist renaissance.

Poyer had yet, in fact, to make an unequivocal statement that his actions supported the king. That, however, was the obvious direction in which he was moving, and was also the general interpretation of his attack on Fleming. As one royalist publication put it to its English readers in early April, 'I tell you againe, Poyer and Powels case is your own, and yours is theirs'.[19] Poyer's bridges back to parliamentary favour had been reduced to ashes, and there was only one constituency which would welcome him now. Sampson Lort, who wrote to parliament on 24 March about Poyer's assault on Fleming, described enthusiastic royalist support for Poyer, noting how 'malignants are very active in these parts, and scattering reports of that nature as may prepare the people for suddaine insurrections'. He also spoke of a royalist declaration for the 'kings common prayer book' which was being prepared by one Colonel Culpepper in Carmarthen, who was shortly to go to Devon or Cornwall to 'advance it there'.[20] This was Poyer and Powell's *Declaration* which would be issued on 10 April and which was indeed sent into Cornwall (and Ireland and France) and is discussed below. Culpepper was apparently William Culpepper, a Kentish man and nephew of the royalist Lord John Culpepper. William had been apprehended in Cardiff in October 1645 as a suspected royalist; he refused to take the Covenant but was monitored rather than imprisoned.[21]

News of Poyer's actions had probably reached the king's ears in his confinement at Carisbrooke Castle on the Isle of Wight, from whence one correspondent wrote on 26 March after hearing reports of 'distractions and tumults in Wales', adding, 'men . . . much feare the west'.[22] Poyer, meanwhile, was said to have 'courted some gentlemen of estates which have been on the kings side to raise men for the king, and they have denyed it; others have promised to raise men for him'.[23] Reports also circulated that a packet of letters from 'some persons of eminency' to Poyer had been intercepted; they were said to 'incourage him with hopes of more assistance'.[24] The implication was that these were from prominent royalists, perhaps even from the royal family itself. Poyer also captured a frigate in Milford Haven, which, it was reported, he had sent to France 'to give advertisement of his successe and resolution'.[25] France was where the young Prince of Wales, the effective leader of the royalist cause with his father in parliament's hands, resided with his mother. Everything was moving towards a public declaration for the king.

Parliament recognised the threat Poyer's revolt represented and the need to suppress it. However, while there were calls for a 'great power' to be sent to defeat the rebels, Oliver Cromwell, Fairfax's second in command in the New Model Army, believed that drawing down a significant number of soldiers would leave other, potentially vulnerable, parts of the kingdom 'much weakened & left naked'.[26] These anxieties centred on a feared invasion by the Scots and also leaving a restive London insufficiently protected and policed.[27] Such concerns help explain the delay in mobilising more significant resources to address the Pembrokeshire threat, a delay which allowed the revolt to gain important momentum. MPs and the army's high command perhaps also felt that the two companies of Colonel Overton's regiment which had been dispatched from Bristol would be sufficient to address the revolt. This small force landed in Pembrokeshire on 28 March, but, as we shall see in a moment, it soon faced the fury of Poyer's rebels. It was only on 30 March, three days after it had received reports of Fleming's defeat, that the Commons ordered

Fairfax to deal with the threat by land and the Derby House Committee to organise the necessary mobilisation at sea.[28] It was not until 7 April, after news of a further defeat to parliament's forces in the county, that significant additional forces were sent against Poyer.

On 28 March, however, the Commons did take an interesting initiative, sending into west Wales Captain Thomas Wogan, who was to 'use his best indeavours to appease the distempers and settle the quiet and peace in Pembrookeshire'.[29] One source reported that Wogan was to be the commander of 2,000 foot and 1,000 horse which were being sent against Poyer, although 'they are not forward to march or hasty to fight'.[30] Wogan was a Pembrokeshire native, a younger son of the deceased county MP John Wogan who had supported Poyer in 1642. Thomas Wogan had served under Essex but became a vigorous supporter of the New Model. He was a radical who would become infamous as one of the 'regicides' who signed Charles I's death warrant in 1649. Elected as MP for Cardigan in August 1646, Wogan was probably friendly with Pembrokeshire's London agent, John Eliot, and we know he was an opponent of the Pembrokeshire MP, and intimate of Poyer and Laugharne, Arthur Owen.[31] As parliament dithered over how best to respond to the rising in the west, Poyer gathered strength and took the fight to his enemies.

Two companies of Overton's regiment landed near Henllan on the southern shore of Milford Haven on 28 March. They were billeted in the church of Pwllcrochan, but the day after their arrival John Poyer appeared at the head of some 100 foot and two troops of horse. After a sharp engagement parliament's forces were defeated, although they were allowed to retreat to Cardiff upon an engagement not to land again in the Haven. Later the same day, Poyer marched on to Henllan, the house of his adversary Griffith White. There, with Colonel Thomas Butler, Poyer surrounded his long-standing enemies, Roger Lort, John Lort, Griffith White himself, and also Adjutant General Fleming who was recuperating from the wounds he suffered in Poyer's attack of 23 March.[32] This group had met together to arrange the quartering and accommodation of Overton's forces. Despite Poyer's advantageous position, 'by a strategem' they managed to evade capture and boarded parliament's ship *Expedition Regis* then riding in the Haven.[33]

When reports of this engagement reached London, they were accompanied by deeply troubling warnings about the country's rallying to Poyer's rebel standard. He was said to be 'dayly raising more forces both of horse and foot', and was also gathering significant taxes to supply his men.[34] An army newsletter of 4 April claimed that Poyer had 'declared for the kinge' and was 500 strong in two foot troops and that Laugharne's cavalry were coming to him.[35] A royalist correspondent observed that Poyer's victories allowed parliament's enemies a free passage into Wales, 'wither divers well affected to his Majestie doe resorte'.[36] Some believed the number of Poyer's rebels were 'not so great as is reported', and were perhaps only 1,000 strong, but other reports claimed that 4,000–5,000 had come in to him.[37] As with all such contemporary reports, it is difficult to gauge the true number accurately, but it probably lay somewhere between these two estimates. Several of Laugharne's companies subscribed a resolution that they would not join with Poyer, but reports came in that many disbanded after receiving their pay and then joined Poyer anyway.[38] From Bristol, a correspondent wrote that 'affairs here are in a very sad condition, our feares dayly increase, and the country is divided; for the malignant party gives out high speeches and divers of the cavalry resorts to Pembroke Castle for the assistance of Col. Poyer'.[39] Poyer's example of resistance to other areas, as much as his own strength and support around Pembroke, caused serious concern about the stability and political reliability of the west of England and not just of Wales.[40] Expectations of a new war were now commonplace as parliament belatedly resolved to mobilise a significant force under Thomas Horton to 'suppresse those Welsh rebels'.[41]

As Poyer looked with satisfaction upon his military successes and the myriad of difficulties he was posing for his local enemies, so he recognised the need to make his rising part of a wider political and military mobilisation against the Independents and the New Model. Some statement of the 'cause' for which Poyer and Rice Powell were fighting was required as a means of identifying the basis of their rebellion and as a standard around which others could rally. This came in a printed text dated 10 April entitled *The Declaration of Col. Poyer and Col. Powell*, which the title page declared was 'to be published to the whole kingdome'.[42] As a statement of Poyer's political credo and a text circulated to mobilise other discontented parties, it is worth considering in some depth.

An important point about this pamphlet was, once again, stated on the title page. Here, Poyer and Powell declared that their position on religion, monarchy and the liberty of the subject was the cause of their rising, but it was also 'the ground of their first taking up armes'. Poyer was thus asserting that his position had not altered from his undertakings of 1642, but rather that the parliament had fallen away from him. Elsewhere in the tract, the two men maintained that 'wee doe still continue to our first principles', which is to say, the undertakings articulated for 'King and Parliament' at the beginning of the civil wars. In this sense, then, their statement was something of a piece with Poyer's answer to Colonel Fleming of a month before. Such looking back to earlier principles and undertakings formed the initial part of this short pamphlet, in which the authors described how, in the early stages of the war, the faults of government were laid open, true reformation was promised and the privileges of parliament and the liberty of the people were placed at the core of parliament's case. They now asserted, however, that parliament had 'runne into those evills which wee fought against' and had produced only an arbitrary government that trampled on religion and the law. Interestingly, the two men described 'our party' as having been in power for the last three years, which argues that they still considered themselves to be 'parliamentarians', but perhaps only as that term had been understood before its corruption by the Independents.

In the tract, Poyer and Powell's attack on the Independents was given a local twist. The authors claimed that parliament's excesses had been only to 'satisfie the avarice and ambition of a few men who, by accusing their brethren, have already gotten too much power into their hands, and doe now labour to disband, not to ease the country (as is pretended)'. Roger Lort and John Eliot thus lurked menacingly behind this text. While the *Declaration* was framed in general terms, then, it arose very much from local circumstances which were still in the forefront of Poyer's mind as he devised a statement of general principles. The tract used the Pembroke committee's own declarations against them to prove that they wished to bring in external forces (that is to say, the New Model) to subject the local gentry to parliamentary sequestration and to impose 'intollerable charges' such as the excise. Here the authors deftly linked together widespread resentments about taxation in a county exhausted by war with fears that the New Model was a force of arbitrary government, a machine for imposing unjust laws and suppressing any dissent against a distant and uncaring government of radicals.[43] This rhetorical move also silently aligned Laugharne's (unfairly) disbanded military units with the forces of local community, legitimate authority, responsive government and just taxation.

One of the *Declaration*'s most interesting sections concerned religion. The authors asserted – probably with men like Sampson Lort in mind

– that the Independents wished to 'destroy our soules as well as our bodies', by suppressing the Book of Common Prayer in south-west Wales as they had done elsewhere. In fact, outlawing of the prayer book had been parliamentary policy since before the rise of the New Model, but the strength of royalism in most parts of Wales meant that the directive to replace it with the Presbyterian *Directory of Public Worship* took a long time to be implemented. It was only in early 1647, for example, that moves to remove the prayer book were made in counties such as Radnorshire and Breconshire, while parliamentary attacks on its use gave rise to a violent backlash in Glamorgan in February 1646.[44] Rowland Laugharne, who suppressed these Glamorgan disturbances, found it necessary to allow the continued use of the prayer book in order to placate the revolters. The prayer book was also an important cultural artefact in Wales because it had long been translated into the Welsh language. There was no such provision with parliament's texts such as the *Directory*. Although south Pembrokeshire was a largely Anglophone community, there was still an important presence for the Welsh language here, and probably also a particular cultural resonance for the text, even in its English version. Moreover, Poyer's *Declaration* had an intended audience beyond the confines of the Pembrokeshire Englishry, and was fashioned to motivate populations in Carmarthenshire, Cardiganshire and Glamorgan, as well as north Wales, areas which were largely monoglot Welsh and deeply attached to the vernacular prayer book. Such local cultural loyalties were key to the pamphlet's defence of the prayer book as 'the sole comfort of the people here, and their way to attaine the knowledge of God'. As we have seen, Poyer was no Presbyterian much less an Independent in religion. His commitment to the prayer book was sincere and of long standing. Such a public declaration of an attachment to and defence of the prayer book would provide crucial common ground with ex-royalists for whom defence of the Established Church was often a core component of their political motivation. As is discussed below, however, the *Declaration*'s message would later be modified somewhat for consumption by religious Presbyterians.

One can imagine that the *Declaration* was a text with popular appeal in Pembrokeshire, south Wales, and many parts beyond. It described a set of values and ambitions which were common to many royalists and most Presbyterians too. The *Declaration* seems to have been produced in some numbers and purchased fairly widely if the numerous remaining copies in major libraries is any indication.[45] It also made a splash in the newsbooks, which reproduced parts of the text.[46] One London-based correspondent noted the tract's appearance in a letter of 11 April, the day after its publication. He described it as 'in vindication of the king', adding, 'what numbers they [Poyer and Powell] have wee are not certain, but are assured the whole contrey is for them, and 'tis sayed they are at least 2,000'.[47] Notice was also taken of the *Declaration* by a royalist newsletter writer on 13 April, who observed that 'Coll. Poyer and Powell of Tenby Castle are still very resolute & have sett out their declaracion against the Parliament point blanck, in as high and malignant termes as any cavalier could doe (& indeed some doe conceive Jenkin had a hand in it)'.[48] 'Jenkin' here was Judge David Jenkins of Glamorgan, a bullish theorist of monarchical power who had recently been imprisoned on a charge of sedition for his contemptuous writings against parliament. To say the *Declaration* was akin to a Jenkins production was going too far. The text was not as stridently royalist as Jenkins's works and not as full of 'malignant termes' as many publications supporting the king. However, it is instructive that this commentator interpreted the *Declaration* in this manner.

The *Declaration* was clearly recognised as a thoroughly royalist text which was reaching out to the swelling constituency of the discontented.[49] It is notable that the royalist newsletter writer who discussed the publication immediately went on to describe how 'the people resort to them [Poyer and Powell] very fast, as well gentry as others, both out of England and Walles & it is said they will have shortly forces sent them out of Ireland from Inchequin'.[50] Powell and Poyer were thus drawing in considerable support, and were also contributing to parliament's many headaches because of the situation developing in Ireland. Here one of parliament's commanders, Murrough O'Brien, first earl of Inchiquin, had very recently defected to the king's cause.[51] A newspaper claimed that Inchiquin was 'expected . . . [at] every houre to land with his armie' at Pembroke.[52] Reports that one of Poyer's prominent supporters, Colonel Thomas Butler who had served under Essex, had a brother in Munster who held a correspondence with the rebels under Inchiquin, can only have enhanced anxieties in London.[53] The prospect of royalist invasion from Ireland through Milford Haven which was largely controlled by Poyer now became a very real, and very frightening, prospect for parliament.[54]

Another aspect of the *Declaration* which has received no attention but was crucial to its widespread circulation and importance in the risings of

1648, is that part of the text was adopted as a form of 'oath' (also, confusingly, called a 'declaration' and a 'protestation'), and seems to have been used for the purposes of subscription to a royalist 'association'. In his letter to parliament of 24 March, Sampson Lort mentioned that Colonel Culpepper was at Carmarthen preparing a declaration for the prayer book which he was to advance in Cornwall or Devon. Lort also spoke about the scattering of 'reports' to 'prepare the people for suddaine insurrections'. It is possible that the 'declaration' and the 'reports' he mentioned being distributed were, in fact, one and the same. The *Declaration* finished with a basic statement of 'first principles': to bring the king to a personal treaty;[55] to establish him in his just prerogative; to maintain the liberties of the people and privileges of parliament in 'their proper bounds'; and to defend the Protestant religion 'and the Common-prayer as it is established by the law in this land'. This same formulation turned up elsewhere and was the basis for an 'oath of association'. In mid-April 1648 it was reported that 'the west, as Devon & Cornwale looke upon the successe & constancy of the Welch; they are willing & ready to ioyne with them'.[56] We know from a letter from Plymouth on 12 May 1648 that 'malignants' in Cornwall were understood to be mobilising and 'that there had bin endeavour made in the county to get hands to Poyers declaration'.[57] Colonel Culpepper, one of the *Declaration*'s architects, was destined for the West Country in late March, and around this time discontented soldiers in Cornwall 'were accused of holding out a hand to the governor of Pembroke'.[58] That the *Declaration* was one of the bases for the Cornish revolt against parliament and the army in May 1648 is further suggested by the fact that rebel leaders told some of their supporters that they were fighting 'for kinge & parliament', the formulation from 1642 which was also to be found in Poyer's text.[59]

Culpepper was also known to have distributed papers, again probably related to Poyer's *Declaration*, to the royalist turncoat Lord Inchiquin in Ireland. It was also said that he 'carried letters from Wales to his highness the Prince of Wales', which describes his presentation of the *Declaration* at St Germains, to which the Prince gave a positive response.[60] This is discussed further below. When Horton marched into Wales in mid-April, he reported that officers who had engaged for Rice Powell were 'displeased to see Culpepper and other Cavaliers rule all'.[61] Culpepper, who was taken by New Model forces after the fall of Tenby in June 1648, was clearly an important cog in the wheel of the royalist mobilisation in Wales and the South West during March–May 1648, and was intimately involved in the drafting and distribution of the *Declaration*. Moreover, the letter from Plymouth suggests that Poyer and Powell's *Declaration* was intended as the basis for a wider mobilisation in the county and 'hands', or signatures, were being sought in the manner of an association.

Further pieces of this jigsaw concerning the *Declaration* as the basis for a wider association can be found in a newsbook issued after the collapse of the south Wales revolt. This produced evidence which related to 'the Confederate Welshes . . . attempted association'.[62] The newsbook reproduced Poyer and Powell's *Declaration*, as well as a text from late March or early April 1648 which encouraged communities to associate behind Poyer and Powell's revolt. This text described Pembrokeshire as 'wasted with the late war', but maintained that there were some who 'have a designe to make the seat of a new war here'.[63] It claimed that the gentry would be sequestered by a rampant parliament and army and, 'worse then all the rest', the prayer book would be removed. It mentioned the soldiers then besieging Pembroke Castle, a probable reference to Fleming's force, and maintained that more troops were shortly expected. The text continued, 'if we be once subdued, your turn is next, and therefore, if to prevent this mischief in the beginning you will associate your selves with us, we doubt not but other counties will doe the like'. The text then directed the recipients to arrange meetings whereby associations would be formed and asked them to 'communicate the same to other such counties as you shall think fit, and to desire their association with us'. The basis upon which this appears to have been done was either Poyer and Powell's *Declaration* in its entirely or, more likely, the passage of 'first principles' with which it concluded. This was picked up in London, and a royalist newsbook of mid-April reported that the counties of Pembrokeshire, Carmarthenshire and Breconshire had 'unanimously declared to adhere unto Colonell Powell and Captaine Poyer . . . according to their late Declaration'.[64]

A hitherto unnoticed pamphlet also from early May tells us more. It is entitled *The Declaration and Protestation of the Kings Army in South-Wales*, although much of the text is taken up by reports of royalist activity in the north of England.[65] However, at the end is a report of the engagement between Poyer's forces and those at Henllan. The text then rehearses a version of the 'oath' found at the end of the Poyer and Powell's *Declaration*, albeit with an important modification to the wording on religion which is discussed below. The text begins with the words 'Wee whose names are subscribed do declare . . .'.[66] Along with the evidence from Cornwall of an effort to 'get hands' to Poyer's *Declaration*, this indicates that we are looking at a subscription text designed to be sworn and/or signed.

Another pamphlet from mid-May reproduces this 'Protestation' and offers additional evidence about its operation as an oath of association.[67] The 'Declaration' is described as being taken by Poyer, Laugharne, Powell and 'the rest of the officers and souldiers in South-Wales'. After reproducing the 'Declaration' itself, the pamphlet provides further undertakings which run: 'You will either give consent to this Declaration and joyne with us in effecting it, or [if] you shall not . . . then not to reveale or prejudice our Oath'. If the swearer agreed to take the 'oath' they were bound not to reveal 'our secrets' except to those who could advance the cause's interests and who were 'such as you do believe to be well-affected to us'. This evidence comes from a pro-parliamentarian pamphlet, so it is uncertain whether the author wished to convey the impression of dangerous Welsh forces coming together under a veil of secrecy and sinister designs. However, the remainder of the text is rather sober reportage from Wales and the north of England; it also reproduces accurately letters between Laugharne and Horton before St Fagans. It seems unlikely, then, that the undertakings which accompanied the oath were mere invention. This material thus bolsters the case for seeing Poyer's *Declaration* as the basis for an oath of association for promoting the royalist rebellion in south Wales and beyond.

Significantly, the text in some of these pamphlets is described as 'The Protestation', a term which probably deliberately recalled parliament's own Protestation oath which it had issued in 1641. This was subscribed to in a mass campaign throughout the country (although not, it seems, in Wales) and was enormously significant in mobilising early parliamentarian support.[68] In 1648, one pamphleteer called Poyer's oath 'the Protestation of the Brittish forces in Wales', with 'British' being a contemporary synonym for 'Welsh'.[69] Parliament's 1641 Protestation certainly had resonances with Poyer's with its emphasis on defending the privileges of parliaments, the subject's lawful rights and Protestant religion. These are what might be called the unobjectionable basics of the parliamentarian cause. Indeed, it seems likely that Poyer first rose for parliament in defence of these basic positions, and his 'Protestation' in 1648 was an attempt to restate such a political doctrine albeit on the king's behalf. Attempts were made in the civil wars to reformulate or reinterpret the Protestation in defence of Church and Crown, so what Poyer was doing was not entirely novel.

The *Declaration and Protestation of the Kings Army in South-Wales* describes how this 'Protestation' was 'assented to and taken by Col. Poyer, and the rest of the kings party in South-Wales, and is now dispersed into the severall counties of North-Wales, where it is now taking [sic] by the Cavaliers'.[70] This possible connection between Poyer's revolt and that which broke out in north Wales under Sir John Owen, around a month later, has not been noticed before. There are indeed some echoes of Poyer's 'Protestation' in the Anglesey declaration for the king of 14 July 1648 which, while a much lengthier document, had at its heart an undertaking to 'maintain the true Protestant religion by law established, his Majesty's royal prerogative, the known laws of the land, just privileges of parliament . . . and our own . . . legal properties and liberties'.[71] This had obvious conso-nances with Poyer and Powell's text, although this might simply be because both groups sought to repurpose parliament's original 1641 Protestation. In any event, this new source indicates that the text of the 10 April *Declaration* was being dispersed widely to rally supporters to Poyer's standard.

Taken together, then, these pamphlets demonstrate that Poyer and Powell's *Declaration* became the basis of a royalist oath of association. A manuscript newsletter written from London to a Scottish noble on 28 April discussed how south Wales 'is now associating to oppose all power that is not from King and Prince'.[72] The word 'associating' suggests a pol-itical cause coming together around a text or statement of principles, and the evidence points to this being Poyer and Powell's *Declaration*. It also seems telling that shortly after the *Declaration* was issued, the Commons considered the 'evill consequence [that] might follow if malignants & [et]c were let alone to gather a head in some other place or to joyn with or be assisting to Col. Poyer and the party he hath already'.[73] This dem-onstrates their awareness of the need to stop Poyer's rebellion spreading through the mechanism of the *Declaration* oath.

Despite the evidence that Poyer's *Declaration* was mobilising men and women behind his cause, a problem seems to have arisen from the 'Cavalier' influence of Culpepper and the robust defence of the prayer book in the original text. While a strong defence of the prayer book might have been agreeable to Poyer and Powell, it was unacceptable to many of their prospective allies. In a letter written on 17 April while he was at Neath in Glamorgan, Thomas Horton observed that Powell (and Poyer) had 'declared so positively for the king, that it is hoped the great-est part of the officers and souldiers (they having taken the Covenant) will fall off from him'.[74] The *Declaration* with its emphasis on the prayer book did indeed leave very little room for religious Presbyterians. As a result, it seems the text was altered to produce a less 'episcopalian' oath. A version of the text circulating in early May, for example, which the Presbyterian Rowland Laugharne adopted, changed the original wording of the *Declaration* on religion. This now read that subscribers would defend religion as established by law, 'with such regard to tender consciences as shall be allowed by act of parliament'.[75] Such a construction would allow Presbyterians as well as prayer book Protestants to subscribe to the oath. This modified text was also the one reproduced in a pamphlet of August 1648 about Poyer's revolt, while the newsbook version, also from August, simply had the 'oath' as protecting religion 'as it is established by law in this land'.[76] It appears that Presbyterians like Laugharne required a more flexible construction on religion without reference to the Book of Common Prayer, and it was only on this basis that they would join the royalist revolt. A parliamentary newsbook of mid-April seems to support this interpretation. It described Powell as 'absolutely joyned' with Poyer and added that 'hee tells some he is for Presbitery; others that he is absolute for the king and common prayer booke'.[77] It seems, however, that the emphasis on the prayer book was attractive to the 'greatest part of the commonalty', which flocked to Poyer and Powell in 'great numbers' after their *Declaration* was issued.[78]

Another fascinating aspect of this pro-royalist mobilisation is offered by yet another pamphlet which has not previously been considered. Entitled, *A Fight*, it was produced in mid-June and was concerned principally with the royalist rising at Colchester.[79] However, the work also reproduced a submission dated 10 June which bears all the hallmarks of a John Eliot production. It was entitled 'A Declaration by the well-affected gentlemen of South Wales', and Eliot almost always used the phrase 'well-affected gentlemen' to refer to himself and his confrères. This part of the pamphlet also oozes contempt for Poyer, demonstrates a close knowledge of events in Pembrokeshire, provides a defence of the 'well-affected gentry' in the county whom Poyer had plundered, and called for Poyer to be denied mercy or indemnity. These were all themes which Eliot played on repeatedly in other publications, and which argue for his authorship of part of this pamphlet.

In this counter-'Declaration', Eliot maintained that he wished to rebut a newsbook report from the week before that Poyer, then under siege in

Pembroke, had not assisted Laugharne in his offensive against Horton, an argument Eliot claimed was 'purposely given in by some of Poyers agents . . . to extenuate the foulenesse of his rebellion'.[80] He continued by offering evidence of Poyer's complicity in providing Laugharne with troops, but also mentioned how, 'to amuse the people of the counties of Pembrook, Carmarthen, and Glamorgan as instruments to raise an army for Laughorn', Poyer and his associates 'made several declarations to the said counties'.[81] Fascinatingly, Eliot then claimed that Poyer had tailored his 'declaration' for each county. In Pembrokeshire 'they declared for king, parliament, Covenant and against the Lord Generals Army'; in Carmarthenshire it was 'for king, parliament and against the army'; and in Glamorgan 'for the king & against the army'. He concluded, that their 'juggling with God and man, thrived accordingly'.

This is a remarkable set of observations but, unfortunately, there is no surviving evidence to support his claim about this targeted 'marketing' of the declaration in these counties. Moreover, it is difficult to see why their cause in Glamorgan would be promoted by an oath that did not mention parliament, while those in Carmarthenshire would respond to an oath that did. However, Eliot's mentioning of the Covenant does recall Poyer's initial response to Fleming when he mixed king, parliament and Covenant together. It is possible, then, that the details of this adaptation of Poyer's *Declaration* were wilfully garbled. However, Eliot's basic message might well have been true: that the 'oath' or 'declaration' was modified to appeal to different audiences, principally by mentioning the prayer book in some versions, and the line about 'tender consciences' in others. What is interesting, too, is that Eliot connects the circulation of the *Declaration*(s) with Poyer's cause 'thriving' in south Wales.

Clearly, then, Poyer and Powell's *Declaration* was a crucial text underwriting the broadening of their insurgency against parliament and the New Model. It has not previously been recognised that it also provided a subscription text which circulated in south Wales, Cornwall (and perhaps other parts of the West Country), Ireland and possibly in north Wales also. We have not been aware of this attempt to create a royalist association in the west on the basis of Poyer's text. That this association never established itself and developed a formal structure is unsurprising because of the speed with which the New Model was able to crush its military pretensions. Less than a month after the *Declaration* was issued, the nascent association was destroyed in embryo at the Battle of St Fagans.

As something of a 'follow-up' to the issuing of their *Declaration* on 10 April 1648, Poyer and Powell resolved to demonstrate their military readiness to serve the king. A correspondent from Carmarthen wrote that Poyer and Powell 'are joyned and have declared for the king [and] . . . are now in the field and upon their guard'.[82] Poyer mustered troops on 11 April, the day after the *Declaration* was issued. He did this in his own name, perhaps as he was yet to receive a commission from the king or Prince, although that was not to be long in arriving. He made a symbolic choice in the site of his muster: Colby Moor in the heart of Pembrokeshire. This was the site of Rowland Laugharne's most notable battle in August 1645. It was probably chosen to revive memories of the martial victories Poyer's associates had won, but also to connect his cause with Laugharne's name and prowess. The day following, he mustered somewhere in Carmarthenshire and the day after that at Llanbadarn Fawr in Cardiganshire. It seems that Poyer was making a statement that the three counties of south-west Wales, which had been associated together by both royalist and parliamentarian military administrations, were now under his authority and command (or possibly that of Rowland Laugharne for whom Poyer acted as proxy).

The impact of Poyer and Powell's *Declaration* and their mustering of south-west Wales can be seen in the fact that on 19 April John Eliot produced a pamphlet in the name of 'Divers Gentlemen' of Wales which constituted a rancorous assault on Poyer's personal and political history.[83] The pamphlet was printed by one 'H. Becke' and issued under the imprimatur of Gilbert Mabbott, a licenser with a close relationship to the New Model Army.[84] Although not an Army production, such connections suggest how Eliot was operating within an Independent political network sympathetic to his and the Lorts's aims. Indeed, a royalist news-sheet linked the publication with the Eliot–Lort faction, and further alleged that it was 'contrived purposely (upon direction of the Houses) by a privat hand to asperse and slander him [Poyer], it being first showne to the faction in the Houses, and by them allowed of as authentique'.[85] That Eliot's pamphlet was designed to address some of the excitement and expectation generated by Powell and Poyer's tract is indicated by Eliot's initial address. Here he discussed the 'ordinary crime among the vulgar discontents of these times', to seize on news relating to one's interests and 'instantly cry it up' as though assured of future successes. However, he warned that such hopes were often built on 'deceitfull shallow grounds of revengefulnesse and malice', adding

neither can I much blame such who know not the condition of the party
they so much elevate, or his principles. If they did, sure no rationall men
would ever betray their own judgements and the cause they so much
affect, as to place their confidence upon one who will appear like a flash
of lightning, soone gone out . . . which frustrates the expectations of
the beholders.[86]

Eliot was shaken by Poyer's military successes against Fleming and probably also the popularity of his *Declaration* among the 'vulgar'. To suggest,
as he did here, that Poyer was a flash in the pan was nonetheless to acknowledge that there was a flash which had attracted attention in the first place.
Poyer had clearly made a significant impact on public opinion in London
and Eliot believed this demanded an answer. Indeed, his royalist critic in
the press maintained that this pamphlet was published 'with the intention
to loppe off friends from assisting him [Poyer]'.[87]

Eliot had the tools to hand for the job of character assassination; he had
been publishing material hostile to Poyer since 1645, and he reproduced
much of it in this text. Thus he enlarged once more, but now for a royalist
audience, on Poyer's low birth and poor connections. In this pamphlet he
significantly ratcheted up the level of vituperation, however, suggesting
that Poyer's mother and his wife were whores and his children bastards.
Drawing liberally from the palette of his earlier publications, Eliot painted
Pembroke's governor as a vindictive plunderer, a drunk and a quarreller.
In other words, Poyer was a man without lineage and without honour,
two qualities which were perhaps of particular significance for a royalist
rather than a parliamentarian readership. Eliot also rubbished any idea that
Poyer had 'raised this rebellion out of affection to any publique interest',
but rather maintained that it was his 'base guiltinesse' in owing thousands
of plundered pounds to the state that had occasioned his revolt. This
'viper', he asserted, would drag the kingdom into a new war for purely
selfish reasons.

Such an analysis was repeated elsewhere, for example in the assessment
of one army officer guarding the king on the Isle of Wight, who maintained
that Poyer and Powell's 'design and engagement' was 'to no other end
of principle but a meere selfe-end, for the advancements of their owne
wretched & mechanick ambition'.[88] Indeed, this view of Poyer remains
evident in much modern scholarship too. Commentators have tended to
see him only as an ambitious, frustrated and self-centred individual who

rebelled against parliament for essentially petulant reasons. While there is an element of truth to such characterisations, we should not think of Poyer only as a selfish individual empty of ideology and conviction. His *Declaration* of 1648 articulated his political creed, and it was one, he would argue, that he had stuck to since 1642, not invented *in extremis* in 1648. Some of these points are discussed further in a review of the scholarship on Poyer in Chapter 9.

Eliot concluded his pamphlet by addressing the 'kings party who perhaps hath through ignorance applauded him'. He hoped his publication would allow them to recognise the weak foundation upon which they built their 'fond hopes'. If monarchy was to rise from 'such a well-spring of impiety as Poyer is', then Eliot assured his readers that 'the sequell can prove but fatall and destructive to this kingdome'. He was confident that the next 'newes' in London would be of Poyer's being blockaded at land and sea, and unable to fight because of a lack of support from neighbouring counties. Thereafter, Poyer and 'his sattalits' would be 'cub'd up to feed at rack and manger upon their purloined provisions' by the New Model, and would ultimately be brought to justice. His confidence proved well placed and his predictions accurate.

Eliot's poison pen letter was rushed into print on 19 April because by this time another, perhaps even more disturbing, Poyer and Powell production was rolling off the presses.[89] This was a reprint of their *Declaration*, but it was introduced with a letter to the Prince of Wales and concluded with a direct appeal to the people of England, and to the inhabitants of London in particular. Again, this seems to have been a popular publication, and was reproduced in royalist newspapers which lauded 'glorious Collonel Poyer and Powell' who were, 'with the assistance of God and the loyallists of Great Britaine, to pull down the usurpers at Westminster to reduce their sectarian army and to restore' the Prince and king 'to a capacity of governing'.[90] With the king in parliament's hands at Carisbrooke Castle, his young heir now became the active figurehead and putative leader of the revived royalist cause throughout the three kingdoms.[91] Indeed, Poyer and Powell's letter mentioned that they had already addressed themselves to King Charles but had not received any response, something they attributed to his 'close restraint'. As a result, they had turned to his son who was understood to have power of commission.

Poyer and Powell needed to tackle their uncomfortable parliamentary history in this text, and they did so by arguing that they had believed parliament intended 'to make you both greate and glorious'. It was only 'of late' that they realised that parliament was instead set on 'cleane contrary wayes'. While unconvincing, such formulations did duty to allow them to present themselves as the Prince's loyal servants and to request instructions and a commission under which they could operate. For his part, it is doubtful that the Prince was too choosy about his supporters as long as they were prepared to fight and support his father's full restoration. Perhaps buoyed by a positive response to their rebellion in London, which was known to have a Presbyterian majority, Poyer and Powell also exhorted the kingdom in general and the capital in particular to resist parliament and deliver King Charles 'from that horrid and trayterous oppression under which he hath so long suffered'.[92]

In addition to this pamphlet, Poyer and Powell also sent the Prince a set of manuscript propositions and instructions about the nature of their engagement, the understanding upon which they would champion the king's cause and the support they required to make such an undertaking a success. These were not circulated in print at the time, but they were published in August 1648 after their revolt had collapsed.[93] As is discussed more fully in the next chapter, the documents may have been published at the instigation of the radical preacher Hugh Peter.[94] In these 'propositions', Poyer and Powell first requested Prince Charles to 'own them for his army and to be their generall'. Secondly, they asked for an act of oblivion and indemnity for things they had done in the war, 'and to be freed from suits in law' arising out of the conflict. This was a clear reference to Poyer's entanglements with the Lorts and was a consistent element of his post-war public statements. The third and final proposition was another familiar request of Poyer's: that the Prince provide for a settling of his and Powell's arrears. In addition, they asked to be maintained in the positions they currently occupied 'until they be preferred to greater'. Backing the right side in the coming conflict, they hoped, would bring favour and preferment.

One can imagine why these propositions were not publicised along with Poyer and Powell's *Declaration* and their *Letter* to Prince Charles. They concerned some of the private and personal elements behind their royalist declaration which would not have played well in the court of public opinion where their undertaking for the king's cause centred instead on lawful government and moderate religion. It is fruitless to speculate whether Poyer *really* engaged for the king because of ideological or personal and financial reasons. He was consistent in his support for moderate reformation and, as far as we can discern, for a political settlement in which the king was restored within a balanced polity with his parliament. His concern for arrears, indemnity and future financial security can easily be portrayed as a grasping low-born merchant's priorities taking precedence over purer ideals of political commitment. Yet this would be to treat his ideological motivation as mere pragmatic cover, which it clearly was not. One can understand how Poyer's meagre dividend for his faithfulness during the war led him to seek these assurances from the Prince. We can surely recognise that his desire to lay to rest the demons of his wartime service operated alongside, rather than instead of, his commitment to the Church and Crown.

In addition to these propositions, the two men also forwarded to the Prince 'Instructions' which would facilitate a close working relationship and assist in the prosecution of their cause. These included matters such as sending arms and ammunition to Pembrokeshire; an agreed cipher for secret correspondence; for ships to be sent to Milford Haven; that officers and commanders be sent to west Wales, and, perhaps with the bitter memory of Gerard's depredations in the county still fresh, they also asked that none be sent 'that may give offence to the souldiers or country here'; 'to consider of correspondency and intelligence' with sympathetic elements in Scotland, Ireland, 'and other parts of England and north Wales'; and also to request 'proclamations of pardon for all such as shall adhere to them', a necessary insurance policy for wary potential converts to the cause. This was a comprehensive programme for expanding and maintaining their rebellion and for its integration within the wider mobilisation against parliament not just within England, but in alliance with Scottish and Irish interests too.

Prince Charles responded positively to these overtures. It was clear from the intelligence he was receiving that Poyer's revolt was striking a chord with discontented communities across England and Wales, and the Prince doubtless saw the propaganda value of backing a prominent parliamentarian who had 'seen the light' and come to support his and his father's cause. The Prince thanked Poyer and Powell for their *Declaration* and *Letter* and expressed himself 'extreamly satisfied with . . . your great zeale and affection to the King . . . and to us'.[95] He further described the 'seasonableness of your appearing in armes' at a time when 'good concurrence of others with you . . . may give us more than ordinary hope of good successe'.[96] He provided answers to their 'Propositions' (which we do not possess) and hoped these would satisfy them of his willing support and 'encouragement to proceed chearfully & constantly in this cause'.[97]

The first practical fruit of this correspondence was a commission from the Prince as 'highest captain generall under his majesty of all the forces by sea and land' in England and Wales, for Poyer to be governor of Pembroke and to hold the town in the Prince's name. He also directed Poyer to obey the individual he appointed as his general in south Wales, and it was an open secret that he was negotiating with Rowland Laugharne, then in London, to assume this role.[98] The Prince's positive response soon became public knowledge, with one newsletter reporting that he had 'sent a commission, great civilities, and offers to [the] Welsh and Lanhorne'.[99] This all sounded very heartening, but, as we shall see, there was little in the way of practical support provided beyond making encouraging noises. Prince Charles viewed the Welsh uprising as positive primarily in encouraging the Scots to invade England on the king's behalf sooner rather than later. As this did not happen, Poyer and his associates were effectively left high and dry to face the New Model on their own.

Poyer and Powell had promulgated their 'association' in the hope that other localities would follow their lead. There is plentiful evidence that 'malignants from many places . . . c[a]me in unto Poyer', with opponents suggesting that 'many lyes and fictions' were circulating to encourage them, such as that London had already declared against the parliament.[100] The Derby House Committee acknowledged in early April that the business of Pembrokeshire was a 'growing evell'.[101] One correspondent wrote later that month how the Welsh 'gayne upon theire enemies', and suggested that they were 4,000 strong with 10,000 more listed; this was an exaggeration but probably reflected significant numbers nonetheless. It was also suggested that 'most of the considerable persons of those parts' were declaring for the royalist cause, including several notable gentlemen of south-east Wales such as the Stradlings and Sir Charles Kemeys, both from Glamorgan.[102] Poyer's revolt was thus spreading throughout south Wales with several counties demonstrating a resurgent royalism, while resistance to parliament's authority was also becoming an issue in Cornwall, Bristol and other parts of south-west England. However, there were notable refusals to join Poyer, including his old enemy the earl of Carbery who withdrew himself from south Wales and declared that he would not assist the rebels or provide them with any support.[103] But other reports described much of south Wales as 'universally bent to opposeth the parliament and army what forces soever comes'.[104]

And a force was coming, although it had taken a long time to mobilise. On 1 April the senior New Model officer in south Wales, Thomas Horton, was directed to move against Poyer with Vice Admiral John Crowther supporting his efforts from the sea.[105] On 7 April the Derby House Committee wrote to the commissioners for disbanding in south Wales that it believed Horton's forces were 'sufficient' for reducing Poyer and his rebels, hoping their imminent defeat would 'make their disobedience soe farre exemplary as others will have small encouragment either there or in other parts to interrupt and trouble the publique peace'.[106] The same day, however, they wrote to Fairfax that 'the streingth of Poyer may bee encreased' and recommended that Horton's forces be augmented.[107] This order was soon repeated with even greater urgency. Horton marched from Brecon towards south-west Wales while Colonel John Okey mobilised from Cardiff; they rendezvoused near Neath in western Glamorgan. In late April, Horton encountered a rebel force commanded by Rice Powell near Carmarthen and, without waiting for reinforcements, engaged them. Colonel Fleming, 'the designed governor of Pembrock Castle', was part of Horton's army and became separated from the main body.[108] According to reports of the time, he could not face falling once more into Poyer's hands and shot himself with a pistol. Horton retreated back to Brecon. Throughout these encounters Poyer guarded Pembroke.

Horton's defeat was happily reported in the royalist press which inflated grossly the number killed and wounded and trumpeted up Fleming's demise as a major victory.[109] However, even parliamentary commentators acknowledged that this was a 'rout' and a setback.[110] The Venetian ambassador reported that the 'royalists . . . remain masters of practically the whole country [of Wales] without opposition'.[111] Consequently, the Derby House Committee wrote to Fairfax on 29 April about the 'doubtfull condition of the countrey of south Wales & of the parliaments forces there'. Belatedly recognising the scope and significance of the rebellion, they once more argued that a 'greater force than is yet there' needed to be sent to suppress the insurrection, adding 'the coninueance of it [the revolt] soe long without suppression is of very bad & dangerous examples & that which gives great encouragment to the like attempts in other places'.[112] Two days later, Fairfax wrote to the Commons Speaker about the 'growing strength of your enemies in south Wales'.[113]

He resolved to send 'a considerable part of the armie into those partes', and also determined that the bulk of the army should remain closer to Wales than it did at present. Two regiments of horse and three of foot were ordered to augment the effort to suppress the rebels. This would bring the number of parliament's forces in the area up to an impressive 8,000 men.[114] Their commander was to be Fairfax's Lieutenant General, Oliver Cromwell. This caused the royalists some pause, as they feared that Cromwell could 'quell the Welch . . . going with such a number of resolute & expert men & he himselfe a stout & good commander'.[115]

Although the appearance of the future Lord Protector would ultimately spell doom for John Poyer and his rebellion, an apparent fillip to his cause was the reappearance of Rowland Laugharne, who had escaped from London, and was first reported in south Wales on 29 April.[116] He seems to have held the Prince's commission as royalist general in south Wales, and had 'gon downe to his troopes . . . to command them (as wee hope) for his Majesties service'.[117] In his famous *History of the Rebellion*, the earl of Clarendon wrote an account of the contacts between the Welsh dissidents and the Court at Paris. Perhaps because Rowland Laugharne remained a notable figure after the Restoration, when Clarendon revised his *History* and wrote some of its later sections, the narrative attributes all the initiative (and all the restraint) in the south Wales revolt to Laugharne, while Poyer and Powell are seen as 'freaks' (that is to say capricious and inconstant individuals) whom Laugharne would 'reduce . . . when it would be time, to sober resolutions'.[118] Laugharne, Clarendon wrote, would not engage until he 'first sent a confident to Paris to inform the Prince of what he had determined and of what their wants consisted . . . desiring to receive orders for the time of their declaring'.[119] In this account, which has been followed by many historians, Laugharne is the leader of the group and orchestrates contacts with Paris. However, the first evidence we have of contact between the rebels and the Court comes from mid-April and seems to have been the initiative of Poyer and Powell with little mention of Laugharne.[120] Moreover, Poyer and Powell had independent communications with the Prince before Laugharne did. It may well be that the three men had agreed to approach Paris and coordinate their actions, but the idea that Laugharne was somehow directing matters does not stand up to scrutiny. A plausible reading of Clarendon's account is that Laugharne was reluctant to engage but that his hand was forced by the precipitate actions of Poyer and Powell; heads less 'sober' than his. Such a scenario may help explain the divisions between Laugharne and Poyer which were reported later on, and which perhaps arose out of disputes about the timing of their declaration for the king. Clarendon's account offers one way of explaining how the men entered the field without logistical support from the Prince of Wales, but it is problematical in portraying Poyer as a bit-part player in these undertakings.

Whatever the details of his communications with the Court, Laugharne had decided to join the south Wales revolt, and probably landed near Powell's forces in the west, joining with them and moving eastwards to engage Horton's army.[121] As we have seen, his political engagement was that promulgated by Poyer and Powell in their *Declaration* of 10 April, with the crucial amendment regarding tender consciences in any religious settlement.[122] On 4 May Laugharne was at St Nicholas in the Vale of Glamorgan some seven miles west of Cardiff. He wrote a pre-emptory letter to Horton asking, 'by what power you first came in and still remains [sic] in these counties of my association?'[123] He raised the issue of disbanding his troops without pay and requested that Horton withdraw from the country. In his reply, Horton informed Laugharne he had come to address Poyer and Powell's refusal to disband for which they were adjudged traitors, and also for their 'issuing out warrants 'without the least colour of authority for the tumultuous raising of the counties of Southwales', and joining disbanded soldiers 'with the most active Cavaliers both in these and other parts, into a body . . . [and] laying the foundations of a new war'.[124] Following the exchange of some ill-tempered letters with parliament's commissioners, whom he accused of being 'affected to your own ends in promoting a faction', Laugharne, perhaps forced into fighting by the overly eager actions of a Glamorgan commander, Major General John Stradling, engaged Horton's forces at St Fagans on 8 May 1648.[125] Laugharne led an army of some 8,000 men, drawn from Pembrokeshire, Carmarthenshire, Cardiganshire and Glamorgan as well as from parts of England, probably predominantly from the South-West.[126] The ensuing battle was a disaster for the Major General and the royalist cause in south Wales.[127] The insurgent forces were routed and some 3,000 royalists were taken prisoner. Laugharne was wounded but escaped and fled to the stronghold of Pembroke where Poyer awaited.[128] Poyer's absence at St Fagans generated suspicions of cowardice.[129] The royalist rising in south Wales had received a punishing body blow, but worse was to follow.

CHAPTER 7

The Siege of Pembroke, May–July 1648

The defeat at St Fagans was a bitter pill to swallow for Poyer and his fellow rebels. The hopes and enthusiasm of the insurrection's early days evaporated quickly. As *The Moderate Intelligencer* put it after reports of the battle were circulated in London, 'thus are at present the high flown expectations of the disaffected to parliament disappointed and withered'.[1] Another newsletter described 'the strange alteration the defeating of the Welsh hath made in all sorts . . . When the lettres were read in the house of the defeate, how many Royalists hunge down their heads, & went out, nott staying the conclusion'.[2] Their hopes had indeed been buoyant before this crushing reverse, with supporters rallying to the royalist banner in south Wales in impressive numbers, driven on by their subscriptions to the positions laid out in Poyer and Powell's *Declaration*. Even the Derby House Committee recognised that Horton's victory came 'in a very seasonable tyme, when the malignants were growen very high and upon the expectacion of a contrary event and had the boldnesse to threaten destruction to all that had beene faithfull to the Parliament'.[3] Although the prospect of Cromwell and his troops coming into the region was a sobering one, royalist satirists, by contrast, were happy to predict his downfall, and also to play on a universal symbol of anti-Cromwellian caricature: his large nose supposedly made red through too much drink: 'King Cromwell into Wales is gone/To deale his angry blowes:/But valiant Poyer and his boyes,/Will cuffe his copper-nose'.[4] Such jests did not flow so easily following St Fagans, however, and royalist humour turned more bilious and caustic as the spring of 1648 turned into a long summer of royalist hopes crushed. One royalist newsbook soon after reporting the loss at St Fagans, for example, made light of Horton's 'vaunted' victory 'over the poor naked Welch', adding that it was 'an easie thing to whip a man's arse when his breeches are down'.[5]

Following the debacle at St Fagans, Laugharne and Powell raced back west to their strongholds in Pembrokeshire. They were hotly pursued by Horton's forces, which were soon augmented by Cromwell's troops.[6] News of the defeat in Glamorgan gave succour and encouragement to parliament and the army's supporters in south Wales and beyond. On 11 May, Horton's letter relating his success at St Fagans was read out in the Commons, and a day of thanksgiving was ordered to be held in London on 17 May and again on 31 May throughout the rest of the country.[7] Many royalists refused to believe the reports of the battle, seeing Laugharne's defeat 'as a spoil to that universal design laid of rising in all parts of the kingdom', and so a rumour that Poyer and Powell had, in fact, killed 1,100 men spread rapidly as a kind of emotional prophylactic.[8] Given the Presbyterian sympathy for Laugharne in London, it is perhaps unsurprising that the day of thanksgiving on 17 May was 'punctually observed' by those in parliament, 'but only very slightly in the City'.[9] As one commentator wrote, the thanksgiving was 'so meanely observed that I beleeve they are almost ashamed of it'.[10]

Despite their victory, the parliamentary forces in Wales remained in deeply hostile territory and faced a struggle to reduce and pacify the local population. Thomas Horton wrote to Fairfax shortly before the engagement at St Fagans that

> It hath been formerly represented to your excellency by our most know-ing and faithful friends in these parts, how improbable it was that one party [that is his own regiments] though more considerable then ours is, should of itself be able to subdue the enemy in the field, reduce Pembroke, and keep all Southwales from rising, being generally inclined to it, by reason of the malignity of the most of the gentry, which lead the common sort of people which way they please, which we find by every days experience; and without doubt, tumults will grow greater and their numbers increase, if such a strength be not assigned to these parts as may attend both the motion of the enemy and to awe those places which are most apt to rise.[11]

Horton, then, was very conscious of the royalist sympathies of south Wales and the resources which would be required to address the many challenges he faced there. Individuals in parliament and the army were mindful of the need to press home their advantage, particularly as the example of rebellious south Wales seemed to be encouraging dissent and recalcitrance in neighbouring areas such as Bristol and Cornwall.[12] The Derby House Committee, for example, discussed south Wales's dangerous example and the necessity of a 'thorough' and effectuall prosecution of this most happy victory that all the remaynders of it may be rooted up in that place & the country quieted . . . and all other places be deterred to make the like attempt'.[13] As Horton's 3,000 men pursued Laugharne and Powell, Cromwell crossed into Wales and moved through Cardiff to Carmarthen, entering Pembrokeshire on 23 May.

The lack of coordination in the various plots, risings and diplomatic initiatives which constituted the 'Second Civil War' were becoming clear.[14] While agitation was building in Essex, Norfolk, Kent and the South West, the Scottish Engagers were not ready to invade, and the Prince of Wales was unable to provide much in the way of material support. The defection of the navy to him in late May 1648 did hold out the promise of logistical assistance to Pembroke, but this never materialised.[15] As one correspondent wrote to a Scottish Engager, the forces in Wales 'declared too soon in hopes of your assistance and appearance in England, which must be destroyed unless your unexpected armie prevent the opinion of your march'.[16] The delay in bringing the Engager army south, and thus dividing the New Model's forces, gave parliament 'tyme to oppresse the honest Welsh, the greate designe of Crumwell'.[17] St Fagans had shown that the Welsh insurrection could not contend with the New Model without external aid and assistance. While logistical support from the sea and an influx of men and *matériel* would have been welcome, reducing the New Model's presence in south Wales by drawing off regiments to meet threats elsewhere was the most viable strategy for an ultimate victory. Unfortunately for Poyer, Powell and Laugharne, the uncoordinated nature of the provincial revolts and the Scottish invasion, the failure of disaffected elements in London to rise, as well as an inability adequately to mobilise resources by the Prince of Wales whose gaze was drawn to Scotland rather than the west, meant that Fairfax's forces had the time and resources to address the Welsh threat. As Clarendon wrote, the Prince of Wales promised the rebels support but 'when Pembroke was not supplied with provisions for above two months . . . [they] were never thought of after'.[18]

Despite these enormous challenges, royalist hopes after St Fagans were not wholly extinguished. As one cavalier had it, 'since Laughorne is escaped, you must not looke upon Wales as dead, though they have received a blow'.[19] However, the Welsh rebels' backs were against the wall. They retired into their strongholds in Pembrokeshire where they had been successful in seeing off royalist invasions during the first civil war. They placed 'a good garrison' in both Pembroke and Tenby, and one newsletter noted that 'the country is defensible, and the Welch say they will loose it (if they must) by inches'.[20] Rice Powell resumed his command of Tenby while Laugharne and Poyer found themselves once again thrust together in the garrison at Pembroke. A parliamentarian newspaper reported on 20 May that 'there hath bin and still is some devision between Laughorne and Poyer'.[21] The two men had fallen out in May 1645 over command of Pembroke's forces, and perhaps old tensions were exacerbated by the timing of Poyer's declaration for the king. We may also speculate, however, whether there was a power struggle between the two men for the leadership of the nascent south Wales royalist association, which had risen under Poyer's *Declaration*, or whether the differences arose from the different conceptions of prayer book or Presbyterian undertakings that were found in the alternative versions of the rebels' 'oath' which was discussed in the previous chapter. Disunity, however, would not help them face down the most formidable military force to have appeared in Pembrokeshire since the civil wars began.

As they moved towards their opponents in south-west Wales, Thomas Wogan, the man given a special commission by parliament to assist in suppressing the south Wales insurrection, wrote an informative letter to Speaker Lenthall on 11 May.[22] He had been tasked with finding out 'who they are that have beene the countenancers and abettors of Poyer in the holding of Pembrooke Castle contrary to the expresse comands of both Houses of Parliament', and while military events might have overtaken this aspect of his duties in recent days, he nonetheless wrote partly to inform Lenthall about the 'civilian' side of his mission.[23] In his search for Poyer's 'countenancers and abbetors', Wogan pointed the finger at Arthur Owen, the Pembrokeshire MP, brother of Sir Hugh, and long-time associate of both Laugharne and Poyer. He stated that Owen's 'late arrival here to disband the souldiers give [sic] great encouradgdement [sic] to their disobedience'. As we saw in Chapter 5, Owen was indeed accused by John Eliot of having tried to keep Laugharne's supernumerary forces together as a bulwark against New Model influence. Wogan also mentioned that four-teen servants and retainers of Arthur's brother, Sir Hugh, had 'voluntarily put themselfes into Poyers service'. He further indicated that Arthur Owen had had 'many close consultations with Button and Mathewes the ring leaders of this rebellion'. These were two Glamorgan men, Miles Button (who was also Poyer's brother-in-law) and Colonel Humphrey Matthews of Castell-y-Mynach.[24] Both men were involved in the rising of the so-called 'Peaceable Army' in Glamorgan in September 1645, a clubman-style reaction against parliament and its local Independent agents, and both had fought at St Fagans.[25] They were now sitting (perhaps rather uncomfort-ably considering Button had fought with Gerard in Pembrokeshire in 1645) alongside Poyer and Laugharne in Pembroke Castle.

Wogan continued by providing a list of reliable men who should be appointed in south-west Wales as commissioners for the militia and sequestration. This was necessary, he said, because 'the rest of the comitee have adhered to Poyer'. This list read, as might be imagined, as a register of Poyer's long-standing enemies. They included the three Lort brothers, Roger, Sampson and John, John Eliot, Henry White of Henllan, Arthur Annesley (Roger Lort's brother-in-law), and Herbert Perrot, the man the Lorts had tried to install as county MP in opposition to Arthur Owen in 1646.[26] Purging the local commissions of Poyer sympathisers, he believed, would help raise soldiers for parliament and discourage 'the disaffected to rayse forces'. He also sent a list of four officers from Laugharne's army who had refused to join the insurrection and brought their troops with them into parliament's service.[27] These loyalists, he hoped, would have their arrears satisfied out of the estates of those who were in rebellion 'and that the comittee might make sale thereof and pay the same'. The parlia-ment picked up on this suggestion, for an ordinance was soon introduced for sequestrating Laugharne, Powell and Poyer's estates as well as other 'delinquents' then in rebellion.[28] The ordinance was passed on 19 June.[29] Perhaps wary of the spiteful infighting which had characterised the politics of the local committee since its establishment, however, parliament placed the sequestration of these estates in the hands of outsiders, apparently New Model officers, many of whom had been in Sir William Waller's army.

Shortly after Wogan completed his letter to the Speaker, he and the other New Model forces sat down before Tenby under Thomas Horton to commence a siege. Tenby's governor, Colonel Rice Powell, faced some 1,200 men of Colonel Overton's regiment as well as two foot companies under Colonel Constable. In the town with him, according to one publication, was 'most part of the gentlemen in Southwales that were in this rebellion against parliament and their armie'.[30] On 27 May, the attackers stormed the town's suburbs and caused a good deal of destruction; then, on 31 May, a breach was made in the town walls by their ordnance and this led in short order to the garrison's capitulation. Tenby's townsmen and women had seen a great deal of hardship during the recent conflict, and likely had little sympathy for the officers and soldiers in their midst, many of whom had come from Carmarthenshire, Monmouthshire and Glamorgan. A report of the surrender made to parliament averred that the townsfolk 'seeing nothing but ruine, brought the desperate officers and country gentlemen to a compliance', while another dispatch had it that it was the rebel soldiers who were ready to 'mutiney' and who forced their officers to come to terms.[31] Powell surrendered along with several hundred soldiers and many officers, including 'Mr Culpepper', probably the author (or co-author) and distributor of Poyer and Powell's *Declaration*. Elements of the parliamentary press rounded on 'proud, sad, insolent' Rice Powell as 'that shameful apostate who . . . deserves not mercy at all but that he should be cast into that current of the fludgate of justice, and made exemplarie to posteritie and to all perfideous villains'.[32] This kind of anger on the part of the army against men like Powell who had plunged the country back into war, was, ultimately, the sentiment that brought the king to trial in the search for 'exemplarie' justice. There were rather more sympathetic elements within the town of Tenby, however, for Powell was given 'one pottle of sack and one pottle of white wine at his goeing away a prisoner' by the town's bailiffs.[33] He was conveyed to gaol in Carmarthen.

While Horton was engaged at Tenby, Oliver Cromwell had taken on the larger and much more difficult proposition of Poyer and Laugharne in Pembroke Castle. He arrived about 24 May and established his forces to the south of the town. Cromwell himself took up residence in Captain Walter Cuny's house at Welston, near Carew. Cuny would later claim that it had cost him nearly £200 to accommodate the Lord General and his troops for the seven weeks of the siege. In 1653 he received £150 from the state for his pains.[34]

Cromwell's army was considerable, numbering perhaps 6,000 men. A contemporary report enumerates the forces in addition to his own regiment as, 'Colonel Pride's regiment of foote, Colonel Deanes and Colonel Hortons horse, part of Colonel Scroops and Colonel Okeyes dragoones'.[35]

Inside Pembroke, meanwhile, it was reported that Poyer had 300 horse and perhaps 700 foot.[36] Poyer's wife later recounted that he was 'necessitated to maintayne a thousand men for nyne weekes'.[37] The contest was one of minnows against sharks. However, as its history during the first civil war demonstrated, Pembroke was a difficult nut to crack, even for well-provisioned and numerically superior forces. After the quick successes at St Fagans and Tenby, parliamentarian supporters were hopeful that Poyer's last bolthole would crumble quickly. The Derby House Committee wrote in early June to the New Model Colonel John Lambert in the north of England that Tenby had fallen, adding 'it is hope[d] that Pembrooke will soone be had alsoe'.[38] Around the same time, a parliamentarian news-book averred that 'Pembroke Castle is not so impregnable as some report, besides what may be done with granadoes, a flanker of it on the north side may be easily battered, the wall rotten, nothing so strong as Chepstow'.[39] Even Cromwell was recorded as saying that 'he doubts not but the business of Wales will soon be over', and that he would be able 'in a short time to retreat with part of his army'.[40] This was wishful thinking. The preacher, Hugh Peter, who accompanied Cromwell to Pembroke, described the town and castle after having sat through the siege as 'the strongest place that ever we sate down before, and the castle even impregnable'.[41] The weather was also very poor, with 'constant rain' adding to the besiegers' difficulties, while Cromwell wrote of the neighbouring countryside as 'so miserably exhausted and so poor, and we [having] no money to buy victuals' so that his infantry had to survive largely on bread and water.[42] Cromwell had several pieces of ordnance before the castle but a ship which was to bring up heavier guns foundered near Berkeley in the Bristol Channel, and the siege cannon were delayed in arriving. The strength of Pembroke's defences required larger artillery to breach the walls, but this would take time to transport; as Cromwell had it, 'this place not being to be had without fit instruments for battery, except by starving'.[43] No quick victory over Poyer was in the offing.

If things were bad for the besiegers, however, conditions quickly become even worse for the inhabitants and soldiers in the town itself. It was reported that those inside could not get grass for their horses and so used thatch from the houses' roofs instead.[44] As the siege wore on, things deteriorated further. On 16 June, Cromwell wrote of the town and garrison being 'in extreme want of provision, so as in all possibility they cannot live a fortnight without being starved'.[45] This must have been extraordinarily difficult to endure, but the siege lasted longer than most anticipated. This suggests that there was some resolute, and perhaps inflexible, leadership within the town. One of our problems in assessing Poyer's role during these weeks is that we are constrained to look almost exclusively through his enemies' eyes. While this is something of a problem for the assessment of his entire life, it is particularly acute during the siege where we possess no corroborating or independent evidence. Despite these difficulties, weighing the different accounts critically still suggests that Poyer's hold over the garrison and town was forged from discipline rather than love. In a letter to Speaker Lenthall, Cromwell reported rumours that the besieged population of Pembroke 'mutinied about three days since; cried out, "Shall we be ruined for two or three men's pleasure? Better it were we should throw them over the walls." It's certainly reported to us that within four or six days they'll cut Poyer's throat, and come all away to us'.[46] Three days later, a separate report described the town as 'almost at the last gaspe being much discontented & divided' because of a lack of food.[47] Such reports argue for fierce internal dissension and a simmering resentment against Poyer behind the town's walls.

And yet the inhabitants of Pembroke did not cut his throat; they did not throw him over the walls. The siege continued for nearly a month longer. The following line of Cromwell's letter perhaps gives us a glimpse as to why this was: Poyer told the townsmen and women that 'if relief did not come by Monday night, they should no more believe him, nay they should hang him'.[48] Relief did not come, but neither was Poyer hung. Cromwell's report is possibly inaccurate, but it does suggest Poyer to be an individual of considerable charisma and conviction who was able to at least put on the appearance of hope; it also implies a leader willing to claim responsibility. We should remember that this was the man who had stood almost alone for parliament in a region that was largely royalist at the beginning of the civil war; this must have counted for much in that wet, starving summer of 1648. Poyer had also held out in sieges against Carbery and the rapacious Gerard between 1643 and 1645, and, on all these occasions, he led his fellow townsmen and women to liberty and safety. Under such extreme circumstances as Cromwell's siege it would be unsurprising if there were not discord and conflict within the town. What is surprising, and needs a better explanation than has previously been offered, is how Pembroke managed to stay as united as it did for as long as it did in resisting Cromwell's overwhelmingly superior force. A hostile report in the early stages of the siege called for parliament to be severe against the rising's ringleaders 'to whom the people are pure slaves'.[49] While this suggests some kind of subjection on the part of the common people, it does not necessarily follow that the author considered them to be simply oppressed. The report might rather be understood as portraying the people as slavish adherents to men like Poyer and Laugharne, and perhaps there was a greater sense of genuine loyalty and support for Poyer and his cause than comes through in our highly partisan sources.

Although Laugharne was present in the town with Poyer, he had been wounded at St Fagans and was described as 'very sicke of body and minde'.[50] Cromwell reportedly allowed Laugharne's wife and a doctor to visit him in the Castle.[51] Perhaps because of this incapacity he was not as prominent as we might expect for the putative leader of the royalist forces in South Wales.[52] The siege was largely understood to be against 'Poyer', and he comes across in the evidence as the town's leader. Although post-Restoration reports of the siege are to be treated as suspect, they nonetheless present Poyer as the driving force in the town, organising the defence and keeping up morale; it was even said that 'for the supply of the common souldiers [he] did beate out all his plate to a considerable sum, paying them therewith & thereby keeping them from mutiny'.[53]

Poyer must have hoped that time would be his best weapon in this fight as he hoped for rescue, probably in the shape of a relieving naval force under the banner of the Prince of Wales; a 'Richard Swanley, 1644' *redux* with, Poyer would hope, a more amenable liberator. The Prince did indeed send a commission to one Colonel Foxe on 4 June to sail to Tenby or Pembroke and deliver Laugharne a letter assuring him of 'the esteem in which the Queen and Prince hold him' and to convey the same to Poyer and Rice Powell. Foxe was also to inform them of the Prince's own intention to come to England, when, he promised, 'he will have particular regard to the good of the Welsh'.[54] Perhaps such assurances from the exiled Court managed to get through to Poyer, and helped stiffen his resolve. Yet ultimately these hopes were built on air. The Prince never arrived in England in 1648. His intelligence was hopelessly out of date as he conveyed his esteem to Rice Powell who was already languishing in gaol and considered Tenby a friendly port when it was in parliamentarian hands. We know that Poyer used the prospect of royal assistance as leverage with Pembroke's inhabitants, telling them when parliamentary vessels in the Haven fired their cannon for a victory over rebels in Kent, that it was

'"Prince Charles and his revolted ships"' who was 'coming with relief'.[55] And while there was indeed a navy revolt in the Prince's name in late May 1648, there was no sign of royalist ships on the Pembrokeshire horizon that summer. One can imagine the seductiveness for Poyer of the Prince's assurances of assistance and statements of moral support; but assurances which did not translate into concrete military and logistical aid were not much use in the face of Cromwell's ordnance.

Poyer, then, was the effective leader of Pembroke garrison despite Laugharne's presence, and there are some reports of the political and personal positions he espoused, although these are all from unfriendly sources and need to be treated cautiously. An interesting letter from Pembrokeshire of 21 May described how Poyer 'holds to his first resolution of such and such things as he demanded', while another dispatch reported that 'Poyer pretends his old principles still'.[56] These letters suggest that he remained fixed on securing his arrears and indemnity as he had demanded from Christopher Fleming.[57] We might read these letters alongside another report of a Cromwell dispatch to the Derby House Committee from late June. In this letter, Cromwell related that Poyer had sent him a message 'admiring that a David should be so persecuted by a Saul, having been alwayes faithfull to the parliament of England ever since the beginning of these wars'.[58] As we shall see in the next chapter, Poyer consistently emphasised his faithfulness to parliament after his surrender. Such a strategy might look like him turning his back on the royalist revolt, and doubtless it was politic to put some distance between himself and the diehard royalist wing which he had never occupied. He was probably looking to 'play both ends against the middle' to a degree and emphasise his parliamentarian credentials from the first war to save his skin.

Additionally, it is interesting that Poyer turned again to the example of Saul and David from the first Book of Samuel as he had done in his response to Fleming on 13 March 1648. This suggests that Poyer saw himself as a constant and faithful servant of God and parliament who had a troubled relationship with power and authority, as did David with Saul. However, he was playing with fire by equating Cromwell with the persecuting Saul. Cromwell was increasingly convinced that his campaigns with the New Model were revealing the will of God in granting His chosen instruments victories over the wicked. Poyer's equating himself with David does suggest a considerable degree of hubris, but it also reveals his conviction that he was holding firm to the principles for which parliament had called him to serve in 1642.

Throughout this period Cromwell's forces bombarded the town and castle. Food and supplies were running low and morale, as we have seen, was fragile. Glimpses of Poyer emerge trying to encourage his troops and fellow townspeople with prospects of relief and the promise that some kind of liberation was at hand. Presumably news reports about uprisings against parliament in places like Essex, Kent and the north of England, as well as the apparently imminent Scottish invasion, must have been used to rally the besieged population and maintain their fighting spirit. The argument that the New Model would be required elsewhere and the siege lifted (or at least weakened to the point where it could be challenged) was likely deployed. Indeed, around 25 June, acting at the request of the Derby House Committee, Cromwell dispatched four troops of horse and two of dragoons to join Colonel John Lambert to protect the north from the Scottish threat.[59] However, Cromwell wrote that he could not spare more troops without 'manifest hazard to these parts'. This was largely because of a hostile and recalcitrant countryside which, Cromwell acknowledged, had already experienced two or three insurrections 'and are ready to do it every day'.[60] In another letter around this time, he described an 'insurrection . . . near the siege' of '500 country men' who had gathered together under the pretence of stopping the earl of Inchiquin landing, although they were, in fact, a 'royall party'. Pembroke town was 'much discontented' when some of Cromwell's cavalry put them to flight.[61] A country hostile to Cromwell would have been a source of encouragement and succour to those besieged in Pembroke. Poyer may have suggested to his fellow sufferers that they were the epitome of the kinds of resistance being shown by their neighbours, friends and families in surrounding parishes.

Cromwell anticipated the rapid reduction of the town in a letter to Fairfax of 28 June, particularly, he said, if he could obtain the heavy ordnance required to breach Pembroke's sturdy walls. The missive also noted one aspect of his enemies' resistance which we should remember when considering Poyer's plight and the nature of his leadership. Cromwell described his opponents as 'a very desperate enemy who, being put out of all hope of mercy, are resolved to endure to the uttermost extremity'.[62] Poyer's resolve, and indeed probably that of Laugharne and many of the other officers in Pembroke, was strengthened by the knowledge that they would almost certainly face death if they fell into Cromwell's hands. Such a fate was particularly likely for Poyer, who was publicly proclaimed a traitor and had become the figurehead of the royalist rebellion in south Wales and a hate figure of the Independent press.

At the end of June, Cromwell at last received the heavy artillery he needed. These weapons caused considerable damage to Pembroke town, destroying a number of houses and causing some thirty deaths. On 7 July, Poyer reportedly sallied out of the town at the head of eighty horse and 150 foot, but his brave assault was to little effect.[63] This was something of a last gasp as men were by now leaving the garrison under the cover of night and either escaping or joining Cromwell's forces. The town was broken and even Poyer now despaired of any assistance materialising. A later account described how the town and castle had 'neither ammunicion nor provisions left & noe hopes of releife'.[64]

At first, Cromwell demanded Pembroke's complete surrender and would not consider articles or capitulation.[65] However, the pressing need to meet the Scots who were about to invade the north softened his position, and he composed articles for the town's surrender. One report had it that these articles were more lenient than many had wished because of the need quickly to resolve this already over-lengthy siege.[66] The New Model chaplain Hugh Peter went into Pembroke with the terms of surrender, 'at [viz: "as"] a hostage . . . to wait upon Major General Langhorn and Poyer'.[67] He stayed at Poyer's house where, as is discussed in the next chapter, he came across Poyer's commission from Prince Charles and their correspondence. A tense negotiation began on 9 July, with one correspondent noting that the articles Peter carried were 'long disputed, theirs [i.e. the Pembroke officers' counter-articles] sent out, rejected; some danger of breaking off'.[68] Initial offers of articles were often rejected by garrison commanders; to be seen to capitulate too readily could be construed as a blot on their honour and possibly a form of treachery. Revised articles were drafted by the besieging Council of War, and Cromwell wrote to Poyer with an ultimatum on 10 July: 'I have considered your condition and my owne duty; and (without threatening) must tell you that if (for the sake of some) this offer be refused and thereby misery and ruine befill [sic: 'befall] the poore souldiers and people with you, I know wher to charge the blood you spill'.[69] Cromwell was thus offering terms or a devastating assault on the town and castle with no quarter being given. His letter reveals that a stumbling block with the original articles had been the handling of a select group of individuals ('for the sake of some'); this clearly meant Poyer, Laugharne and a group of officers who had hoped for more lenient treatment.

Poyer and his associates received the revised articles 'at which', one report runs, 'the Governour [Poyer] and Laughorne [were] much displeased, being surrendered to the mercy of Parliament; but [they were] overswayed, and the articles accepted of'.[70] The rebellion's leaders had desired assurances of their own safety, but were overruled by their fellow officers who only saw death at the New Model's hands if these terms were rejected. Thus it was that, under the terms of the final articles, Laugharne and Poyer along with Colonel Humphrey Matthews, Captain Philip Bowen and Poyer's younger brother, Captain David Poyer, surrendered themselves 'to the mercy of the parliament'. Additional clauses provided that Miles Button and sixteen other officers, who mostly hailed from Pembrokeshire, Glamorgan and Monmouthshire, be banished from the kingdom for two years; other officers and soldiers had liberty to return home after engaging to 'live quietly and peaceably'; and Pembroke's townspeople had guarantees of freedom from plunder and violence.[71] Perhaps in an indication of his continued opposition to these terms, the articles were signed not by Governor John Poyer but by his brother, David.

Poyer's rebellion was over, as was the royalist rising in south Wales. Revolts elsewhere in England were soon extinguished. Cromwell himself marched northward to meet the Scottish Engager army. He left orders that the defensive 'workes of the towne and castle' of Pembroke be demolished.[72] After a major engagement at Preston between 17 and 19 August 1648, the Scots were roundly defeated and the king's (and the Prince's) hopes were crushed. The Second Civil War was at an end. Cromwell, convinced that the New Model's victories were signals of God's favour towards their cause, moved north to settle Scotland. Behind him, many of his radicalised soldiers demanded justice against those who had plunged the nation into war once again. Revenge and retribution were on the minds of New Modellers and Independents. As Poyer travelled east under close military guard, he must have pondered what such 'justice' would look like for him.

Revenge and Revolution: Poyer, Print and Parliamentary Justice, August 1648–April 1649

Following Pembroke's capitulation, the five prisoners, including John Poyer, who had 'surrender[ed] themselves to the mercy of parliament' remained with Cromwell's forces as he left south Wales. They were joined by others who had been taken at Tenby: Colonel Rice Powell, Colonel Culpepper, Colonel Edward Kemeys and Captain Henry Addys. On 23 July, Cromwell left his prisoners at Gloucester where 'some or all of them, it is said, will be tried there by a Council of War'.[1] This would have been a garrison court martial, one of which had sat at Gloucester during the first war. After the taking of Tenby was reported in the Commons on 7 June, the House ordered that Cromwell 'do proceed against . . . the prisoners . . . by a Council of War as are so tryable according to the course of war in some place of safety'.[2] The parliamentary press had it that those who were 'so perfidious to the parliament' such as Rice Powell, were to receive the exemplary justice of a court martial rather than being turned over to the civil authorities.[3] Clearly, this was to be an exemplary form of military justice against 'perfidious' rebels like Powell and Poyer, and so, in leaving his charges at Gloucester, Cromwell was following the orders parliament had laid down a month before.

However, on 21 July, as Cromwell was still approaching Gloucester, the Commons passed a new order that 'such persons as have been for the parliament and are revolted from the parliament, that have been taken prisoners, be sent to the General [Sir Thomas Fairfax] and be tried by a Council of War'.[4] It is unclear why the prisoners were not to receive a swift military trial at Gloucester, and why their cases were referred to Fairfax rather than being handled locally. The initiative appears to have been designed to deal specifically with the Welsh rebels who had just been defeated. It may be that there was some squeamishness about proceeding too fast and too quickly against prominent figures in a royalist rebellion while the country remained uneasy and agitated. Parliament did not, perhaps, wish to make martyrs too quickly in south Wales. An alternative, of course, is that parliament wished to have a set piece trial and a highly visible set of executions in London to terrify the population and demonstrate the fate of rebels on a national stage.

Discussions of 'justice' were pervasive following the Second Civil War, particularly as that concept related to King Charles I himself. There were sections among the New Model soldiery in particular who considered Charles I implicated in the blood guilt of the civil wars and demanded an atonement for his constant betrayals and the misery and sufferings he had caused.[5] Others argued that Charles needed to be politically neutered but still retain his throne as a kind of constitutional monarch. Some even suggested that his guilt could be assuaged by having senior advisers executed on his behalf. There remained the Presbyterians and royalists, of course, who considered him their divinely anointed monarch and thought that none on earth could judge him. The road towards putting the king on trial and, ultimately executing him, was a long and complex one in which the nature of retributive justice was frequently under discussion.

The cases of Poyer, Laugharne and their fellow prisoners were caught up in these wider discussions of justice, but they were, of course, of a very different tenor from those concerning the king. These were military prisoners taken in battle and there were recognised codes of conduct which applied in such situations.[6] They had surrendered at mercy instead of quarter, and thus had no guarantee of their lives. However, while they were military prisoners, they had surrendered themselves to the mercy of *parliament* rather than of the army or Cromwell himself. They may have been thankful in this regard as the royalist leaders taken at the bloody siege of Colchester, Sir Charles Lucas and Sir George Lisle, were subject to the summary justice of Lord General Fairfax, who had them both shot immediately after the town was taken.[7] It may be, then, that the Commons order of 21 July was designed to show parliament's authority over their legal position, although it deferred to the requirements of military justice by handing the men over to Fairfax.

The fact that Cromwell relinquished his responsibility for meting out justice to Poyer and his associates did not stop him from advising others on the course they should follow in such cases. His assessment of how to deal with Pembroke's rebels is revealing of wider army sentiment towards such side-changers in the wake of the Second Civil War. In a letter to Fairfax of 28 June, Cromwell hoped that parliament and the army would be able to discern 'what the mind of God may be in all this, and what our duty is'.[8] He was convinced that God's purpose was not 'that the poor godly people of this kingdom should still be made the object of wrath and anger, nor that God would have our necks under a yoke of bondage'. In the 'things that have lately come to pass', Cromwell discerned 'the wonderful works of God . . . who will yet save His people and confound His enemies'. Cromwell's conviction was that God was with the 'poor godly people' of England such as himself and his zealous soldiers, and that He wished their designs to triumph, even though they were tested by trials such as renewed war.[9] As the instruments of God's work, Cromwell and the army recognised that a form of judgment was required on those evil and deluded persons who stood in the way of Providence and confounded His designs.

This line of thinking about the 'wonderful works of God' and the need to deal rigorously with His enemies, also came through in a letter Cromwell wrote to Lenthall immediately after Pembroke's surrender.[10] In this dispatch, Cromwell dilated on the five 'persons excepted' (including Poyer, of course) under the articles of surrender. The men were, he wrote,

> such as have formerly served you in a very good cause, but, being now apostatised I did rather make election of them than of those who had always been for the king, judging their iniquity double because they have sinned against so much light, and against so may evidences of Divine Presence going along with and prospering in a righteous cause, in the management of which they themselves had a share.

So Cromwell had chosen to make examples of those who had once fought in parliamentarian colours but had rejected its righteous cause and thus betrayed God's manifest design. These were apostates who demanded exemplary treatment to demonstrate the perils of resisting (and particularly in turning one's back on) God's revealed plan for the kingdom.

Poyer and his fellow inmates were moved from Gloucester to Nottingham Castle where they were soon joined by other high-profile prisoners from the defeated insurgency in the north, including the leader of the uprising there, Sir Marmaduke Langdale.[11] In November

1648, Cromwell, who was then camped near Pontefract, received a letter from the Governor of Nottingham concerning a former rebel who had approached parliament's committee for compounding with delinquents, the body which dealt with royalists by determining a fine they should pay as punishment for their disloyalty. In his own letter to the compounding commissioners, Cromwell expressed astonishment that such a rebel should be considered for the leniency of a mere fine, and his comments are interesting not only for understanding his attitude towards insurgents like Poyer, but also because he discussed one of those taken alongside Poyer in Pembroke who, like him, had surrendered to parliament's mercy.[12] Cromwell asserted that 'their fault who have appeared in this summer's business is certainly double to theirs who were in the first, because it is the repetition of the same offence against all the witnesses that God has borne, by making and abetting to a second war'. He was disgusted that when parliament had such men in custody 'and it will cost you nothing to do justice . . . after all this trouble and the hazard of a second war, for a little more money all offences shall be pardoned!' Cromwell then spoke of Colonel Humphrey Matthews who had been taken at Pembroke, stating 'this cause we have fought for has not had a more dangerous enemy, but he apostatised from your cause and quarrel'. He had been a parliamentarian lieutenant colonel in Gloucester during the first war, but then became 'the desperatest promoter of the Welsh rebellion amongst them all'.[13] Despite his history of disloyalty, Matthews had petitioned parliament, been released from custody, and was allowed to compound for his royalism, 'by what order', Cromwell thundered, 'I know not'.[14]

The letter reveals Cromwell's attitude towards Matthews but also, by extension towards Poyer, Powell and Laugharne, who had demonstrated a similar history of parliamentary service followed by wicked betrayal, or 'sinning against the light'. Cromwell finished the letter by remarking on the army's sense of grievance that such turncoats, whose defeat had been purchased with so much death, were effectively being freed by civilians in parliament who did not respect the army's sacrifices made in their name: 'I find a sense amongst the officers concerning such things as these, even to amazement; which truly is not so much to see their blood made so cheap, as to see such manifest witnessings of God (so terrible and so just) no more reverenced'. Such attitudes towards the rebels of 1648 were echoed elsewhere, as at Colchester where the besieged royalists were told to expect a 'taste of the fury of an exasperated soldiery . . . justice must be done on such exemplary offenders who have embroiled the kingdom in a 2nd bloody war'.[15] These attitudes would determine John Poyer's fate, and they mirror the growing sense in the army that the search for justice against the king himself might need to be taken out of the hands of a parliament which seemed too willing to deal meekly with traitors and turncoats. As one parliamentarian soldier lamented, 'of their [parliament's] clemency we have had sad experience'.[16]

Although Poyer had been surrendered to parliament's mercy, then, there was not necessarily a unity of purpose between parliament and the army, or even within parliament itself, as to what his and his fellows' fate should be. Humphrey Matthews's case suggested that some kind of deal might be possible if Poyer could exploit these differences between his captors. Perhaps he did not have to die, particularly if he managed to tell a convincing story of the nature and longevity of his parliamentary service to sympathetic ears. However, as the Second Civil War was climaxing with the invasion of the Scots, so parliament sought to bring his case to a conclusion. On 14 August the Commons ordered that Fairfax 'take a course for the speedy trying by martial law' of those taken at Pembroke and Tenby.[17] This decision to move to a prosecution of the case may have been encouraged by an intervention from the man who had carried the treaty articles into Pembroke, Hugh Peter.[18] In early August, Peter produced a pamphlet entitled *A Copy of his Highnesse Prince Charles his Letter*.[19] The pamphlet reproduced a letter which Peter had sent from Swansea on 23 July. In this dispatch he related how, while he waited in Poyer's house in Pembroke as a 'hostage' during the treaty negotiations, he found 'in a vault there' Poyer's commission from the Prince as well as the Prince's letters to him and Powell. In addition, he claimed to have discovered 'all the transactions betwixt the Prince and them, together with many other letters of theirs, manifesting the whole designe of this years trouble'.[20] Peter only reproduced the commission and the letter to Poyer in the pamphlet, but he was clear that Poyer was engaged in a design that was thoroughly royalist in its inception and execution. Moreover, Peter placed Poyer's actions at the heart of the troubles and tumults which still raged around the country. He asserted that his evidence 'shewes they fought not for arrears'. In other words, Peter alleged – despite Poyer's pleas about money to parliament in 1647 and to Fleming in 1648 – that this was, in fact, a thoroughly *royalist* revolt. Such a conclusion is deeply tendentious, of course, for Poyer's rising was initially a mutiny over arrears and indemnity, which snowballed into a royalist insurgency. Peter thus publicised Poyer and Powell's particular culpability for the disorders in south Wales and rejected the claim that they were anything other than royalist supporters who sought the destruction of the parliamentary state.

That this was a coordinated publication exercise is indicated by the fact that a letter from an army officer at Gloucester dated 27 July, probably when Poyer, Laugharne and Powell were still incarcerated in the town, and containing the material Peter recovered from Poyer's house, was published across two issues of the newsbook *The Moderate Intelligencer*; the first issue appeared at the same time as Peter's tract.[21] The unnamed officer spoke of having to leave too many of his fellows behind in Wales while they were needed against the invading Scots, 'but the disaffection [there] is still great, the plot was laid deep and the people cunningly wownd in'.[22] He demonstrated that this was the case by reproducing not only Poyer's letter to the Prince and his commission, but also his set of instructions and propositions which requested, for example, coordination with the Prince's supporters throughout the three kingdoms. In an echo of Peter's words, the Gloucester correspondent remarked how the Poyer material demonstrated his 'handsome contrivance of a new war through the kingdom'.

It may be hypothesised, then, that parliament's decision to move to the 'speedy' trying of Poyer and his fellow rebels was encouraged by the disclosure of this material, with its evidence not only of Poyer's duplicity in claiming that he rose to demand arrears, but also that his rising was tied into and coordinated with the other revolts of the Second Civil War. As Peter described it, through the material found in Poyer's house one could discern 'the laying every peece of them [the royalist revolts] in all parts of Scotland, England, and Wales'.[23] The production of this material, then, seems to have been designed to render Poyer more deserving of swift and severe justice. The army connection is important here. Peter was close to Cromwell who, as we have seen, pushed for judgment against 'apostates' like Poyer and his fellow rebels. Peter's pamphlet was published by Robert Ibbitson, a printer with close connections to the New Model. The *Moderate Intelligencer* letter and copy of the Poyer material also came from within the army. Taken together, this looks like evidence of an army-inspired (perhaps even a Cromwell-inspired) attempt to expedite the trial and eventual execution of the men seen as the main perpetrators of the spring's insurrections. Although it cannot be proven that the production of this material occasioned the Commons order of 14 August, it probably increased pressure on parliament to move against Poyer and his allies.

The Commons' order swiftly to begin the rebels' trial spurred the men's allies into action, however, and on 19 August 1648, the Prince of Wales himself wrote to Lord General Fairfax about their cases.[24] The Prince told Fairfax that he had been informed 'that some rigorous course is intended' against the three men 'for things done under the authority of my commission'. He described himself as 'extreamly sensible of such a proceeding, as well in regard of the merit of the person[s] as of my owne honour, which I take to be highly concernd in their preservation'. He claimed that executing the rebels would require him to execute any parliamentarians who fell into his hands. He requested, therefore, that 'such moderation may be used towards them as becomes soldgers to one another, and as I conceive to be due to them'. It is noticeable that Prince Charles was prepared to own Poyer's case as one that engaged his honour, and also to praise his merits. Although Poyer was not known personally to the Prince, the royalist rebellion had yet to be suppressed entirely in England, and it would have been poor public relations to allow a highly visible adherent like Poyer to be sacrificed without some kind of intervention or plea for his life. For his part, Fairfax replied that he had passed the letter to parliament, but that it was 'not in my power to act further, the parliament having ordered in what way they shall be proceeded against'. He continued that the prospective severity of their punishment was 'not so much that they were in hostility against them . . . as that they have betrayed the trust they reposed in them to the sad ingageing this nation again in war and blood'. He concluded that it was 'not in my power to interpose their justice'.[25] There were echoes here of Cromwell's letter to Fairfax at Pembroke's surrender which argued that the rebels were doubly guilty for betraying God and the parliamentarian cause, and thus required exemplary punishment.

Perhaps because of the Prince's intervention, but perhaps also because of the febrile and rapidly changing politics of autumn 1648, Poyer and his associates were not, in fact, brought swiftly to trial. The struggles between Presbyterians and Independents within parliament, and indeed between parliament and the army, intensified after the end of the Second Civil War.[26] The Presbyterians became very wary of an unbridled soldiery in alliance with radical Independents, and what this might mean for the

future of Church, state and monarchy. Part of Cromwell's frustrations
with the parliament, as seen in his letter concerning Humphrey Matthews,
was that the assembly did not seem to understand the necessary course of
action in moving against those who had been shown as enemies of right-
eousness. This sentiment was widely shared in the army, and soldiers'
representations in the autumn asked why justice had yet to be done on men
like Poyer, Laugharne and Powell.[27] The more moderate Presbyterian caucus within parliament still had a considerable presence, and they acted as
a brake on the courses advocated by the army. It was likely a Presbyterian
initiative, then, that produced the Commons order of 10 November 1648
for banishing Major General Laugharne along with several others (but not
Poyer) rather than their facing a military trial.[28] However, this was another
parliamentary order which came to nothing.

The failure adequately to prosecute and punish those responsible for
the renewed fighting by parliament, including Charles I, was the cause of
considerable resentment in the army. Negotiations between parliament
and the king continued at Newport on the Isle of Wight, but many radical
Independents considered this a fool's errand. As parliament pressed for
a settlement with the king on the basis of lenient proposals, the army's
patience broke. On 6 December 'Pride's Purge' saw the army exclude those
MPs whom it considered unfriendly to its cause from sitting in parliament; among them the Presbyterian Arthur Owen of Pembrokeshire.[29]
The remnant, the so-called 'Rump Parliament', was a pliable instrument
of the army, and it was the Rump that ultimately resolved to put the king
on trial. It established a High Court of Justice in which the case against
Charles was put by John Poyer's onetime legal counsel, John Cooke. The
commissioners who placed Charles on trial for his life were desperate
that he should plead to the charge of treason, recognise the authority of
the court, and thus acknowledge the new political dispensation in which
he might be spared his life; he might even remain king, albeit stripped of
most of his power.[30] If this was the case, however, their tactic failed and
Charles remained steadfast in refusing to acknowledge that the court had
any authority to sit in judgment on him. As he refused to plead to the
charge, the court could only move to sentence. Finding him guilty, fifty-
nine commissioners of the court signed his death warrant, among them
Thomas Wogan. On 30 January 1649, Charles I was beheaded outside the
Banqueting House in Whitehall. For the first and last time in its history,
England and Wales became a republic.

It is unsurprising given these momentous events that the trial of John Poyer and his fellows was not a priority. However, they remained in custody and certainly had not fallen off the radar entirely. On 19 December, reports circulated that the three men were shortly to be shot at Windsor, and that they had supposedly taken this news with magnanimity, replying 'Gods will be done, thank God, we have made our peace with him and shall without fear undergo what he shall be pleased to suffer men to doe unto them'.[31] Nothing happened, but expectations of such exemplary punishment were certainty in the air, and on 26 December 1648 a letter of intelligence observed that the king was expected at Windsor and that 'a huge scaffold is prepared to destroy some of his freinds upon his owne sight as soone as he comes thither & 'tis thought Laughorne, Powell & Poyer shalbe those for I am told the council of war have condemned them to dye'.[32] The report was inaccurate in that the council of war (or court martial) had yet to sit on this case, but the three men were indeed brought to Windsor Castle around the same time as Charles I. It is interesting to speculate whether Poyer saw the king, or perhaps even had a conversation with him, in the short time before his death. In late January 1649, the leader of the Scottish Engagers the duke of Hamilton, escaped his captors at Windsor, although he was soon recaptured. Several other royalists managed to slip the leash too, and it was rumoured that Poyer, Powell and Laugharne had also escaped, although these reports proved false.[33] Thus it was that on the day following the king's execution, 31 January 1649, worries about these escapes produced a debate in the Commons about bringing 'chief delinquents', including Poyer, Powell and Laugharne, 'to a speedy tryall'.[34] The House appointed a committee to produce an act setting up a court to try these 'enemies of the state'.[35] Despite this initiative, the wheel of parliamentary justice still only turned slowly, and it would be more than two months before such a tribunal convened.

It was probably around this time that Elizabeth Poyer, John's wife, wrote a letter to her sister, and wife of Rowland Laugharne, Ann.[36] It is a heart-rending document which suggests the terrible privations Elizabeth suffered as she waited for her husband (and her brother-in-law's) trial. Elizabeth thanked her sister for 'all yor unspeakable favors' since she arrived 'to this place', adding 'next to God yow have ben my seporte [support] undoubtedlie elce [else] I had starved'. However, she was still constrained to ask for a loan of five shillings, 'I am verie much ashamed in regard I have ben troublesom to yow'. She promised to repay the money at the first opportunity, but 'the Lord knowes my condicion is most stranglie sad'. Elizabeth was reduced to such straits that she was borrowing money from her landlady and did not have any 'shoues [shoes] to goe forth a doore'. This pathetic letter shows how far the Poyers had fallen. John had asserted his own pressing need for funds in his numerous representations for compensation and arrears, and although we might be sceptical as to some of the sums claimed, his persistent concern with money does suggest that the family's finances were in a parlous state. Poyer's business interests must have been severely disrupted by the war, and latterly by the siege of Pembroke. Moreover, since June 1648, Poyer's properties had been sequestered and under parliamentary control. Elizabeth likely had no source of income and it must have been difficult readily to obtain loans as the wife of a high-profile 'rebel'. In all of this, we should remember that she also had four young children to look after. Her letter offers a very human perspective on the consequences of Poyer's momentous decision to stand against his former parliamentary masters.

As part of the ongoing assault on the rebels' financial interests, Poyer, Powell and Laugharne, were all included in the Act of 23 February 1649 concerning the sequestration of delinquents in south Wales.[37] The Act recognised that much of south Wales (including Pembrokeshire) was, from the beginning of the wars, 'under the command of the kings forces and so continued for many years'. However, parliament acknowledged that there were different kinds of 'delinquents' among the population. On the one hand there were 'divers desperate malignants that have maliciously endeavoured the subversion of parliaments', while on the other there were those 'forced in some things to comply with them to preserve themselves and families from spoil and ruine'. Hence the Act wished to make 'some distinction' whereby 'exemplary justice may be done on the most capital offendors and the more moderate punishment be inflicted on the lesser, now involved in a general guilt'. The Act thus imposed a fine of £20,500 on the counties to be paid by the 'lesser offendors', or ex-royalists, the collection of which was to be overseen by commissioners who included Walter Cuny, Roger and Sampson Lort, Thomas Wogan, James Philipps and John Eliot. This would not be a pleasant experience for those who had sided with Poyer and Laugharne through the 1640s, and it would also mean the continued misery of Elizabeth Poyer and Ann Laugharne. The three Pembrokeshire rebel leaders of 1648 were excluded from a general pardon and the Act was a reminder that 'exemplary justice' for the leaders of the recent rebellion was still in MPs' minds.

The following month the business of Poyer's trial appeared finally to be moving toward a conclusion. It seems that parliament waited until the highest-ranking rebels of the recent war, the duke of Hamilton, the earl of Holland and Lord Capel had been dealt with. They were executed on Friday 9 March, and on Monday 12 March the Commons moved to consider the remaining 'grand delinquents of the kingdome under restraint and prisoners of war'. A newspaper reported that in this debate, 'Major General Lanhorn, Poyer and Powell were first insisted upon'.[38] This suggests a sense within the House that these were notorious capital offenders whose cases had been unresolved for too long. It is also possible, of course, that they had particular enemies in the Rump who insisted on the rapid conclusion of their case: Thomas Wogan would be an obvious candidate to press for this. The House confirmed their order of 14 August 1648 referring the Welsh rebels to the army 'to be tryed by a court martiall', and a warrant was sent to bring them from Windsor to Whitehall to face trial. On 14 March, Poyer appeared with Laugharne and Powell as well as one 'Major Phillips', and they were committed to the custody of the Marshal General of the Army to await their trial. The press reported that

> Poyer is very poore, and had a little used some practise of his glovers trade while hee was prisoner at Windsor, he did ride to London without boots, in a paire of corse gray cloath stockins and shoes, with a paire of spurs upon his shoos; they are all of them very reserved in their speeches.[39]

It seems this was an attempt at satire, playing on Poyer's trade and his reduced circumstances which meant that he could not maintain the apparel of a gentleman's boots, but had been forced to fashion shoes with spurs, a sign of gentility. Nonetheless, in concert with Elizabeth's letter, this image of an impoverished and cowed Poyer provides us with graphic evidence of the family's rapid fall and parlous straits.

The following day, the Council of State appointed Colonel John Okey, Laugharne's second-in-command from April 1647, Colonel Thomas Pride (of 'Pride's Purge') and Hugh Peter to draw up the charge against Poyer, Laugharne, Powell, Major Phillips, David Poyer and Captain Philip Bowen, 'and to send for papers and persons in order thereunto and to expedite the whole'.[40] Okey had local knowledge, having served as the New Model officer in south Wales, while Peter's presence suggests that his publication of the communications between the Prince of Wales and Poyer would be utilised against the latter. These were clearly unsympathetic prosecutors, but the process of deposing witnesses and obtaining documents would take time, hence there was a further delay of three weeks before the court martial actually sat. The same day that Okey and the others were appointed to draw up the charge, a parliamentary committee ordered that Roger Lort, Sampson Lort, John Eliot and James Lewis, who had been under investigation for suspicions about their early royalism, should be discharged, 'they having surrendered and taken the benefit of the parliament's declaration of 1643 and since borne arms and held office for the parliament and have been active in opposing Langhorne, Poyer and Powell in the last insurrection'.[41] There was a terrible symmetry in the issuing of this order at the same time as Poyer faced a trial for his life; it underlines how total the Lorts's victory was.

The hiatus between the establishing of the court martial and its convening gave Poyer time to try to explain his position to a wider audience through the medium of print, although he was to be crossed in this, as in so many other things, by his nemesis John Eliot. A pamphlet was produced entitled *The Grounds & Reasons of Coll: Poyer Takeing Armes in the Second Difference*. Historians have not noticed this work because no printed copies survive, but someone transcribed the pamphlet and this remains among the papers of William Clarke, secretary to the Council of the Army.[42] It can also be reconstructed from the pamphlet John Eliot published to answer it, which has also remained largely unused by scholars.[43] The pamphlet was supposedly authored by 'Wm. Gr. gent', one who 'was present & an eye witness in all these accions'. This indicates someone called 'William Griffith[s], gentleman', a very common name in south Wales, but we may hazard a guess that the author was William Griffith of Penybenglog in Pembrokeshire. He was an antiquary and historian whose family had a similar political record to Poyer's, having supported parliament at the outbreak of war and been plundered by Gerard's royalists; he was also connected to the Owens of Orielton.[44] Little more is known, unfortunately, about any relationship this individual might have had with Poyer. It is possible, of course, that Poyer wrote the tract himself and was simply using Griffith's name to afford his account a degree of authorial distance.

The pamphlet itself was a review of Poyer's actions in the war and his diligent service for parliament. It emphasised that he was called to service by parliament's declarations but that his 'enemies' by 'their malice & false informations (after they had longe endeavoured) brought him in dislike with the parliament & army'.[45] Through the agency of these 'enemies' (clearly the Lorts and Eliot) his commands were taken from him long before his public breach with Fleming. Thus Poyer, via Griffith, was at pains to present himself as constant and faithful to parliament, and to argue that he was betrayed by others, rather than being wholly culpable for his role in the 'second difference'. Poyer also renewed his claims that the Lorts sought to murder him. For this reason, he said, he sought refuge in Pembroke Castle where his enemies besieged him. Poyer asserted that he requested arrears and indemnity without which he could not live because of the 'great power & comands which his enemies were intrusted [with]'. They despised him, he said, because he forced them to abandon their early royalism and adhere to the parliament.[46] In this version of events, Fleming arrived at Pembroke but was seduced by the silken lies of the Lort brothers and so 'refused to treat, proclaimed him [Poyer] rebel and besieged the Castle for seven weeks'. Poyer hoped that parliament might be truthfully informed of his services and provide him relief, but 'too much creditt was given to his bloody enemyes' who 'disperses [sic] abroad lyinge pamphletts to strengthen themselves in the opinion of the people, to defame & make him odious to the parliament & army as possible [sic] they could devise'.[47] The pamphlet then skips over the inconvenient truths of his declaration for the king, rallying the people of south Wales, his assault on Fleming in Henllan, and his dogged resistance to Cromwell's siege.

After his surrender, Poyer stated that he has been 'a close prisoner, having nothing to mayntayne himself, his wife and foure poore children but the charity of his fellow prisoners'. His dishevelled appearance before the Commons on 14 March does not simply seem to have been the invention of the newsbooks. He lamented that 'his enemyes cries [sic] out for justice' against him, but they were getting off scot free for their own royalist pasts and many subsequent betrayals of parliament's cause. Poyer averred that he would be able to give details of their crimes and misdemeanours 'if a resonable tyme bee granted him'.[48] The pamphlet concluded with a list of Poyer's services to parliament, beginning with the fact that he 'was one of the first that declared in armes for the parlyament in south Wales'.[49] Time, however, was something that Poyer did not have. The pamphlet may have been an attempt to buy some, but it is not exactly clear who would accept such a story or support his calls for an investigation of his enemies. The publication appears to have been designed to elicit pity and to explain the manner in which his actions had been forced by a group of devious local enemies who now controlled all the levers of power in the region. While, as we have seen, there was a very considerable seam of truth running through all this, neither parliament nor the army would be disposed to open up these local intrigues or investigate too closely the political histories of their supporters, particularly in Wales where many parliamentarian officials had not-so-hidden royalist pasts. The pamphlet was perhaps a despairing attempt to gain some leverage over sympathetic elements in the Rump and the army, but it is doubtful whether they would pay much attention to the desperate pleas of so notorious a turncoat.

To make certain that no such sympathy was generated among the public, parliament or the army, Poyer's tract was soon answered by yet another broadside from John Eliot. *A Short Comment upon the Grounds and Reasons of Poyers Taking up Armes* pointedly described the risings of 1648 in its title as 'these second *insurrections*', to challenge Poyer's characterisation of them as the more emollient 'differences'.[50] Eliot asserted that his intention was to 'undeceive the reader' and vindicate the 'wel-affected' gentry of Pembrokeshire whom Poyer had abused. He began, however, with his tried and tested tactic of character assassination. He ran through a familiar litany of Poyer's mean origins, his attacks on the clergymen Nathaniel Cradock and Evan Roberts, and his being a 'notorious lewd liver . . . a common drunkard, a great swearer and a quarreller'. Eliot claimed that such points were relevant for understanding that it was not affection to parliament which had encouraged Poyer to take up arms, but rather that his flawed grasping character induced him to take 'advantage of the unsetlednesse of the time' and to wrest possession of Pembroke Castle from Captain Walter Cuny (a man who, for the moment at least, was one of the Lort–Eliot circle).[51] Poyer's new position allowed him to plunder and pillage the surrounding country, his only interest was his own, while good men like Roger Lort tried to rein in his excesses. Eliot concluded that Poyer's resistance to Fairfax's orders in August 1647 gave 'first rice [sic: "rise"] to the late insurrections'.[52] The pamphlet then proceeded to answer Poyer's text at every turn with a commentary that undercut Poyer's original intention. These comments hammered on the point that Poyer had been proclaimed traitor by parliament and refused to deliver

Pembroke Castle when summoned. This was clearly a tactic designed to bring back into focus the reason why Poyer was on trial rather than raking over the ashes of personal grievances in distant Pembrokeshire. Indeed, Eliot sneered that Poyer had shown particular impudence in complaining about being prisoner and having no money when 'in justice he should have been adjudged first according to the height of his crime, for he rebelled before any part of this Common-wealth stirred'.[53] Seeing Poyer as the initiator of the 1648 risings echoed the position of Hugh Peter, and it is likely that Eliot sought to endorse and perhaps help direct the court martial's case against him.

This rather desperate pamphlet battle continued with the publication in late March 1649 of *Poyer's Vindication*, which was framed as an answer to Eliot's *Short Comment*.[54] Poyer attempted to address Eliot's 'monstrous false lies scattered abroad to uphold the reputation of a poor solicitor' in a rather longer and more detailed pamphlet than his last effort. He fought back by stealing some of Eliot's tactics, offering scandalous snippets about Eliot's dalliances with women and his loose living, but he lacked Eliot's barbed wit and satirical eye and this section of the text falls flat. Elsewhere, Poyer vindicated at length his own background, character and actions in the war, and lost no opportunity to rehearse his attacks on the Lorts and Eliot for their royalism, inconstancy and duplicity. In some ways this was the battle of the turncoats, as both men played on the other's chequered and inconstant political histories to score points. Poyer's pamphlet became a sustained attack on his enemies, which he must have felt would serve him well, but it is difficult to see how such an approach would play positively with the Rump or the army. He concluded by stating that he thought it 'good to set [the pamphlet] forth, lest falshood (for want of reply) should be taken for verity; the innocent guilty and knaves shot free'.[55]

Eliot was not one to let Poyer have the last word, however. Hot on the heels of Poyer's tract, Eliot hurried out yet another pamphlet as his bitter struggle with Poyer moved towards its fatal climax. *A Just Reply to a False and Scandalous Paper Intituled Poyers Vindication* was published under Eliot's name but, unfortunately, as of 2008, the only copy, which was once in the library of Worcester College, Oxford, has been lost.[56] We know this was a small quarto volume of four pages, so was of a piece with Eliot's previous contributions to this 'debate'.[57] The text was consulted in the early twentieth century by the priest and scholar James Cornelius

Morrice, who merely informs us that this text, like *Poyer's Vindication* 'indulge[s] in the vilest recriminations' and is 'worthless as literature'.[58] This indicates that it was much of the same from Eliot, a personal and vindictive attack designed to diminish Poyer's claims and deny him an unchallenged moment in the public eye.

To whom was Poyer talking with his pamphlets? It is difficult to be certain. His *Vindication* may have been a tract to posterity, designed to clear his name when all hope was gone. However, it is possible that clearing his name was a genuine hope which he thought would play well in the upcoming trial; indeed, Poyer would shortly rehearse a version of this text's arguments before his military tribunal. Perhaps Poyer had a very particular readership in mind. Only a single copy of *Poyer's Vindication* is extant; similarly, only one copy remains of *A Short Comment* and only a transcript of Poyer's original *The Grounds & Reasons* and the ghost of the single copy of Eliot's *Just Reply*. This would suggest that few copies of these texts were produced or purchased, and thus it may have been a fairly 'closed' printed discussion. Perhaps these pamphlets were circulated only among interested groups in parliament and the army, and what we have here are lobbying documents in the politics of Poyer's fate.[59] It might be notable, for example, that Poyer described his anxieties about being disbanded without assurances of arrears and indemnity in his *Vindication* as 'having a former president by his Excellencies army'.[60] This was a reference to the New Model's own struggle to secure arrears and indemnity from a hostile parliament in 1647, and indicates an attempt to suggest that their causes were not so dissimilar. It is also worth recalling in this regard that the only copy we have of Poyer's *The Grounds & Reasons* (and of Eliot's lost *Just Reply*) are to be found among the papers of the Army Council's secretary. Someone in the high command was reading this material.

Less than a fortnight after *Poyer's Vindication* was published, on 2 April, the court martial sat at Whitehall to consider Poyer's case along with those of fellow defendants, Rowland Laugharne, Rice Powell and Philip Bowen.[61] There seems to have been a good deal of public interest in the case. As we saw, theirs was the example of grand delinquents 'first insisted uppon' by parliament, and the trial occupied a decent amount of space in the newsbooks. Moreover, a version of the court's charge and the defendants' answers was produced quickly for a readership which evidently wanted to know about the case.[62] One newspaper reported that it would not detail the particulars of the trial 'in regard there will shortly be a particular narrative of the whole proceedings published'.[63] If this was indeed produced, however, it is now, sadly, lost.

Courts martial were not uncommon in the early days of the republic as the Rump and the army sought to deal with those who had fought against them the previous spring and summer.[64] The use of martial law had, in fact, been a feature of the civil war period, with military courts sitting in several garrison towns as well as London. Military courts were seen by parliament as bodies which could establish stability through exemplary justice. These tribunals did not have grand or petty juries which might hand down sentences other than those expected by the parliamentary state or the army command. It was believed that the courts inspired terror and conformity through swift and brutal verdicts. Judges, who could be a mixture of army officers and civilians, proceeded by written informations and generally the courts operated through written evidence rather than oral testimony, although the latter often supplemented written submissions.

On 2 April each of the Welsh defendants was called in individually to the court martial and had their charges read to them.[65] Poyer was first brought to trial. He faced three charges. First, that he was entrusted by parliament with command of Pembroke Castle and 'did most trayterously and perfidiously betray his trust'. Secondly, that he 'joyned with the publicke enemies of this Mation [sic "Nation"]'. Thirdly, that he did 'in a hostile manner' sally out of the castle against those sent to reduce it and 'killed and put to death Col. Fleming, Capt. Spooner and others'.[66] The charges against the other defendants were similar, and the court provided them with copies and gave them two days to provide answers.

Poyer was the first to respond, and his answer reads like a precis of *Poyer's Vindication*. He had considerable practice in defending himself and spinning an exculpatory narrative, but the version he offered here had notable weaknesses before this particular tribunal. First, he denied that he ever was entrusted by parliament with the command of Pembroke Castle 'as the castle was his own and he the captain of the trained band, and major [sic "mayor"] of the town of Pembroke'.[67] In fact, he maintained, it was in this unofficial capacity that he raised troops for parliament and fortified the town and castle upon his own charge.[68] He then proceeded to round on the 'treacherous combination' of the Lort brothers, Eliot, Thomas Bowen and James Lewis who, as commissioners of array (the parliamentary newsbook report carefully interpolates 'as he saith' here) proclaimed him rebel and traitor against the king.[69] He denied that he

ever had communication with the Prince of Wales and averred that he
would have surrendered the town to Fleming if he had assurances about
his soldiers' arrears. He denied knowing the New Model soldiers he was
charged with killing, and claimed he stayed in the castle for his own safety,
'it being his own house'.[70] He tried some legal footwork by asking for the
same 'liberty of the articles' granted by Cromwell as they had been applied
to Humphrey Matthews, well knowing that Matthews had been allowed
to compound for his delinquency. He denied acting maliciously against
parliament or the army but if 'out of a misguided zeal and judgement, or
forced upon by his adversaries, who hindered his appeal to his Excellency
[Fairfax], he humbly desires the clemency of the court, and that his former
services may not be forgotten (alledging that in death there is no mercy)'.[71]

Thus we see that Poyer based his defence very much upon his
parliamentary service in the first war and the nefarious designs of his
Lort-inspired enemies. This was a reworking of arguments he had been
deploying since 1645, with some additional tweaks. It formed a coherent
narrative but not a particularly convincing one, especially when a good deal
of the army's anger, as we have seen from Cromwell's correspondence, was
directed at men such as himself *because* they had been zealous defenders
of parliament in the first war and had rebelled against the 'cause'. Poyer
simply does not seem to have recognised this fact, and he continued to
see his bold, early declaration for parliament as testimony of his faithfulness and zeal, and something which might help to save his skin. The
point about Matthews was a canny one, but had Poyer been able to read
Cromwell's own correspondence, he might have recognised that suggesting he be allowed to compound was unlikely to wash with the army high
command. His claim that he had never had any communication with the
Prince of Wales rings particularly hollow and was brutally exposed in a
kind of cross-examination which followed. In sum, Poyer's defence almost
certainly angered the court rather than mollified it.

Laugharne, Powell and Bowen responded at far less length than Poyer.
Laugharne claimed that he had waited in London for his arrears but, when
he could no longer survive for lack of funds, he went into Wales but took
up no commission. Bowen simply denied engaging against parliament.
Powell, meanwhile, was ordered to bring in a fuller answer as his response
was considered insufficient.

Poyer's answer to the court was widely known; courts martial were
open proceedings like criminal trials, and the newspapers took a keen

interest. His attempt to distance himself from the king's cause received a negative response in the few illicit royalist news-sheets which maintained an outlaw existence under the early republic. The author of *Mercurius Pragmaticus* was particularly vitriolic.[72] Poyer's denials that he had engaged for the king or had correspondence with the Prince were seen simply as forms of cowardly disloyalty. The newsbook maintained that if Poyer was executed, 'he will be reproached, scorned and laught at by those who lov'd, aplauded and honor'd him for his supposed loyalty'. Poyer all along had clung to the 'rebels', and so deserved a 'mercy which . . . will prove fatall to him . . . of a bullet'. Poyer and his fellow 'supposed royalists' had shown themselves to be 'dastards . . . traytors and rebells' for denying 'their master for feare of death'. Poyer was thus vilified by both parliamentarians and royalists for betrayal and inconstancy. These were allegations he would have rejected, for he considered himself to have held firm to his original undertakings while others shifted about him. However, inflexibility in a period of such dramatic flux as the civil wars was often a dangerous trait.

On 6 April, the defendants requested that they be permitted to bring forward witnesses, which was allowed, and the court reconvened the following day. A newsbook report suggests, however, that their witnesses did more harm than help. It described how they 'hath made the matter appear much clearer against them than it was before . . . giving in evidence to prove divers things which were not witnesses to bee found to cleare before'.[73] As a result, the court was adjourned until Tuesday 10 April when a further charge was to be brought in. As though this were not bad enough, Poyer's bitterest enemy John Eliot appeared in court like some Shakespearean villain to pronounce the *coup de grâce* against him. Eliot submitted a paper to the court to clear himself and his associates of the charges Poyer had levelled against them in his evidence of 2 April. Eliot's 'declaration' stated that neither he, Roger Lort nor James Lewis had ever been commissioners of array 'which Mr Arthur Owen hath often urged in the House of Commons against us, and Sir Hugh Owen his brother in severall other places, but could never prove it'. He maintained that he knew nothing of Poyer being proclaimed a traitor for his service to parliament, but rolled out a claim from his earlier pamphlets that Eliot, his son, Herbert Perrot, Griffith White, James Lewis and the three Lorts were proclaimed traitor by the notorious royalist judge David Jenkins at Carmarthen in 1643 for bearing arms against the king. It is interesting to see Arthur and Hugh Owen's names brought into this discussion about Poyer's guilt, which underlines again how these men had operated as something of a political cadre during the 1640s.[74] However, the very fact that Eliot was allowed to present his paper suggests that the court martial was more sympathetic to his position than Poyer's. Indeed, it seems that Poyer's tactic of defending himself by attacking those who had close ties to the army had spectacularly backfired.

The court reconvened on Tuesday 10 April, when Poyer's case was to be brought to a determination, although the hearing took 'many hours'.[75] Witnesses on both sides were heard. Despite his assertions that he had received no commission from the royalists, 'a commission from Prince Charles was found in his chest', which was then 'produced amongst other papers found in his house', although Poyer claimed that this was the first time he had ever seen them.[76] Evidently Hugh Peter had brought the material from Poyer's cellar to the trial, and the fact that he had published these texts the previous summer shows how hollow and misguided Poyer's denials must have sounded. In addition, Peter also produced several warrants under Poyer's signature directed to constables for provisioning Pembroke in 1648, as well as letters to the officials of other towns 'incouraging them to raise what forces they could and joyn with him'.[77] Finally, a 'printed *Declaration* set forth in his name, shewing the grounds and reasons of his fortifying the Castle of Pembrok' was produced for the court. This was, of course, his and Powell's *Declaration*, the key text for the south Wales revolt, which had been published one year ago to the day.

Poyer was required to speak and answered that the charge was long and complex and so he desired further time to prepare his defence. The court president, Colonel John Barkstead, responded that he would not permit further delay and that Poyer had had plenty of time to respond to charges he had first seen eight days before.[78] After a brief recess, Poyer then spoke to his defence, rehearsing his answers of 4 April, that he was not governor of Pembroke by a parliamentary commission, had never 'revolted from his trust', that the castle was 'his own house' and that he had defended it against the king's forces. The court was unimpressed. It was objected that 'this kind of plea was matter of circumstance, the thing he was to speak to was matter of fact', and he had 'little to speak to those things more than what he had formerly pleaded'.[79]

Several (unnamed) witnesses then provided testimony that Poyer had commanded the castle when Captain Spooner and Major Potts were killed by shots from its towers. The court acknowledged that Poyer had not received a particular commission, yet as mayor he was a captain, and had acted on that authority, took pay for the same and submitted accounts to parliament for his arrears.[80] It considered the charge thus proven that he 'acted upon that [royalist] interest against the parliament and joyned with that party'. Poyer was found guilty and was sentenced to death.[81] The same sentence was passed against Rowland Laugharne and Rice Powell two days later for holding intelligence with and harbouring the enemy; the fate of Captain Philip Bowen is unknown, although it seems likely that he was acquitted.[82]

The royalist author of *Mercurius Pragmaticus* rejoiced in Poyer's fate. He described the death sentence as a 'just reward for his double dealings', and that those Cavaliers who thought he had 'some loyalty and become a convert . . . now . . . have found how his pulse beats'. He spat his hope that no royalist would 'harbour one good thought of such a base degenerate rebell or . . . ever yeild him the least of pity for his sufferings', because he denied his loyalty to the king when faced with death.[83] Such bitter recriminations must have fallen on a benumbed Poyer, by now unable to doubt that he was to meet his end in a few short days. Admittedly he was faced with an impossible task to defend himself given the overwhelming evidence of his complicity with and support of the royal cause the previous spring. However, he surely did himself no favours by demonstrating little contrition, but rather, almost by reflex, dredging up the history of his factional struggles with the Lorts and John Eliot; men who were now the face of the republic in Pembrokeshire.

While this seemed like the final act for all three men, precedent meant that this might not, in fact, be the case. Mercy was sometimes granted after a sentence of death was handed down, and clemency was still an option for the new republican state which was widely disliked, and so was keen to win over people's hearts and minds. A demonstration of clemency might be one way to accomplish this. As a result, there now began a fevered lobbying campaign with the three men (and their wives) petitioning prominent figures to intervene and have their sentences commuted. The first to plead for mercy was Ann Laugharne, who presented a petition to Fairfax and the court martial on Thursday 12 April.[84] Justice had already been shown in the sentence, she claimed, so pardoning and mercy did not diminish the scope of Laugharne's crimes but rather demonstrated the army's capacity for compassion: 'such acts of mercy making your Excellency and Army as much renowned, beloved and feared as their greatest victories'. She implored him that Laugharne's 'one unadvised act might not cause all his former eminent services to be forgotten' and mentioned how his loss would affect her and her eight children, but also her two sisters, of whom Elizabeth Poyer was one, of course. One commentator demonstrated how such pleas even at this eleventh hour might not be hopeless: 'doubtlesse his Excellency [Fairfax] (who is so famous for acts of clemency and civility) will in judgment think of mercy and spare his life, who once gave life to the dying cause of the parliament, when their friends were almost extirpated out of South-Wales'.[85]

On 16 April, Poyer himself petitioned the Rump Parliament pleading for mercy.[86] His script was a familiar one, but he deployed it here in the hope of a reprieve. He again led with the argument that he was 'one of the first that appeared in arms in South Wales against the common enemy', and, as captain of the trained bands, fortified Pembroke Castle by his own hand and kept the garrison against the king's forces for the next five years. Despite the unlikelihood of it playing well with his intended audience, Poyer nonetheless felt compelled once more to allude to his 'enemies which he had subdued [who] became seekers of his destruction' by distributing 'false and scandalous reports against him' to the Commons and also to Fairfax. He attempted again to explain that he had occupied Pembroke in the spring of 1648 only for his own defence and security. Poyer recounted surrendering the castle to Cromwell 'upon mercy, which your petitioner conceives cannot be mercy in taking away his life'. He thus asked for mitigation so that he might be serviceable to the Commonwealth 'and so his poore wife and children may not absolutely perish, nor one miscarriage of his may not exentuate all his faithfull services'. This last section played the part of contrite petitioner well, and he had perhaps learned from Ann Laugharne's representation of a few days before. The promise of future service and the introduction of the damage done to his innocent family were recognised means for attempting to obtain the indulgence of sentencing authorities. Most were unmoved, however, and one newspaper repeated the Cromwellian position against Poyer's claim for being one of the first to declare for parliament: 'first services are made worse by apostasy, for he that runs to the end shall have the Crown'.[87]

Poyer also appealed to Colonel Charles Fleetwood on 21 April. Fleetwood had been a member of Essex's lifeguard and was possibly known to Poyer through his Meyrick connections, but he was now a major figure in the New Model. Poyer requested that he 'cast your eye over these few lines and present the truth to his Excellency [Fairfax]'.[88] He pleaded that he had 'served the parliament in their lowest ebb of affairs' and withstood the attacks of Gerard and other royalists stoutly. He tried to press home the points made at his trial that he had not been commissioned by parliament 'nor receiving a penny from them', but, in a perhaps unfortunate echo of his *Declaration* of the previous spring, he claimed 'I stood firm to my principles'. He stated that he was proclaimed traitor without proof of disaffection to parliament, and averred, rather unconvincingly, that he never intended to desert parliament, as was shown by his release of Fleming's captured soldiers and a private offer of surrender he sent to Cromwell. He concluded the letter with a heart-rending line: 'Pardon my boldness, for life is sweet, and all lawful means are to be sought after to preserve the same.' At around this time also, further petitions were directed to Fairfax by Elizabeth Poyer, Ann Laugharne and three sisters of the presumably unmarried Rice Powell.[89]

These representations evidently had an effect on Fairfax. The Venetian ambassador reported that the three rebel leaders had been condemned, 'but the sentence has not yet been carried out because of the numerous petitions in their favour'.[90] The royalist historian James Heath would later describe how the 'importunity of their wives and friends' moved Fairfax to clemency.[91] On 21 April, the day of Poyer's appeal to Fleetwood, Fairfax wrote to the Marshal General of the Army about the three Welsh prisoners in his custody. He ordered that 'for divers causes me moving, these are to require you that lots be prepared, and that but one of them be shot to death, upon whose lot it shall fall, and the other two to be kept in your custody'.[92] Three army officers including the man who presided over the court martial, John Barkstead, were to witness the drawing of the lots, while Fairfax's own chaplain prayed with the prisoners before they drew.

While this may seem an extraordinary way of proceeding, drawing lots was not as striking a departure from standard military practice as it might appear, although it remained unusual. Military tribunals wished to see justice administered fairly and, in armies, this sometimes required selecting individual victims to atone for a crime perpetrated by a number of men (although usually more than three). In situations where there was equal guilt, as in cases of mutiny for example, it was acceptable to apportion blame through casting lots such as drawing slips of paper or rolling dice.[93] Thus it transpired that, on 21 April, the three condemned Welshmen gathered in Whitehall to determine their fate. They were 'unwilling to draw their own destiny' and so allotted the task to a child, an innocent unsullied by the world. On two slips of paper were written the words 'Life Given by God', while a third was left blank. According to a contemporary account, 'the childe gave the first to Colonel Powel, the second to Maior Generall Laughorn, in both which "Life" was written, and the third (being a blank) to Colonel Poyer, so that he is designed to be shot to death'.[94] The Army secretary William Clarke wrote a few days later 'it is observable that the lot should fall on him who was the first beginner of the second war'.[95] God's judgement was clear to those who wished to see it. Rice Powell and Rowland Laugharne were released from custody on 7 May 1649, although they remained under surveillance by the suspicious republican authorities.

Despite the apparently final decision as to Poyer's fate, on 23 April Elizabeth Poyer petitioned parliament on her husband's behalf; she had been importuning Fairfax for 'some few dayes that she might have liberty to petition the parliament for mercy'.[96] She appears, however, to have presented Poyer's petition rather than one of her own. He petitioned for remission on the basis of 'his good services formerly for this Common wealth'. To support this claim, he submitted a list of his services to parliament which was lifted from his *Grounds & Reasons*, although there were some notable changes. In this representation the references to Poyer's local enemies which had been in the original text were omitted, while a paragraph was added which placed Poyer at practically all the civil war engagements in Pembrokeshire and Cardiganshire, adding that he 'never received any pay or sallary for his pains for the Parliament'.[97] He was hoping that the impression of his active military service would play well with army sympathisers, while the point that he had done all this with no salary showed his zeal, but also perhaps raised the point as to whether the army should be executing someone who never had a commission. However, these points had been addressed at length at his trial and must have been widely known at Westminster too.

It is also worth noting also that Arthur Owen had presented a series of royalist warrants signed by John Eliot to the House on 21 April as well as the original commission of array for Pembrokeshire which included the names of many of Poyer's enemies. He had perhaps hoped that a desperate rearguard action which demonstrated that Poyer had been telling the truth about his enemies' royalist pasts might have done him some good.[98] John and Elizabeth Poyer's petition and Owen's submission were despairing gambles with little chance of success. After a 'short debate', the

Commons laid Poyer's petition aside. For them, Providence had spoken, and it would be folly to revisit the case. Fairfax granted a day's stay of execution; Poyer would now be shot on 25 April. Being told this, Poyer supposedly remarked that 'he had but one life to lose and in sacrificing of it in this world, hee hoped to have a blessed and joyfull restrauration thereof in the world to come'. While this sounded like so much conventional Protestant piety and stoic suffering, a grain of veracity is introduced in the detail that he also called on God to 'forgive them who were the causers of it [his death] and that for his part he freely forgave them, being in peace with all men'.[99] It reads as though Poyer's enemies were never far from his thoughts; the 'causers' of his death were not the military judges at Whitehall, but the black cabal of the Lort–Eliot interest who had blighted his service and who, in his eyes, finally succeeded in their design to take away his life.

The place chosen for the final act of Poyer's life was Covent Garden near St Paul's Cathedral, a place some New Model regiments had been using to stable their horses.[100] Several ministers visited him on the morning of his execution. Around two o'clock in the afternoon he was transported from Whitehall in a coach guarded by Colonel Thomas Hewson's regiment.[101] He was said to be 'very penitent' and uttered 'condoling speeches in relation to the bleeding and dying condition of this poor, distressed & languishing nation'. He further desired that his death 'might close up the breach of the people, and that his bloud might be the last that should issue forth in streames within the bowels of this Common-wealth'.[102] After arriving, he was accompanied by Fairfax's chaplain and 'Mr Cradock', who might have been the famous Independent preacher from south Wales, Walter Cradock (one hopes it was not Nathaniel). After speaking with them for a while, he proceeded with 'teares in his eyes' towards the piazza of Covenant Garden.[103] He made a short speech as was traditional for those condemned to be executed. He forgave all men and asserted 'that he ever acted for the liberty and freedom of the subject', and that he died 'a true Protestant according to the discipline of the Church of England, and that he desired a speedy period might be put to the present distractions between prince & people'.[104] It is interesting that he again affirmed himself as a member of the Church of England, and at a point when the purest honesty between the condemned man and God was paramount. Moreover, the reference to the continued distractions between 'prince' and people is telling as it suggests that Poyer anticipated a future political settlement involving the Prince. This was a striking thing to be saying when the whole institution of monarchy had been abolished by the Rump in March. This seems, then, to be a restatement to the political creed of 'King and Parliament' which had energised him in 1642, sustained him through the war, and which he restated in April 1648.

After praying with 'great zeale and fervency', he spoke to the soldiers present as he stood before the wall of Bedford House which abutted onto the piazza. He confessed to have lived 'very loosely' and repented of his sins. He reminded his auditors to keep their minds on heaven, for things on Earth were uncertain:

> I have had experience of changes; though I was once low, yet I came to be very high; I was advanced but now I must leave all; and though my fortunes changed, yet my affections to the parliament did not alter, I was alwayes honest to them untill this unhappy disaster which hath brought this misery upon me.[105]

To the last, Poyer asserted that he was a faithful servant of parliament, although the mutability of the world had rendered his constancy a liability. He took off his doublet, placed a cap over his face and then held up both hands, crying out, 'Come Lord Jesus, Lord receive my soule'. A line of three soldiers with firelocks 'did their office, who at one voley bereav'd him of his life'.[106] His corpse was carried away by coach through St James's to Tothill Street. Upon examination it was found that he died by two bullets to the heart, 'both . . . so near that the one almost tore into the others hole'.[107]

CHAPTER 9

Afterlives

The dramatic scene in Covent Garden piazza on 25 April 1649 was the last act of a remarkable life. John Poyer made no impression upon the public consciousness for his first thirty-four years, but his final decade was one of incident, controversy and struggle which brought him local and national notoriety. His resistance against Fairfax and Fleming in 1647–8 and his subsequent declaration for the king, electrified the country and pulled the nation's gaze westward as Poyer fired the starting gun for the Second Civil War. This chapter will consider how these events, and Poyer's life more generally, have been understood and interpreted after his demise. It examines Poyer's posthumous reputation and discusses some of the ways in which his move from parliamentarian stalwart to royalist rebel caused problems for those remembrancers of the war who preferred their subjects to be singular and steady in their political devotions. It will also trace the way he was discussed by later authors including the influential treatment provided by Thomas Carlyle in the mid-nineteenth century. The chapter concludes with some analysis of Poyer's presentation in modern historical scholarship. Before we turn to Poyer's legacy, however, we need to consider briefly the fate both of his enemies and of those who were most profoundly affected by Poyer's death, his wife and family. We begin by examining the post-war lives of Poyer's principal antagonists: the Lort brothers and John Eliot.

The defeat of Poyer and Laugharne in 1648 opened the door for Roger Lort and his associates to capitalise on their status as Poyer's leading adversaries and, by extension, the foremost supporters of parliament and the New Model in south-west Wales. They thus readily assumed roles as principal figures in local administration under the early republic. Sampson Lort served as sheriff of Pembrokeshire in 1649 and was followed in turn by James Philipps, Roger Lort and John Lort; all of these men also sat on the county's commission of the peace.[1] In addition, they were prominent as members of the major parliamentary commissions which implemented republican policy in the provinces, including those for sequestrating delinquents, assessing taxation and for the militia.

Roger Lort maintained his position as head of the family throughout the 1650s. During this time he, along with Sampson Lort and John Eliot, had to face down articles brought by Presbyterian opponents which sought to drag their royalist pasts into the light and question their political reliability. They were also accused of misappropriating parliamentary funds and lining their own pockets.[2] With their newly elevated status and powerful connections, it seems they were able to head off these threats without much trouble. That Roger Lort enriched himself through his new offices, however, seems certain. He was, for example, able to loan large sums to local gentlemen during the Protectorate, while the estate he bequeathed at his death was much expanded from that he had inherited.[3] The capacity he showed for political flexibility in the 1640s did not abandon him with the return of monarchy, although he was ailing by the end of the republic, being described as 'sickly and infirm' in 1659.[4] Perhaps because of his physical disabilities, it was his eldest son, John, who was described as being active for the king in 1659 and 1660, and he was even nominated to become a member of the ultra-loyalist Order of the Royal Oak.[5] This strategic royalism doubtless reflected his father's ability adeptly to manoeuvre towards the royalist side when he saw cracks appearing in the republican facade. Despite his role in helping to defeat the royalist rising of 1648 and his impeccable republican credentials, then, Roger Lort secured a pardon for his actions during the civil wars in July 1660, and, in 1662, even received a baronetcy from Charles II![6] Local Restoration commentators were caustic about his political survivalism, however, and one pen portrait of the gentry of south-west Wales described Lort as 'a man of any principle or religion to acquire wealth . . . Lortt's selfishness is incompatible with publick employments unless yt addeth to his private profitt'.[7] He enjoyed his baronetcy for only a brief period, however, as he died in 1664.[8] The scale of his wealth is suggested by the fact that he left legacies to his four daughters which amounted to the huge sum of £4,700. His demise triggered off a series of lawsuits within the family over possession of Lort's estate, however, and these appear to have preoccupied the family for several years.[9] The Lort male line died out at the end of the seventeenth century and the heiress married into the Campbells of Cawdor in Scotland. The Campbells of Stackpole became one of the leading landed interests in south-west Wales during the eighteenth century.

Turning from the head of the family to his brothers, the post-war career of Sampson Lort, is particularly interesting. As noted above, he was a thoroughgoing republican and occupied several important local offices in the 1650s. In 1660, local opponents described how 'during the late eleven years of persecution . . . Mr Lort was a potent & a most violent actor under several changes'.[10] Particularly noteworthy was his appointment to the Commission for the Propagation of the Gospel in Wales in February 1650. This was a radical religious body designed to eject unworthy ministers and puritanise a country which was seen as dangerously infected with the disease of royalism. Sampson Lort was not a member of this body, but he became one of its most active and enthusiastic commissioners.[11] He was, then, a convinced religious Independent who was remembered as a close ally of the radical Hugh Peter, and was vilified for his enthusiasm at the Restoration. He was described as a man who had 'destroyed almost as many ministers as . . . [the Biblical Sampson did of the] Philistines . . . [he] [h]ates the church, huggs the profitts of it . . . [is] ambitious of publick employment, but in pure order to enlarge his fortune'.[12] He was also said to have been a 'most impetuous instrument for ejectinge of orthodox and godly ministers', and to have supported men 'with the denominations of barking doggs', as well as 'schismatickes' and 'phanatickes'.[13]

In 1659, Sampson Lort stood for election to parliament as member for Pembroke boroughs. One can only imagine what the Poyer family in the town thought of one of the leading architects of John Poyer's downfall attempting to secure this seat. Sampson was encouraged to stand because his brother, John, was serving as mayor at this time, and had allegedly said that he would 'choose his brother if he had but six voices for him'.[14] There was evidently dissention in the town, however, likely among a group loyal to the old Poyer interest, for Sampson Lort's candidacy was crossed by none other than Arthur Owen of Orielton. John Lort as mayor returned his brother as the victorious candidate but the bailiffs crossed him and returned Owen. It does not seem that the dispute was resolved before the parliament was dissolved. Lort tried again to get elected to parliament in March 1660, this time for the borough of Haverfordwest. However, the political winds had changed, and his opponents in the town made much of his alleged fanaticism in the 1650s to stymie his candidacy.[15]

Sampson Lort did not possess the political flexibility of his elder brother; he was too much of a convinced religious radical to flourish under the restored monarchy. As a result, he lost all his positions in local government, although, like his elder brother, he took advantage of a pardon offered by Charles II for his activities during the civil wars and interregnum.[16] He made his will in 1663, describing himself as a 'most unproffitable servant of God'. He bequeathed properties across south Pembrokeshire to his heir, Thomas.[17] His daughter, Elizabeth, married the noted Quaker Charles Lloyd of Dolobran in Montgomeryshire, suggesting that Lort's own radical religious sensibilities may have moved towards this sect in his last years.

We know the least about the third of the Lort brothers, John of Prickaston near Castlemartin. As with Roger and Sampson, he sat on local committees under the republic such as those for the militia and assessing local taxes.[18] He married Alice, the sister of Thomas Bowen of Trefloyne, Roger Lort's close associate during the 1640s. As we have seen, he became mayor of Pembroke in 1658–9 (he held property in Monkton) and attempted unsuccessfully to get his brother elected to parliament for the town. His rather lesser political profile perhaps allowed him to make the transition to the Restoration without too much difficulty. He was, however, presented by the Pembrokeshire grand jury in March 1661 (along with Sampson) for receiving public monies in the 1640s and 1650s for which he had yet to account.[19] He died in 1673 and an inventory of his moveable goods and debts amounted to some £1,662.[20]

Perhaps the most notorious of Poyer's enemies was John Eliot of Amroth. Along with his Lort patrons and associates, he too flourished after Poyer's demise.[21] However, under the Commonwealth he was subject to some very uncomfortable scrutiny from a sometime preacher of Pembroke and ally of the earl Essex, William Beech. Beech orchestrated something of a personal campaign against Eliot, accusing him of systematic corruption and financial peculation as well as of being an old royalist and turncoat. In 1650 he described Eliot's 'very mix and compounded good affection to the state . . . that . . . hath in it more of revenge upon parliament's friends for beating him and his friends when he was an active enemy to them, then it hath of intireness to the parliament by whose power he was beaten'.[22] He was investigated for the sale of forged debentures (war bonds given to soldiers) amounting to some £10,000; the Lort brothers were also deeply implicated in this alleged fraud.[23] At this point Eliot was still acting as Pembrokeshire agent in London, and appears to have been able to use his position and his contacts to face down the allegations thrown against him by Beech and others.[24]

It seems, however, that the accusations of financial wrongdoing and the investigation which followed either damaged Eliot's position in the capital or caused him to keep a lower public profile. In any event, he seems to have returned shortly after to his Narberth estates.[25] Here he appears as party to several important Lort land transactions in the early 1650s, and in 1653 was appointed by Roger Lort as his attorney to receive several properties which he had purchased.[26] Although he appeared on parliamentary commissions in the county and retained his place on the commission of the peace, Eliot made little impression in the historical record. It seems likely that he died around the period of the Restoration. A bill in a lawsuit brought by his son (also John), is only dated as having been presented during Clarendon's lord chancellorship (1658–67), but this mentions his father's demise five years previously.[27] Eliot was alive in July 1660 when a motion was made in parliament that he be added to the commissioners for collecting the poll money in Pembrokeshire; the same year he was also appointed as a commissioner for raising money to disband the army.[28] It appears, therefore, that Eliot died at some point between 1660 and 1662. Whatever the exact date of his demise might be, John Poyer's chief persecutor, who had revelled in the civil war atmosphere of print and publicity, evidently left the world quietly and with little fanfare.

We now turn from Poyer's adversaries to the afterlives of his immediate family. In 1649 Elizabeth Poyer had battled valiantly for her husband's life. She endured poverty and privation in London waiting for his trial and was energetic in trying to obtain a reprieve after the court martial passed its verdict. As is the case with so many early modern wives of prominent men, however, she remains a shadowy figure who was often only referred to in connection with her husband's case. She does not emerge with much of a personality of her own from the extant records beyond what looks like a fierce devotion to her husband and her children. Her movements and activities during the interregnum are obscure and can only be reconstructed in the most general terms from her later petitions. However, it seems likely that she stayed close to her sister, Ann, in the immediate aftermath of Poyer's execution. Ann Laugharne was described in July 1649 as lodging at Sir Hugh Owen's house in Dean's Yard near Westminster Abbey where, it was claimed, she was 'continually raylinge with most reprotchfyll langwage against the parliament'.[29] Laugharne was released from prison around this time and returned to Pembrokeshire; Elizabeth probably accompanied him.

Elizabeth Poyer emerges from obscurity after the Restoration of King Charles II in 1660. The man in whose name Poyer had rebelled, and who had written supportively to him in the spring of 1648, was unexpectedly returned to the throne after the collapse of the republican experiment. Charles returned to widespread relief and rejoicing, but also to a deluge of petitions and requests for aid and assistance from royalist supporters who had been left out in the cold for more than a decade.[30] Elizabeth was among these early supplicants. In December 1660, some seven months after Charles's return, she presented a petition to the monarch along with her brother Miles Button, who had been taken prisoner in Pembroke, and his wife, Florence, who was the daughter of another casualty of the 1648 rising in south Wales, Sir Nicholas Kemeys.[31] This detailed petition rehearsed how, in their 'severall capacityes', they had suffered in the king's and his father's service. Miles had fought with Charles Gerard (presumably against his brother-in-law, John Poyer, and his sister) and also as a Colonel under Laugharne in 1648. After Pembroke's fall he was banished for two years under Cromwell's articles of surrender, during which time he served the Prince in Ireland under the duke of Ormond and the earl of Inchiquin. He returned home and recounted being imprisoned fourteen times by the republican authorities as well as being plundered after St Fagans, which lay a short distance from his house at Cottrell, before compounding for his delinquency.[32]

For her part, Elizabeth Poyer approached the king in a surprisingly forthright manner. She said she was 'confident' that the king 'cannot be unmindefull of the faithfull service her husband ingaged in' on his behalf and proceeded to rehearse a list of his engagements which could have been lifted from one of John Poyer's own publications. The pressures of Poyer's maintaining the siege on his own for nine weeks, she wrote, had caused 'such a scarcity that hee was forced to deliver the towne upon articles & himself to become a prey to the fury of an implacable enemy'. Strangely for a petition to the king, she also recounted that he was owed £8,000 arrears by parliament for his service as a colonel and governor of Pembroke. This cannot have been a wise move on Elizabeth's part, but it does support Poyer's repeated claims that his arrears were cripplingly large. These disbursements, she continued, had caused 'the losse of his whole estate reall & personall'. Elizabeth then claimed that the Prince, by his own letters, had promised to satisfy him on these accounts, adding that after all these sufferings, 'to fill upp the cupp of your petitioner's misery, her husband was by them murthered in Covent Garden, whereby the inevitable ruine of your petitioner with 4 small children is necessitated without your Majestys gracious comiseracion'. Since his death, she had been forced to live on friends' charity. As recompense, the three petitioners jointly requested the opportunity to have a patent for making a barony which they would confer on a worthy individual who would pay them a significant sum of money in return.

This was quite a bold set of requests from Elizabeth Poyer, although her claim that the king, as Prince, had promised to satisfy Poyer's accounts did have some basis. In his letter to the Welsh rebel leaders of 23 April 1648, Prince Charles had assured them that 'we shall be carefull to supply and assist you in all things to the uttermost of our power'.[33] While this might have been intended as a general declaration of support on the eve of war, nevertheless, the 'uttermost' of his power was now far beyond what he had enjoyed in 1648, and Elizabeth wished him to make good on his promises.[34] It possibly did not help her case that it was mixed up with two others. This blunted its message, immediacy and individuality. Moreover, Ellizabeth's claim for parliamentary arrears from the man whose father parliament had executed seems clumsy and ill-judged. Perhaps as a consequence of these problems, it does not appear that the petition produced any tangible benefit.

After this fruitless attempt, Elizabeth redoubled her efforts in the summer of the following year by petitioning both the king and the (royalist-dominated) Cavalier Parliament for recompense for her sufferings in the royalist cause. In July 1661, Elizabeth once more petitioned Charles II, although this time on her own.[35] She began with a striking statement that she 'hath had her deare husband murthered by the hand of a bloody usurper', as well as her estate and livelihood taken away. She repeated the figure of £8,000 losses suffered in the wars, although wisely did not attribute this to non-payment by Poyer's parliamentary masters, and painted a sorry picture of herself and her four children being 'exposed for these many yeares to exreame hardshipp and misery'. While it was standard practice to emphasise, and even exaggerate, one's suffering in a document of this kind, Elizabeth's petition has the kinds of language and detail which suggest that she and her children had indeed suffered terrible hardships; something supported by her letter to Ann Laugharne asking for money which was discussed in the previous chapter.[36] Elizabeth described how she was forced to be 200 miles from her children, who were in Pembrokeshire, to seek relief, and 'to this end (for the space of 22 monthes and upward) hath walked upp and downe heere [London] destitute and unpittyed . . . Soe that she may truly cry out noe sorrow nor trouble can be like hers'. This did indeed set up a pitiable image which Elizabeth then boldly juxtaposed with Charles's, as yet unfulfilled, promises to her husband:

> yet when your petitioner considers what your majestys encouragements and gracious promises were to her husband, and how meltingly your roy-all heart hath seemed to compassionate her condicion upon all addresses to your majestie. And observing how some supplyants [supplicants] like her selfe (lesse miserable shee is sure, perhaps lesse deserving too) have beene aboundantly supplyed by your royall bounty) your petitioner can-not but be much comforted and still wayte, not daring soe farr to wrong either your excellent Majestie or herselfes as to thinke that your peti-cioners condicion of all others can be the least minded by your Majestie because the most suffering and forlorne.[37]

This was an unusually candid and direct petition. It set up a clear quid-pro-quo which needed to be honoured in a manner that was uncommon in petitionary addresses to the monarch. There was also the clear sense here that Charles's honour was involved in this matter, and that his not keeping the promises he had made to one of his most prominent support-ers in 1648 was something of a stain on his regality, particularly as money, gifts and honours had flowed readily to other royal supporters following the king's return. Although such documents do not give us easy access to

Elizabeth's personality, her petition nonetheless suggests a particularly determined individual who was willing to challenge the king so that she and her family could obtain their due. The petition came with an attachment designed to bolster and give further credibility and authority to the petition itself. This took the form of a certificate attesting to John Poyer's military services for the Prince in 1648, as well as independent testimony of Elizabeth's impoverished state, she being 'in a very low & sad condicion having nothing left to subsist with all'. The certificate was signed by prominent royalists in south Wales in 1648: Rowland Laugharne, Miles Button and Thomas Stradling (a Glamorgan man who was active in the Second Civil War in Pembrokeshire), as well as local justices Hugh Boteler and Hugh Phillips.[38]

Around the same time that this petition was presented to the king, Elizabeth also petitioned the Cavalier Parliament. On 24 July 1661, her petition was read in the House of Commons.[39] Although the text is not given, the report indicates that she had recounted John Poyer's royal service and the circumstances of his death, his 'fidelity, services . . . [and the] expence of his estate to the value of £8,000 . . . and her debts and sufferings'. She requested relief to 'keep her from starving' and to maintain her 'poor family'. The Commons considered her case, and it cannot have been to her detriment that among their number sat Rowland Laugharne, who had recently been elected for Pembroke. Perhaps unsurprisingly, then, her petition was recommended to the king who was requested to grant her relief 'in compensation of her sad sufferings and losses'.

Despite this pressure on the king, however, it appears that it was not until August 1663, some two years later, that Elizabeth received any grant. This was a meagre £100, which the king might have hoped would buy off the vocal Widow Poyer, but which in fact only granted him a temporary respite.[40] A year later Elizabeth petitioned Charles II once more.[41] She attached an annexe to this petition detailing Poyer's 'sad fate' and 'hir sufferings', and reminded the king that her husband's actions were 'warranted by your owne instruccion & commission'. She again raised her and her children's sorry state, for she was £1,500 in debt 'in these 15 years languishment since her . . . husband's death'. She recalled the £100 grant the king had made the year before, along with Charles's promise that she would be further considered if she managed to find an unclaimed royal grant which would assist her. She had become aware of a grant worth £3,000 which concerned the gathering of forfeited recognisances, or promissory bonds, due to the Crown which she wished to obtain. Effectively, Elizabeth petitioned to become a kind of debt collector. If this was not granted, Elizabeth feared that 'shee & her family [will] bee exposed to the streets', and she could see no other way 'to get of[f] of the plunging shee is fallen into'.

There was some discussion in Council about her receiving the grant, but it was indeed made and a year later Elizabeth described herself as 'att her great paines and charge in actuall prosecution' of the grant.[42] Elizabeth Poyer thus seems to have spent the remainder of her life discharging this office and obtaining these defaulted monies.[43] This was hardly typical work for a widow in this period, but Elizabeth Poyer was hardly a typical widow. She was obviously extremely determined, outspoken and not easily cowed; someone who must have been more than a match for the forceful character of John Poyer. It is not clear whether her business kept her in London or whether she managed to return to her family in Pembrokeshire. It is possible that she remarried and changed her name, but her date and place of death are unknown.

The Poyer children continued to live in and around Pembroke as far as can be ascertained. They were evidently not particularly prosperous or prominent individuals and it appears that the devastating effects of the war and the reprisals against their father had fatally compromised the Poyer family's upward climb. John's second son, Thomas, may have been one of Pembroke's bailiffs in 1687 but none of his name again occupied the position of mayor.[44] Perhaps John Poyer's most distinguished descendant was his grandson, Thomas Poyer, son of the 1687 bailiff, who worked as a missionary on Long Island in North America in the early eighteenth century.[45] It is notable that Thomas was a convinced Anglican rather than a dissenter, working for the Society for the Promotion of Christian Knowledge. The Church of England strain was clearly something that ran deep in the Poyer blood.

Colonel John Poyer cast a long shadow over his family, although the records are curiously silent about his posthumous reputation in Pembrokeshire and south-west Wales following the civil wars. The author of a semi-satirical tract produced in 1660 concerning the 'True Character and Deportment' of the local leaders in this region during the civil war years made no mention of him.[46] The squib was concerned with the 'principal gentry', however, and it seems that Poyer's lowly birth did not even make him worthy of consideration. It was doubtful, however, that the author would have known how to satirise Poyer. He was a royalist and a parliamentarian, a figure of notable achievements but also of tragic flaws. As something of an enigma, and a personality often understood through his enemies' assessments, it is revealing to consider the ways in which he was discussed and understood after his death. By considering his posthumous treatment, we can see some of the difficulties contemporaries had in dealing with the conundrum of Poyer's public life; this is also helpful for an understanding of how modern scholarship has tended to reinforce and repeat some of the judgments of the seventeenth century.

Poyer inspired strong and opposing reactions from the moment of his death. In reporting his execution, parliamentarian commentators tended to emphasise his piety and the brave manner in which he faced his end. Most did not dwell on his royalist revolt, which they presumably hoped the public would consider a moment of madness in an otherwise laudable parliamentarian career. The newspaper *A Perfect Diurnall* provided a narrative of his execution before observing that 'hee dyed very humbly and with great penitency, much of God appearing in him'.[47] Similarly, the parliamentarian lawyer Bulstrode Whitelocke observed in his 'Memorials' that Poyer 'died very penitently'.[48] Penitence and remorse were positive qualities for the parliamentarians in Poyer's case, of course. His contrition suggested that he regretted his foolhardy declaration for the king in 1648 and had in his final moments turned his mind back to the enlightened path which characterised much of his career.

On the other side, several royalist newspapers had only scorn and disdain for Poyer, seeing him as a man who renounced his (brief) royalist allegiance when it was put to the test.[49] The news-sheet *Mercurius Elencticus* wrote, 'I pittie not Poyer (I should have done it with all my heart if his behaviour at his death had but rendered him thankefull for the care His (now) Majestie tooke to preserve him by his letters to Fairfax . . .)'.[50] This seems like a remarkable charge: that Poyer, who had never received anything but promises of support from the Prince, should be thankful for a letter praying clemency after his rebellion had collapsed for lack of external aid. However, royalist pamphleteers such as this were reeling from the execution of the king, and several espoused something akin to blind zealotry in their devotion to the cause.[51] The author went on to recount

Poyer's 'catalogue of services for the rebells' which would not save him from their judgment. Men of honour, by contrast would have

> esteemed martyrdome . . . hee will not bee rank'd with those undaunted heroes who with so much Christian courage . . . sealed their fidelity with their blood, and left the sweet odour of their memories admired and pretious (whilst his shall rot and stink) in the nostrils of posterity.[52]

As we will see, Restoration commentators among the royalists were nowhere near this unforgiving, but they needed to erase much of Poyer's life before 1648 to fit him into their worldview.

As discussed in the previous chapter, the royalist newsbook *Mercurius Pragmaticus* had virulently decried Poyer's conduct at his trial. In reporting his death it reflected that Poyer had 'received the reward of his former perfidiousnesse . . . when he endeavoured, in hopes of pardon, to return to the vomit of his disloyalty [rather] than wash away his ignominy with his blood'.[53] Like his republican counterparts, this author saw the hand of Providence in Poyer's downfall, but it was to punish him for denying his royalist allegiance and his debt to the Prince. However, even *Pragmaticus* was not entirely negative in its treatment, for the paper noted that Poyer was 'a man of singular courage both in martiall and private affairs'.[54] Even some of Poyer's most jaundiced commentators, then, recognised positive elements of his character, something that hints at the ambiguities found in later portrayals. We can see such ambivalence in the royalist newsbook *The Man in the Moon*, which produced an account of Poyer's death that injected mischief into the narrative by suggesting the president of the court had interfered with the lots. However, this had meant that 'Poyer, that deserv'd life most, had the lott of death'.[55] Perhaps his early and prominent declaration for the king a year before meant that it was difficult for some of these royalists simply to portray Poyer as a devil and of a piece with the perfidious republican agents like Cromwell and Bradshaw whose hands were imbrued in the king's blood.

After his demise, Poyer remained relatively unnoticed in the political and topical writings of the interregnum period. Few had occasion to remark upon or rake over the ashes of his life and career. One who did, however, was William Beech, a minister presented to the living of St Michael's in Pembroke in 1639, importantly, by the earl of Essex, whose campaign against John Eliot was mentioned earlier in the chapter.[56] Beech had left the county early in the civil war and worked as a chaplain in the parliamentarian army, preaching a sermon before the troops at the siege of Basing House.[57] He was, however, an Essexian who retained a close interest in Pembrokeshire affairs. He lined up with those like Arthur and Sir Hugh Owen in opposing the Lort–Eliot faction and continued this opposition into the interregnum period.[58] In 1650 Beech published a pamphlet against Eliot which had occasion to reflect on Poyer's role in the civil war.[59] He endorsed the 'Poyerian' analysis of civil war politics in Pembrokeshire and presented Poyer as the victim of a vicious and amoral cabal. Beech described how John Eliot was driven 'not by good affection to the State . . . but REVENGE on those that served the state and had good affection before him'.[60] He described those involved in the rising of 1648, who, he said, were 'driven by all his [Eliot's] strong breaths and ropes and ginnes[61] unto revolt by an unheard-of treachery and by many powerfull impulsives . . . One was shot M[r] Eliot knowes it'. Such an account followed Poyer's interpretation of his actions in 1648: that he was driven to such extremes by his local enemies that revolt was his only option.

Beech's endorsement is unique in the contemporary analysis of Poyer's revolt, and indeed in the historical writing on him. However, even Beech was no swooning admirer of the man. He continued his discussion by observing, 'I am sorry he [Poyer] was principled no better. I did once suffer wrong by that man . . . I wish Mr Eliot were better swayed by better ends than the shot man was'. This was yet another individual whom Poyer had alienated, which further endorses the view that he was a difficult, irascible and headstrong character. Beech's troubled history with Poyer, however, means that we should take more seriously his account of the basic veracity of Poyer's claims about the 'plots' laid against him in Pembrokeshire. Beech, however, was a rare voice in a pamphlet which was largely ignored. A broadside ballad published after the dissolution of the Rump noticed 'brave Poyer' who had opposed the parliament's 'trayterous commands' and met a noble end.[62] No others were prepared to stick their necks out as Poyer supporters in the 1650s, while, on the republican side, there was little point in launching into jeremiads against a dead man whose family was reduced to penury.

As is understandable, Poyer featured only briefly in general histories of the civil war when his revolt in 1648 brought him to national prominence, or in panegyric biographies of Oliver Cromwell when Poyer appeared as a brief point on the radar of Cromwell's life before the Lord General moved on to greater and more momentous undertakings. An example of such writing would be Thomas May's authorised *A Breviary of the History of the Parliament of England* which appeared in 1650. His *History* contained a section on 'The Original and Progress of the Second War', and it is here we briefly encounter Poyer. He was said to have constituted a part of the dangers which threatened parliament 'not only from ancient and formerly vanquished enemies, but those who had before been parliament commanders and had now forsaken their side and cause'.[63] In this account it was Laugharne, 'a commander of great esteem in those parts', who was the principal figure in the south Wales revolt, although, as we have seen, he was in fact a relative latecomer to the rebellion.[64] May probably emphasised his role as Laugharne had been parliament's principal military leader and was better known in London than Poyer. The capitulation of Pembroke is briefly mentioned before May concentrates on Cromwell's journey north to meet the Scots at Preston.[65]

An interesting exception to the relative lack of interest in Poyer during the 1650s is a volume produced in 1659 by an author only identified as 'M. H.' This text set out to provide a history of the union of four kingdoms (it, unusually, included Wales as a 'kingdom') to demonstrate how the 'prudence' of the English in conquering the four 'discordant nations', had produced an 'entirely united . . . Commonwealth'.[66] The text argued that a form of English imperialism had overtaken, subdued, but also civilised the 'Celtic' nations.[67] This apologia for an often brutal conquest in Scotland and Ireland under Cromwell also considered Wales, and spent some time examining Poyer's revolt. In this text, Poyer was animated not by his lack of arrears or his religious convictions, but rather by an aggressive Welshness (or 'Britishness'), which was characterised by an 'ancient animosity' against the English. Poyer and his fellows in 1648, convinced that the Welsh had never been conquered, 'now adventured . . . to make trial of their Brittish valour under the commission of Prince Charles', who, of course, was Prince of *Wales*.[68] Their rapid defeat at the hands of 'English' forces under Cromwell gave the lie to the claim that the Welsh had never been defeated, but it also showed how a more perfect union could only be established by settling the militia, establishing colonial outposts, and executing summary justice against rebels.[69] These were all things which the English republic (in imitation of its Roman forebear) had achieved, and so 'ever since, that countrey hath been kept and maintained in peace and tranquility'.[70] It is interesting that Poyer was rendered in this text as a particularly Welsh figure. This is something which does not come across strongly in the contemporary literature or in subsequent scholarship.[71] The absence of this Welsh dimension probably stems from the fact that he hailed from an essentially English part of the county which was predominantly Anglophone. We have seen in his discussion of the prayer book in 1648 that there were some culturally specific dimensions to his character, but Poyer's Welshness is largely absent from contemporary discussion, so this volume is something of an unusual outlier in this respect.

Poyer's profile changed somewhat after the Restoration of monarchy in 1660. As recent scholarship has shown, the treatment of the civil wars in Restoration history was an important element of the culture, offering an ideologically charged view of the recent past by endorsing royalist actions in the war and decrying the impiety and foulness of rebellion, thus helping to cement and endorse the divinely appointed nature of the Restoration.[72] Royalist commentators reviewing and trying to explain the terrible convulsions the country had suffered in the last two decades, needed victories and heroes to illustrate the stout resistance of the royalist cause in the face of overwhelming odds. Poyer thus served a purpose in some of these texts, although his parliamentarian past made such a presentation far from straightforward. A fascinating example of this can be found in James Heath's popular *Chronicle of the Late Intestine Warr* which was first published in 1661. Heath's history of the civil wars was that of a committed royalist who had fled into exile with Prince Charles and despised Oliver Cromwell, who was traduced in Heath's notorious, *Flagellum* (1663).[73]

In Heath's *Chronicle*, Poyer, along with Laugharne and Powell, were described as individuals who had 'done notable service for the parliament in Wales', but who were 'men of better and surer principles' than the New Model could confide in. As a result, the New Model ordered their disbandment.[74] There was evidently some queasiness on Heath's part, then, in settling a thoroughly royalist narrative on these ex-parliamentarians, and he wrote how Horton was sent to reduce 'these new and old royalists'. This was an awkward construction which perhaps helped to explain away Horton's easy victory at St Fagans: they were not thoroughgoing cavaliers and so it was no surprise they failed to stand firm. It also, however, pointed up the men's ambiguous status in a history designed to celebrate royalist fortitude and parliamentarian perfidy. The officers' Welshness raised another issue too, and Heath described how Horton's initial volleys in the battle 'did so gall and terrifie these raw and undisciplined Britons that they could not be made to stand, or to keep any order'.[75] He portrays Pembroke as a difficult nut to crack, but has little to say about Poyer's role at this time.

Later in the text, however, he discusses the Welsh officers' trial and Poyer's execution. Poyer was clearly a notable sufferer for the cause, yet Heath in his self-styled 'martyrology' still has some hesitancy in presenting Poyer as a fallen royalist hero. He noted that Poyer 'dyed in some reluctancy but ought nevertheless to be numbred with other loyal sacrifices, from whom therefore I could not . . . disjoyn him'.[76] Poyer's pleading for mercy, denying his engagement in the royalist cause and emphasising his parliamentary service, were clearly difficult elements to accommodate in a royalist 'martyr'. Interestingly, at this point in his text Heath had cause to reflect on his own narrative methodology and remarked that it was not possible to keep the 'thred of this Chronicle . . . straight in such a diversity and multitude of transcurrencies which weave it up and down in the various confusions of this new-fashioned state'. This aside came hard on the heels of his discussion about Poyer, and suggested that the Welshman, too, was a man difficult to 'keep straight' among the vicissitudes of the times. It is worth noting that a few years later when Heath published (posthumously) a volume dedicated to those who had fallen or been banished by the usurping powers, his treatment of Poyer was again ambiguous. He provides a very brief entry on him, observing, 'I cannot deny this gentleman a room in the martyrology (those that came the eleventh houre, shall find entertainment) though he was formerly for the parliament'.[77]

Poyer did not fit easily into the analytical frameworks that these historians had for understanding the recent war. There is a telling contrast, for example, that Poyer's countryman and Church of England cleric, David Lloyd, produced a volume entitled *Memoires* in 1668 which celebrated those who 'suffered by death, sequestration, decimation, or otherwise' between 1642 and 1660. While he spent a good deal of time with the thoroughgoing cavalier, Sir John Owen, who rose in north Wales shortly after Poyer in 1648, and also the rebel martyrs from Colchester, there was no entry in his catalogue for Poyer or his two colleagues.[78] It seems that an uncomplicated royalism was what was needed for ready inclusion into many of these texts. One such hagiographical work, however, William Winstanley's *The Loyall Martyrology*, produced in 1665, does allow Poyer the reward of a brief biographical entry without caveats and hesitations.[79]

Moreover, it also provides us with our only image of John Poyer, whose face is included among nearly forty other royalists on its frontispiece.[80] Poyer is shown as a man in his early middle age, with respectably long cavalier-style hair, sober dress and a small moustache and beard. The woodcut is of indifferent quality, however, and most of the faces are so generic that it is unclear whether this bore any true resemblance to the living man at all.

In Winstanley's volume, as in practically all of these Restoration works, however, Poyer's life effectively begins in 1648. There is no attempt to delve any deeper as this would dredge up his problematic parliamentarian past. However, even in current scholarship, as discussed in a moment, Poyer arrives fully formed like a thunderclap from a clear blue sky in 1648 with no backstory or deeper motivation beyond his demands for arrears. This actually reflects a thread of Restoration scholarship such as that found in Thomas Hobbes's *History of the Civil Wars of England*. Hobbes introduces Poyer, Powell and Laugharne in 1648 simply as individuals who sought their arrears, refused to disband and, 'the better to strengthen themselves', declared for the king. This gives Hobbes the opportunity to comment, 'I do not much pity the loss of those men, that impute to the King that which they do upon their own quarrel'.[81] Some of our current scholarship rests upon such problematic evidential foundations, and this causes difficulties for integrating Poyer's complex civil war history with his actions in 1648.

Poyer continued to crop up in civil war histories, biographies of Oliver Cromwell and local antiquarian studies produced in the eighteenth and nineteenth centuries. The notable Pembrokeshire antiquarian Richard Fenton gives a fairly full account of the siege of Pembroke in his substantial *A Historical Tour through Pembrokeshire* (1811). This is based on some contemporary evidence, but Poyer once more has no backstory, and Fenton's observation that Poyer and Laugharne, 'thinking themselves ill-treated by the parliament . . . declared for the king', tells us little about the deeper story and motivations at play.[82]

The most influential and most damning nineteenth-century treatment of Poyer, however, came at the hand of Thomas Carlyle who, with a few strokes of his pen, produced a portrait of the man which has become inescapable though it is highly tendentious. The discussion of Poyer comes in the commentary to Carlyle's enormously successful edition of Oliver Cromwell's letters and speeches.[83] Carlyle worshipped Cromwell and the parliamentarian cause, and so Poyer's stubborn resistance to one of the Great Men of history could not be taken without challenge. Carlyle's 'elucidations' to Cromwell's letters provide the vehicle for his own interpretation of Oliver's life and times, and when he encounters Poyer he pulls no punches. In his introduction to the section on the Second Civil War, Carlyle maintained that Wales was, at this time, full of discontentment. Amid this restiveness, a 'confused' Colonel Poyer was described by Carlyle as 'full of brandy and Presbyterian texts of scripture, refusing to disband till his arrears be better paid . . . Drunken Colonel Poyer . . . seized Pembroke [and] flatly refuses to obey parliament's order'.[84] On the next page we again encounter 'Drunken Poyer' who 'defies the Parliament and the world', while Wales is 'smoking with confused discontent'.[85] At the end of the siege 'drunken Poyer' has had to surrender and 'Pembroke happily is down'.[86] With these few comments, Carlyle produced perhaps the most influential portrait of Poyer in modern scholarship. Carlyle's Poyer is drunk, confused, irrational and in pursuit of money. These basic positions have formed cardinal points in discussions of Poyer ever since.[87] The problem is that they are all lifted from allegations made by Poyer's arch-antagonist, John Eliot. Carlyle's key text in this section of the work is John Rushworth's *Historical Collections*. In this volume Rushworth reproduces one of Eliot's attacks on Poyer which was printed in a parliamentary newspaper (Rushworth took many of his documents from such sources), that described Poyer as sober in the morning and drunk in the afternoon and full of plots.[88] This detail was enough to launch Carlyle's bitter characterisation which has indelibly marked Poyer's revolt as one borne out of personal weakness, anger and greed.

Carlyle's propagation of the newsbook attack on Poyer introduces a fundamental issue for his treatment in modern scholarship: that the vast majority of our evidence for his life and actions was produced by his enemies. Carlyle, and the many historians who have followed him, have not allowed sufficiently for the extraordinary capacity of John Eliot to introduce, often anonymously, an unedifying profile of Poyer into a variety of pamphlets, tracts and newsbooks, and even at Poyer's court martial. While we cannot say that his picture of Poyer is fabricated, it is incumbent upon us to be more critical of a good deal of the material upon which our assessments of Poyer's actions rest.

The beginnings of a more 'scholarly' investigation of Poyer can be found in the work of the Tenby-based gentleman scholar, Edward Laws,

who published his *History of Little England Beyond Wales* in 1888.[89] Laws
devoted a substantial part of his *History* to the civil wars, and based his
account on a thorough examination of contemporary printed material,
texts such as Clarendon's *Rebellion* and even some manuscript sources
from the British Museum. He provides an excellent narrative, particularly
of the Second Civil War, which brings a close local knowledge to bear upon
events. Laws was something of a Pembrokeshire patriot, and saw in Poyer a
kindred spirit who appeared to stand up for local sensibilities. His assessment of Poyer, then, is positive, and he described him as 'a great man'. He
actually began to write a biography of Poyer, but it remained incomplete
and was never published.[90] The roots of Poyer's greatness are elusive in
Law's work, however, and seem to be grounded largely in his brave defence
of Pembroke. His assessment of Poyer's motives, moreover, is superficial
and problematic. He maintained that Poyer was 'not straightforward in
money matters' and 'did not hesitate to plunge his native county into all
the horrors of a second civil war for the sake of a disputed account'.[91]
Later in the volume, Laws maintains that the causes of Poyer's 'disaffection' can be 'readily discerned'. Poyer had moved from being a merchant
to a politician and then 'war' became his 'means of livelihood'. He was,
in short, 'a military adventurer to whom war had become a necessity, so
that when the parliament dispensed with his services, these were at once
offered to the royalists'.[92] This is not a helpful reading. While war was
the context in which Poyer's public life was lived, he was no warmon-
ger. Moreover, Laws reduces Poyer's motivations to the purely material
and empties his actions of any ideological meaning. While it is plain that
parliament's shoddy treatment concerning his arrears was a key factor in
inciting Poyer to rebel, to reduce his motivations only to the question of
money is simply to rehearse the allegations levelled at him by his bitterest
enemies. However, the emphasis Laws places on money and self-interest
would remain prominent in later accounts of Poyer's life.

The most significant modern author on Poyer is Arthur Leonard
Leach. Leach published the most influential narrative of Pembrokeshire's
civil war history in 1937. His *The History of the Civil War (1642–1649) in
Pembrokeshire and on its Borders,* was the product of diligent research in
the British Museum's Thomason Collection of contemporary pamphlets
and was supplemented by new finds among the Tanner manuscripts at
the Bodleian Library and the State Papers at the (then) Public Record
Office. This has remained the authoritative volume on this period of

Pembrokeshire's history, and is a remarkable achievement for an amateur historian who produced the work in retirement after a career as a school-teacher.[93] Poyer is a presence throughout Leach's text and he emerges here for the first time in the literature as a man with a history, not simply a sprite who was conjured into being in 1648. The book remains deficient, however, in underestimating the significance and control of the Lort–Eliot group in Pembrokeshire after 1645 and does not do a particularly good job of placing Pembrokeshire into the context of national politics. On Poyer, Leach is drawn to the kinds of moral judgment which one might expect from the period in which it was written: Poyer's actions are described as 'understandable, even if many of them were far from praiseworthy'.[94] He also, moreover, falls prey to believing John Eliot's claims about Poyer rather too easily. Leach's position is not so far away from that of Edward Laws, in fact, in seeing Poyer's revolt as having nothing to do with any ideological motivations, but rather was the consequence of his dishonest dealings over the revenues of Carew Castle, which were about to be investigated.[95]

Leach also follows Carlyle in believing Poyer to be 'confused' in his political positions, and he is vexed that Poyer 'followed no clear and consistent course either for parliament or for king, for prayer-book or for Covenant'.[96] This is fair enough, of course, given the violent political shifts Poyer sought to navigate, but it is to be hoped that the foregoing chapters have suggested that Poyer did have a political lodestar, and it was a moderate and unexceptional kind of 'Protestation-style' undertaking for 'King and Parliament' which he held to throughout the 1640s. His attachment to the Church of England and the Book of Common Prayer were also at the heart of his political outlook throughout this period. That Poyer does not fit readily into the definitional boxes of political allegiance is a problem for our analytical categories as much as for Poyer's 'inconstancy'. Moreover, Poyer was not alone among those who turned to the king in 1648 in insisting that it was not their beliefs which had changed but those of the institutions in which they put their trust. The splendid research of Andrew Hopper on side-changers in the civil war has revealed how individuals challenged their turncoat status by stressing their ideological constancy. The earl of Holland is a case in point. He, like Poyer, was executed in 1649 for a (second) flirtation with royalism. However, he maintained, again like Poyer, that he had always been 'for King and Parliament', and that 'I have never gone off from those principles that ever I have professed'.[97] This echoes Poyer's assertion that he rose in 1648 in support of his 'first principles' and 'the ground of [his] . . . first taking up armes'.

The understanding of Poyer and Pembrokeshire in the 1640s has not moved on significantly from Leach's study in 1937. Its comprehensiveness means it remains the authoritative work for modern scholars who wish to integrate Pembrokeshire into their discussions. The essays by Rowland Mathias on the mid-seventeenth century in the Pembrokeshire County History, while valuable and written with enviable élan, are essentially lengthy summaries of Leach.[98] Important studies have nonetheless appeared which have added much to our knowledge of south Wales during the civil wars. Significant here was Ronald Hutton's *The Royalist War Effort, 1642–1646*, which first appeared in 1982, and which transformed our understanding of the royalist leadership and the political and logistical challenges they faced in Wales and the West of England during the first civil war.[99] Hutton was not particularly concerned with Poyer and the parliamentarians, however, and he acknowledges his treatment of south-west Wales is rather brief partly because, of all the regions he examined, this was 'the most destitute of Civil War records'.[100] A notable and often-overlooked text on the civil war in Wales is Peter Gaunt's excellent *A Nation Under Siege* which appeared in 1991.[101] Perhaps because of its status as a relatively short CADW volume, scholars often overlook this text's impressive breadth and detail but also its insight and acuity. Stephen Roberts's 2003 article on parliamentary politics and religion in south Wales between 1642 and 1649 is essential reading for understanding the political context within which Poyer's narrative sits.[102] His discussion is superb on Welsh contacts with the political centre in this period, but the piece is much more concerned with south-east Wales than the south-west.

The most significant modern work to deal with the events discussed in this volume is Robert Ashton's monumental study of the Second Civil War which was published in 1994.[103] This provides a nationwide examination of the grievances and discontents which brought about the uprisings of 1648, as well as a thorough discussion of the failures of strategy and coordination which blighted the royalist challenge to parliament and the army. Poyer and Laugharne are discussed at some length, and Ashton is at pains to deploy a wealth of manuscript and printed material in his analysis. It is all the more striking, then, that Ashton's Poyer is essentially the caricature constructed by John Eliot. Although some acknowledgement is made of the fact that our impressions of Poyer are largely those of his enemies, these characteristics are nonetheless allowed to define him. Ashton describes him as 'behaving like a cross between a warlord and a robber baron', as often drunk, and even has Poyer calling his men 'bullies', an epithet only ever applied by his Lort–Eliot opponents.[104] Most of the accusations Eliot published against Poyer are here recounted as fact. It is little surprise, then, that Ashton's assessment of Poyer's royalism in 1648 was to see it as 'the product of convenience rather than conviction. What mattered to him was his private interests.'[105] As in the Independent attacks on him, then, Poyer's royalism is understood here as wholly instrumental, a ruse or cover for personal ambitions, and a lusting after filthy lucre: he was a low-born merchant who had risen above his station after all.

Finally in our review of Poyer's historical afterlives, Robert Matthews has produced a careful and detailed study of the second civil war in south Wales which necessarily has much to say about Poyer.[106] A good deal of this is in the Leach mode, and, like Leach, Matthews is also discomfited by the fact that the leaders of the south-Wales revolt were ex-parliamentarians. Here once more, then, Poyer's political position was simply 'pragmatic', which is a kind way of saying 'insincere'. A page after acknowledging that royalism in 1648 was 'a vague concept, meaning different things to different people', Matthews nonetheless states that Poyer's aims as detailed in his *Declaration* could not meaningfully be described as 'royalist'.[107] To suggest that publishing a declaration to follow the cause of the king and prayer book after colluding with the Prince of Wales was not royalist, reveals our hankering after subjects with inflexible and unchanging belief systems rather than our understanding of the malleable nature of political categories in the second civil war. Moreover, Matthew's book problematically imports an outmoded notion of localism into the events of 1648.[108] This was, he argues, a localist revolt of a culturally specific province against an encroaching English state. This would have been surprising news, of course, to Pembrokeshire men like Thomas Wogan, Sampson Lort and John Eliot who were agents of that state.[109]

Much of the historical writing on John Poyer, then, has fallen into something of a pattern. For the most part he is a man without a past before late 1647. When he does appear, Poyer is pugnacious, irrational and divisive.

He is driven largely by a desire for money and personal advancement; his 'royalism' is both tactical and superficial and is easily sloughed off. His ultimate fate is lamentable, but perhaps not unexpected. This book has set out to demonstrate that there is rather more to the picture than this. While Poyer was certainly a divisive figure who alienated many, he was also a complex and enigmatic character who could inspire significant support. His rallying the population of Pembroke behind him time after time throughout the 1640s argues strongly that he was a charismatic and compelling figure who could articulate his cause convincingly to the local population. He made remarkable progress from his origins as a household servant to John Meyrick to the mayoralty of Pembroke, and then becoming the symbol of parliamentarian resistance in royalist south Wales in 1642. His service in the first civil war was crucial for maintaining a vital parliamentarian port on the western seaboard. Yet he was a victim of the parliamentary realignments after the war which meshed with the fracture lines of local factional politics in a manner that ultimately brought about his downfall. This volume has shown how pervasive, powerful and influential the forces ranged against him were, and how Poyer was struggling for his financial and political survival – and even, perhaps, his life – from the moment the fighting ended. His inability to make connections with the political centre which could rival those of Roger Lort and John Eliot after 1646 is crucial in understanding the trajectory of his post-war career. While he did have Presbyterian friends and associates who protected him, he simply did not have the associative firepower to withstand the rise of the Independents and the New Model Army. As this book has demonstrated, there was much in Poyer's life before 1648 which helps us understand his actions in the second civil war.

This volume also argues that Poyer's 'royalism' in 1648 was not cover for something else, simply a set of clothes he slipped on when he could not get money out of parliament. Rather the royalist cause was the best vehicle at this time for his ideological beliefs about the future direction of Church and state. Poyer was a prayer book Protestant, and the rise of Independency and the New Model was terrifying to him not because it denied him money but because it threatened his salvation. Poyer first supported parliament in 1642 in the firm belief that he was defending a Church that needed to be purified but also defended from the Catholic threat. When in 1646–8 the threat appeared to be coming from within parliament itself, Poyer shifted his position. It has been argued here that his public statements in March and April 1648 constituted an ideological basis for his actions which were genuinely held rather than the products of cynical pragmatism. And this volume has also thrown some new light on the way in which Poyer's *Declaration* and its associated oath were used as means of mobilising support in 1648, and for exporting his revolt throughout south Wales and beyond.

Another thread which runs through this book, and which has been an important component in the recent historiography of the English Civil War, is the significance of print to Poyer's story. The new world of newspapers, pamphlets and declarations were crucial in the interconnected world of London and provincial politics. Poyer's first known foray into print in 1645 was a lobby document, and such texts would prove important in the years ahead. As he faced death, Poyer turned to print to plead for his life and broadcast his diligent services to parliament. At this moment, as at many others in the months and years before, however, he faced a significant problem in that his opponents were better connected and more skilled at deploying political print than he was. John Eliot in particular emerges from these pages as a frankly villainous character, one who was determined to stymie Poyer at every turn. This is certainly how he must have looked to Poyer. Eliot was a new beast, a skilled agent and propagandist who was able to introduce his narrative into the public sphere with far greater effectiveness than Poyer could ever muster. Poyer did not die because of Eliot's adroit publicity, but Eliot made it almost impossible for Poyer's version of events, as conveyed in his many petitions and representations, to gain much traction at Westminster when they were answered at every turn by a biting pamphlet or newspaper editorial.

His enemies' skill with print means that we often only glimpse Poyer through a glass darkly. It is frequently difficult to sift the propaganda from the truth. However, this book argues for a greater critical awareness of our sources when assessing Poyer's life and motives. John Eliot was an accomplished operator, and, if we are not careful, we end up telling his version of events afresh. Partly because of the prominence of these hostile sources, Poyer remains a conundrum and a contradictory character; to paraphrase Heath, it is difficult to keep the thread of his life straight amidst such a diversity. Although he was not a 'great man' as Edward Laws asserted, he was nonetheless a remarkable individual, and one whose life touches upon many vital aspects of the vibrant, chaotic and transformative story of the civil wars in England and Wales.

Timeline of the Civil Wars in Pembrokeshire

---------------------- 1641 ----------------------

October 1641 John Poyer elected mayor of Pembroke.

Outbreak of the Irish Rebellion. Refugees begin to arrive in Pembrokeshire ports.

---------------------- 1642 ----------------------

January–July 1642 John Poyer (and John David of Haverfordwest) write letters to parliament informing members of the Irish threat, Pembrokeshire's defensive vulnerabilities and their responses to parliamentary orders.

July–August 1642 Royalist commissions of array and the parliamentarian militia ordinance circulated in south Wales.

---------------------- 1643 ----------------------

May 1643 Dispute over Pembroke mayoralty; Poyer resumes the post.

July 1643 Royalist leader the earl of Carbery summons the gentry of Pembrokeshire to the king's standard.

August 1643 Pro-royalist declaration from many leading Pembrokeshire gentlemen.

Tenby falls to the royalists.

October 1643 Reported capitulation of Pembroke to the royalists; Poyer apparently heads off any such surrender.

——————————————— **1644** ———————————————

January 1644	Arrival in Milford Haven of Admiral Richard Swanley and relieving parliamentarian naval force.
	Appearance of Major General Rowland Laugharne in the field.
January–March 1644	Royalist forces rolled back throughout south Pembrokeshire.
March 1644	Recovery of Tenby for the parliamentarians.
June 1644	Appointment of parliamentary committee to run Pembrokeshire (and Carmarthenshire and Cardiganshire when liberated from royalist control). Poyer omitted from this body.
June–July 1644	First campaign of the royalist General Charles Gerard in Pembrokeshire and south-west Wales.
	Widespread devastation of crops and houses at the hands of royalist forces.
	Haverfordwest falls to the royalists; Tenby and Pembroke remain in parliament's hands.
September 1644– April 1645	Forces under Major General Rowland Laugharne and Captain Rice Powell take the field and clear most royalist garrisons.

——————————————— **1645** ———————————————

March–April 1645	Poyer petitions parliament for supplies and assistance at Pembroke and is crossed by his opponents on the Pembrokeshire county committee.
April 1645	Second campaign of General Charles Gerard who takes Haverfordwest and other garrisons for the royalists, leaving only Tenby and Pembroke in parliament's control.
June 1645	Gerard returns to England in the wake of the royalist defeat at Naseby (14 June).
1 August 1645	Major General Rowland Laugharne victorious at the Battle of Colby Moor; Pembrokeshire is effectively won for parliament.

October 1645	Hearings against Richard Swanley commence in the Admiralty Court, London.
December 1645	Poyer in London to give evidence against Richard Swanley.
3 December 1645	Poyer petitions parliament for arrears.

——————————————— 1646 ———————————————

January 1646	Poyer arrested in London, ostensibly at Richard Swanley's suit.
c.mid-February 1646	Poyer publishes the '*Relation*', attacking his enemies and defending his conduct during the civil war. He is answered by John Eliot's pamphlet, *An Answer in Just Vindication of Some Religious and Worthy Gentlemen of Pembrokeshire.*
c.February–March 1646	Election of Poyer ally Arthur Owen of Orielton as MP for Pembrokeshire.
Spring 1646	Poyer returns to Pembroke.
October 1646	Poyer steps down as mayor of Pembroke.

——————————————— 1647 ———————————————

13 February 1647	Poyer petitions the House of Lords for arrears.
March 1647	Poyer confirmed by parliament as governor of Pembroke. Rice Powel similarly confirmed as governor in Tenby.
c.mid-1647	Poyer brought before the central parliamentary committee of accounts in London and told to account for £6,000 of wartime expenditure.
August 1647	Poyer imprisons his local enemies, Roger, Sampson and John Lort in Pembroke Castle.
September 1647	Charges against Poyer concerning his wartime accounts preferred at army headquarters at Putney.

December 1647	Parliament resolves to disband the 'supernumerary' forces of Rowland Laugharne.
	Poyer ejects the elected mayor of Pembroke, Matthew Bowen, and once again assumes the office.
	Poyer begins to fortify himself against his local parliamentary enemies in Pembroke Castle.

——————————————— 1648 ———————————————

Early January 1648	The New Model officer, Christopher Fleming, summons Poyer to surrender his command at Pembroke. Poyer refuses.
	Rowland Laugharne detained by the army in London. His forces in south Wales are ordered to disband; many refuse.
13 March 1648	Parliamentary ordinance for Poyer to surrender his command arrives in Pembroke. He attacks the besieging New Model forces.
23 March 1648	Assault by Laugharne's men, in concert with Poyer's forces, against Fleming's troops.
29 March 1648	Defeat by Poyer of New Model forces at Pwllcrochan.
10 April 1648	Publication of *The Declaration of Col. Poyer and Col. Powell.*
11–13 April 1648	Poyer musters troops in Pembrokeshire, Carmarthenshire and Cardiganshire.
20 April 1648	Publication of *Colonell Powell and Col. Poyers Letter to his Highnesse the Prince of Wales.*
Late April 1648	Rice Powell defeats a New Model force under Colonel Thomas Horton near Carmarthen; Adjutant General Christopher Fleming killed.
29 April 1649	First reports of Rowland Laugharne's appearance in south Wales.

8 May 1648	The Battle of St Fagans: rebel forces under Rowland Laugharne are routed by the New Model troops under Thomas Horton. Laugharne flees back to Pembrokeshire.
24 May 1648	Oliver Cromwell arrives before Pembroke Castle. The siege of Pembroke begins.
31 May 1648	Rebel forces in Tenby surrender to Thomas Horton.
10 July 1648	Surrender of Pembroke town and castle to the besieging forces of Oliver Cromwell. Poyer, Laugharne and Rice Powell are taken into army custody.
By December 1648	The prisoners from Pembroke and Tenby arrive at Windsor.

———————————— **1649** ————————————

30 January 1649	Execution of King Charles I.
March 1649	Poyer publishes the tracts 'The Grounds & Reasons of Coll: Poyer Taking Armes in the Second Difference' and *Poyer's Vindication*. These works are answered by two texts written by John Eliot.
2 April 1649	Court martial for trying the Welsh rebels of 1648 sits at Whitehall.
10 April 1649	Court martial passes a sentence of death against Poyer, Laugharne and Powell.
21 April 1649	After an intervention by Lord General Fairfax, a child draws lots to determine which rebel should be executed; Poyer is chosen.
25 April 1649	John Poyer executed by firing squad at Covent Garden.

Notes

Preface

1. *Some Particular Animadversions of Marke for Satisfaction of the Contumatious Malignant* (London, 1646), p. 15.
2. Bodl. Lib., Nalson MS 5, fo. 203.
3. *Some Particular Animadversions*, p. 45.
4. A fuller discussion of the historiography can be found in Chapter 9.
5. Although, on his 'turncoat' status, see Andrew Hopper, *Turncoats and Renegadoes: Changing Sides during the English Civil Wars* (Oxford, 2012).
6. *The Declaration of Col. Poyer and Col. Powell and the Officers and Soldiers under their Command* (London, 1648).
7. *Heads of Chiefe Passages in Parliament*, 2 (12–19 Jan. 1648), pp. 10–11.
8. *Perfect Occurrences*, 121 (20–27 Apr. 1649), p. 999.

Chapter 1: The Setting: John Poyer and Early Stuart Pembrokeshire, *c*.1606–1640

1. Ivan Roots (ed.), *Speeches of Oliver Cromwell* (London, 1989), p. 42.
2. John Howells, 'The Boroughs of Medieval Pembrokeshire: Pembroke', in R. F. Walker (ed.), *Pembrokeshire County History, Volume II: Medieval Pembrokeshire* (Haverfordwest, 2002), pp. 68–78.
3. John Gwynfor Jones (ed.), *The Dialogue of the Government of Wales (1594)* (Cardiff, 2010), pp. 81–2.
4. Gwynfor Jones, *Dialogue of the Government of Wales*, p. 179.
5. John Speed, *The Theatre of the Empire of Great Britain* (London, 1611), book 2, p. 101.
6. Nia M. Powell, 'Urban Population in Early Modern Wales Revisited', *Welsh History Review*, 23 (2003), 33–4.
7. Brian Howells, 'The Economy, 1536–1642', in *Pembs. Co. Hist.*, pp. 83–92; Andrew Thrush, 'Pembroke Boroughs', in Andrew Thrush and J. P. Ferris (eds), *History of Parliament: The House of Commons, 1604–29*: <https://www.historyofparliament online.org/volume/1604-1629/constituencies/pembroke-boroughs> (accessed 29 Oct. 2019).
8. E. A. Lewis (ed.), *Welsh Port Books, 1550–1603* (London, 1927), pp. xxxiii–xxxv.
9. George Owen, *A Description of Penbrokshire*, ed. H. Owen (4 vols, London, 1898–1933), I, p. 57.
10. Somerset Heritage Centre, Q/SR/46/99, Q/SR/112/99–100, Q/SR/158/5; TNA, C2/ChasI/B22/14; PROB 11/200/106.
11. NLW, Pontfaen Estate Records MS 58. See also the comments in Owen, *Description of Penbrokshire*, I, p. 148.
12. 'Mayors of Pembroke', *WWHR*, 5 (1915), 121.

13. Huntington Library, Ellesmere MS 7135. For these local initiatives, see *Acts of the Privy Council of England, 1630–1* (London, 1964), pp. 44, 207; TNA, SP16/192, fo. 102r–v.

14. On the need for repair of Pembroke's walls and gates, see 'Tenby in 1621', *Cambrian Journal*, 2nd ser., 5 (1862), 249–50; NLW, Great Sessions 4/786/2/2, 4/786/3/44.

15. Speed, *Theatre*, book 2, p. 101.

16. Owen, *Description of Penbrokshire*, II, pp. 557–9.

17. It may not have been too out of date. The local puritan, Sir James Perrot, incorporated Owen's description verbatim into his discussion with the government about Pembroke's defensive status in 1626: TNA, SP16/6, fos 116–17v.

18. Hugh Peter, *A Copy of his Highnesse Prince Charles his Letter* (London, 1648), p. 4.

19. Lloyd Bowen, *The Politics of the Principality: Wales, c.1603–42* (Cardiff, 2007), ch. 3.

20. Dilwyn Miles (ed.), *The Description of Pembrokeshire* (Llandysul, 1994), pp. 42–3.

21. Leach, *Civil War*, p. 15.

22. Although see now, Stephen Roberts, 'Cardiganshire and the State 1540–1689', in Geraint H. Jenkins, Richard Suggett and Eryn M. White (eds), *Cardiganshire County History, Volume 2: Medieval and Early Modern Cardiganshire* (Cardiff, 2019).

23. *Some Particular Animadversions of Marke for Satisfaction of the Contumatious Malignant* (London, 1646).

24. Robert Matthews, *'A Storme Out of Wales': The Second Civil War in South Wales, 1648* (Newcastle-upon-Tyne, 2012), p. 28.

25. Richard Fenton, *A Historical Tour through Pembrokeshire* (London, 1811), pp. 303–4.

26. [John Eliot], *A Short Comment upon the Grounds and Reasons of Poyers Taking up Armes* (London, 1649), p. 1.

27. [John Eliot], *An Answer in Just Vindication of Some Religious and Worthy Gentleman of Pembrokeshire* (London, 1646), p. 2. Cf. *The Moderate Intelligencer*, 155 (2–9 Mar. 1648), p. 1197.

28. [John Eliot], *A Declaration of Divers Gentlemen of Wales Concerning Collonell Poyer* (London, 1648), p. 2.

29. [Eliot], *A Declaration of Divers Gentlemen*, p. 2.

30. John Poyer, *Poyer's Vindication* (London, 1649), p. 2.

31. TNA, E134/15ChasI/Mich41; British History Online, High Court of Chivalry proceedings, no. 422: Meryricke v. Catchmaye: <*https://www.british-history.ac.uk/no-series/court-of-chivalry/422-meyricke-catchmaye*> (accessed 3 Oct. 2019).

32. NLW, SD1604/108.

33. British History Online, High Court of Chivalry proceedings, no. 422: Meryricke v. Catchmaye: <*https://www.british-history.ac.uk/no-series/court-of-chivalry/422-meyricke-catchmaye*> (accessed 3 Oct. 2019).

34. TNA, E134/15ChasI/Mich41.

35. 'Mayors of Pembroke', 121.

36. Brian Howells, 'Land and People, 1536–1642', in *Pembs. Co. Hist.*, p. 29. See also the depositions of four Pembroke glovers, including John Poyer's brother, David, in a lawsuit of 1636/7: British History Online, High Court of Chivalry proceedings, no. 422: Meryricke v. Catchmaye: <*https://www.british-history.ac.uk/no-series/court-of-chivalry/422-meyricke-catchmaye*> (accessed 2 Sept. 2019).

37. Poyer, *Poyer's Vindication*, p. 2.

38. Howells, 'The Economy, 1536–1642', pp. 74–5.

39. Parliamentary Archives, HL/PO/JO/10/1/225.

40. TNA, E134/15ChasI/Mich41.

41. TNA, E112/277/52.

42. The date of his death is established by TNA, E112/277/51 and E134/15ChasI/ Mich41.

43. J. G. Jenkins, *The Welsh Woollen Industry* (Cardiff, 1969), pp. 100–4.

44. *Acts of the Privy Council, 1630–1*, pp. 44, 207; TNA, PC2/40, fo. 318; SP16/164, fo. 25; SP16/192, fo. 102r–v.

45. Poyer, *Poyer's Vindication*, p. 2.

46. Huntington Library, Ellesmere MS 7135.

47. Lewis Dwnn, *Visitations of Wales*, ed. S. R. Meyrick (2 vols, Llandovery, 1846), I, p. 137.

48. N. M. Fuidge, 'Gelly Meyrick', in J. P. Ferris (ed.), *The History of Parliament: The House of Commons, 1558–1603*: <http://www.histparl.ac.uk/volume/1558-1603/ member/meyrick-(merrick)-gelly-1556-1601/> (accessed 17 Oct. 2019); David Mathew, *The Celtic Peoples and Renaissance Europe. A Study of the Celtic and Spanish Influences on Elizabethan History* (London, 1933), pp. 341ff.

49. TNA, STAC 5/A35/35; 5/A41/40; 5/A45/19.

50. Longleat House, DE/Box VIII/112.

51. Longleat House, Devereux MS 4, fos 223, 235; TNA, E112/277/51.

52. TNA, PROB 11/167, fo. 54.

53. British History Online, High Court of Chivalry proceedings, no. 422: Meryricke v. Catchmaye: <https://www.british-history.ac.uk/no-series/court-of-chivalry/422- meyricke-catchmaye> (accessed 6 Oct. 2019).

54. On this court, see Richard Cust, *Charles I and the Aristocracy, 1625–1642* (Cambridge, 2013), ch. 1; Richard Cust and Andrew Hopper (eds), *Cases in the High Court of Chivalry, 1634–1640* (Harleian Society, new series, 18, 2006).

55. For John's appointment as customer, see Jan Broadway, Richard Cust and Stephen K. Roberts (eds), *A Calendar of the Docquets of Lord Keeper Coventry, 1625–1640* (London, 2004), pt 2, p. 304. Rowland held the post down to Jan. 1644: Bodl. Lib., Rawlinson MS A221, fo. 174.

56. Catchmay had also recently been investigated about an unprovoked assault in Pembroke: NLW, Great Sessions 4/785/3/82.

57. Richard Catchmay's status as an innholder is confirmed by TNA, STAC 8/123/5.

58. *Some Particular Animadversions of Marke*, p. 45.

59. Henry Crouch, *A Complete Guide to the Officers of His Majesty's Customs in the Out-Ports* (London, 1732), pp. 2–3. The searcher was unsalaried but allowed to keep half of their seizures in lieu of payment, an arrangement which provided much scope for undocumented income.

60. Broadway, Cust and Roberts, *Docquets of Lord Keeper Coventry, 1625–1640*, pt 2, p. 304.

61. See pp. 71, 111.

62. Huntington Library, Ellesmere MS 7598.

63. 'Mayors of Pembroke', 127, n. 18.

64. Huntington Library, Ellesmere MS 7600A.

65. Huntington Library, Ellesmere MS 7600A.

66. NLW, Great Sessions 4/787/1/34.

67. [Eliot], *An Answer in Just Vindication*, p. 2.

68. Poyer, *Poyer's Vindication*, p. 2.

69. This was the case with the Pembrokeshire county militia: NLW, Bronwydd MS 3360; Bodl. Lib., Nalson MS 2, fo. 17.

70. Huntington Library, Ellesmere MS 7443.

71. Dwnn, *Heraldic Visitations*, I, pp. 130–1; A. H. Dodd, 'Nicholas Adams', in J. P. Ferris (ed.), *The House of Commons, 1558–1603*: <https://www.historyofparliamentonline

.org/volume/1558-1603/member/adams-nicholas-1565-1628> (accessed 6 Sept. 2019).

72. *The Articles and Charge Exhibited by the Court-Marshall at Whitehall Against Major Generall Laughorn, Col. Poyer, Col. Powell and Captain Bowen* (London, 1649), p. 2; *The Moderate*, 40 (10–17 Apr. 1649), p. 424.

73. Poyer, *Poyer's Vindication*, p. 2.

74. TNA, E179/291/88.

75. TNA, SP29/35, fo. 27; G. T. C[lark] and R. O. J., 'Some Account of the Parishes of St Nicholas and St Lythan, co. Glamorgan', *Archaeologia Cambrensis*, 3rd ser., 30 (1862), 112–13; Thomas B. Lawrence, *The Thomas Book, giving the Genealogies of Sir Rhys ap Thomas* (New York, 1896), p. 472.

76. HMC, *Salisbury MSS, Vol. XXI*, p. 361; NLW, Dynevor MSS A97, B348; Muddlescombe Deeds 1787.

77. Richard Burton Archives, Swansea University, Cawdor (Lort) MSS 13/619, 6/258; NLW, Dynevor MSS B2, B346, B348, B880.

Chapter 2: The Irish Crisis and the Coming of Civil War, 1640–1642

1. The authoritative study of this period is Kevin Sharpe, *The Personal Rule of Charles I* (New Haven and London, 1992).

2. Kenneth Fincham and Nicholas Tyacke, *Altars Restored: The Changing Face of English Religious Worship, c.1547–c.1700* (Oxford, 2007), pp. 227–73.

3. Nicholas Tyacke, *Anti-Calvinists: The Rise of English Arminianism, c.1590–1640* (Oxford, 1990). The historical debates on some of these points is reviewed in Anthony Milton, 'Arminians, Laudians, Anglicans, and Revisionists: Back to Which Drawing Board?', *Huntington Library Quarterly*, 78 (2015), 723–43.

4. David Stevenson, *The Scottish Revolution, 1637–1644: The Triumph of the Covenanters* (Newton Abbot, 1973); Laura A. M. Stewart, *Rethinking the Scottish Revolution: Covenanted Scotland, 1637–1651* (Oxford, 2016), ch. 1.

5. Stewart, *Covenanted Scotland*, ch. 1.

6. Mark Fissel, *The Bishops' Wars: Charles I's Campaigns against Scotland, 1638–1640* (Cambridge, 1994); Peter Donald, *An Uncounselled King: Charles I and the Scottish Troubles, 1637–1641* (Cambridge, 1990).

7. Conrad Russell, *The Fall of the British Monarchies, 1637–1642* (Oxford, 1991), pp. 60–3, 84–7; Joad Raymond, *Pamphlets and Pamphleteering in Early Modern Britain* (Cambridge, 2003), pp. 161–201; David Cressy, *England on Edge: Crisis and Revolution, 1640–42* (Oxford, 2006), *passim*; David Como, *Radical Parliamentarians and the English Civil War* (Oxford, 2018), pp. 62–5.

8. John Adamson, *The Noble Revolt* (London, 2007), ch. 1.

9. For some discussion of the Welsh dimension of these developments, see Lloyd Bowen, *The Politics of the Principality, c.1603–1642* (Cardiff, 2007), ch. 6; Roland Mathias, 'The First Civil War', in *Pembs. Co. Hist.*, pp. 159–72.

10. Bowen, *Politics of the Principality*, ch. 5.

11. Andrew Thrush, 'Hugh Owen', in J. P. Ferris and Andrew Thrush (eds), *The History of Parliament: The House of Commons, 1604–29*: <https://www.historyofparliament online.org/volume/1604-1629/member/owen-hugh-1604-1671> (accessed 14 Sept. 2019).

12. TNA, C219/43, pt 3, fo. 208.

13. Thrush, 'Hugh Owen'.

14. Lloyd Bowen, 'Faction and Connection in Pembrokeshire Politics, 1640–9' (forthcoming).

15. Lloyd Bowen, 'Wales and Religious Reform in the Long Parliament, 1640–42', *Transactions of the Honourable Society of Cymmrodorion*, 12 (2006), 36–56; Bowen, *Politics of the Principality*, ch. 6.

16. Como, *Radical Parliamentarians*, ch. 3; John Morrill, 'The Attack on the Church of England in the Long Parliament, 1640–1642', in *idem, The Nature of the English Revolution* (London, 1993), pp. 69–90.

17. Jacqueline Eales, 'White, John', *Oxford Dictionary of National Biography*: <https://doi-org.abc.cardiff.ac.uk/10.1093/ref:odnb/29254> (accessed 3 June 2019).

18. John Morrill, 'The Unweariableness of Mr Pym: Infuence and Eloquence in the Long Parliament', in S. D. Amussen and M. A. Kishlansky (eds), *Political Culture and Cultural Politics in Early Modern England* (Manchester, 1995), pp. 19–54.

19. Paul M. Hunneyball, 'The Development of Parliamentary Privilege, 1604–29', *Parliamentary History*, 34 (2015), 111–28.

20. *CJ*, II, p. 39.

21. *CJ*, II, p. 40.

22. There is a huge literature on this, but see Raymond, *Pamphlets and Pamphleteering*, chs 5–6; Cressy, *England on Edge*, pt III; Como, *Radical Parliamentarianism*, pt I; Jason Peacey, *Print and Public Politics in the English Revolution* (Cambridge, 2013), *passim*.

23. TNA, E112/275/32. A copy of the bill can be found at NLW, Picton Castle Estate MS 1897. For other references to William Jenkins of Cowbridge and his involvement in shipborne trade in 1638–9, see TNA, C3/415/33; C8/37/57. He also turns up in a Pembrokeshire context in 1636 when, intriguingly, one his sureties for appearing before the local assize court was Poyer's future enemy, John Eliot of Narberth: NLW, Great Sessions 4/786/3/63.

24. TNA, PROB 11/182, fo. 85.

25. TNA, E112/277/56.

26. That the mayoralty ran from October to October is established in the Meyrick *v.* Catchmay case: <https://www.british-history.ac.uk/no-series/court-of-chivalry/422-meyricke-catchmaye> (accessed 3 Oct. 2019).

27. There is no evidence to support Leach's conclusion that Poyer was mayor from October 1640. Indeed, his attendance on Hugh Owen makes that surpassingly unlikely. Other sources inform us that one Philip Thomas was mayor during this period: Leach, *Civil War in Pembs.*, p. 27, n. 1; 'Mayors of Pembroke', *WWHR*, 5 (1915), 121.

28. See Tadhg Ó hannracháin, 'Counter Reformation: The Catholic Church, 1550–1641', in Jane Ohlmeyer (ed.), *The Cambridge History of Ireland* (Cambridge, 2018), pp. 171–95.

29. Eamon Darcy, *The Irish Rebellion of 1641 and the Wars of the Three Kingdoms* (Woodbridge, 2013); M. Perceval-Maxwell, *The Outbreak of the Irish Rebellion of 1641* (Dublin, 1994).

30. David A. O'Hara, *English Newsbooks and the Irish Rebellion, 1641–49* (Dublin, 2005).

31. Ethan Shagan, 'Constructing Discord: Ideology, Propaganda, and English Responses to the Irish Rebellion of 1641', *Journal of British Studies*, 36 (1997), 4–34; Keith Lindley, 'Impact of the 1641 Rebellion upon England and Wales', *Irish Historical Review*, 18 (1972), 143–76.

32. Shagan, 'Constructing Discord'.

33. *LJ*, IV, p. 461; *CJ*, II, p. 331. Sir Hugh Owen was appointed a member of the committee which investigated these reports.

34. *PJLP*, I, pp. 208–9.
35. *CJ*, II, p. 378.
36. *LJ*, IV, p. 548; *CJ*, II, p. 401.
37. Bodl. Lib., Tanner MS 66, fo. 265r–v.
38. Bodl. Lib., Tanner MS 66, fo. 270.
39. Bodl. Lib., Nalson MS 2, fo. 17.
40. Pembrokeshire Archives, HBORO 73/4–6.
41. For the deputy lieutenants, see Huntington Library, Ellesmere MS 7443.
42. Bodl. Lib., Carte MS 3, fo. 72r–v.
43. On Molloy, see also Bodl. Lib., Nalson MS 2, fo. 28.
44. *PJLP*, II, pp. 333–4.
45. *PJLP*, III, p. 16. On Bellings, see the letter from the Lord Justices of Ireland to Poyer: Bodl. Lib., Carte MS 3, fo. 60.
46. *PJLP*, III, p. 16; *CJ*, II, p. 605.
47. *PJLP*, III, p. 243.
48. For an example of his staying an Irish ship and examining the master, see Trinity College, Dublin, MS 838, fos 1r–2v: <*http://1641.tcd.ie/deposition.php?depID<?php echo 838001r002?>*> (accessed 9 Sept. 2019).
49. Pope had petitioned the Commons, presumably about this matter, on 4 Apr.: *CJ*, II, p. 509.
50. *CJ*, II, pp. 642–3; *PJLP*, III, p. 140.
51. Plymouth and West Devon Record Office, 1/359/72.
52. *LJ*, V, p. 304.
53. John Poyer, *Poyer's Vindication* (London, 1649), p. 2.
54. *Some Particular Animadversions of Marke for Satisfaction of the Contumatious Malignant* (London, 1646), pp. 11–12.
55. In 1646, Laugharne would inform Speaker Lenthall 'my commission is from my Lorde of Essex & for the 3 counties [of south west Wales] onlie': Bodl. Lib., Nalson MS 5, fo. 249.
56. For the reparations and military preparations at Tenby, see Tenby Museum, TEM/Box 16; Herbert F. Hore, 'Mayors and Bailiffs of Tenby', *Archaeologia Cambrensis*, new series, 14 (Apr. 1853), 121n.
57. Parliamentary Archives, HL/PO/JO/10/1/225.
58. Andrew Hopper, 'Meyrick, Sir John', *Oxford Dictionary of National Biography*: <*https://doi-org.abc.cardiff.ac.uk/10.1093/ref:odnb/18642*> (accessed 13 Aug. 2019).
59. See pp. 155, 163, 196–7.
60. [John Eliot], *A Declaration of Divers Gentlemen of Wales Concerning Collonell Poyer* (London, 1648), p. 2.
61. [John Eliot], *A Short Comment upon the Grounds and Reasons of Poyers Taking up Armes* (London, 1649), p. 1.
62. [John Eliot], *An Answer in Just Vindication of Some Religious and Worthy Gentlemen* (London, 1646), pp. 2–3; 'Mayors of Pembroke', 121; Bodl. Lib., Tanner MS 60, fo. 22.
63. *Some Particular Animadversions*, p. 12; Bodl. Lib., Tanner MS 60, fo. 22.
64. Bodl. Lib., Tanner MS 58, fo. 724; Lambeth Palace Library, MS 679, p. 155.
65. Bodl. Lib., Carte MS 14, fo. 609.
66. Bodl. Lib., Tanner MS 60, fo. 21.
67. Worc. Coll., Clarke MS 16, fo. 89v.
68. Poyer, *Poyer's Vindication*, p. 2.

Chapter 3: Allies and Enemies: Poyer and Pembroke during the First Civil War

1. *LJ*, V, p. 441.
2. John Gunter occupied the Essex residence of Lamphey Court and was an officer in Essex's army at its formation: TNA, SP28/1A, *passim*.
3. Bodl. Lib., Nalson MS 2, fo. 290.
4. The characterisation of Pembrokeshire as 'strongly parliamentarian', which still appears in textbooks, is highly misleading: Ian Gentles, *The English Revolution and the Wars in the Three Kingdoms, 1638–1652* (Harlow, 2007), p. 133.
5. For Carbery, see Ronald Hutton, *The Royalist War Effort, 1642–1646* (2nd edn, London, 1999), pp. 68–75.
6. *Some Particular Animadversions of Marke for Satisfaction of the Contumatious Malignant* (London, 1646), p. 13.
7. TNA, SP16/492, fo. 262.
8. *Some Particular Animadversions*, pp. 13–14; *The Kingdomes Weekly Intelligencer*, 51 (16–25 Apr. 1644), p. 413. For an account of the depredations he suffered at the royalists' hands, see [Simon Thelwall], *A True Relation of the Routing of His Majesties Forces in the County of Pembroke* (London, 1644), p. 6; *Some Particular Animadversions*, p. 22.
9. William Smith, *Severall Letters of Great Importance and Good Successe* (London, 1643), p. 6. Bristol had fallen to the royalists in July 1643.
10. *Some Particular Animadversions*, pp. 14–15.
11. *Some Particular Animadversions*, p. 14.
12. TNA, SP16/492, fo. 262.
13. [John Eliot], *An Answer in Just Vindication of Some Religious and Worthy Gentlemen of Pembrokeshire* (London, 1646), p. 2.
14. *Mercurius Aulicus*, 37 (10–17 Sept. 1643), pp. 512–13.
15. *The Agreement of the Major, Aldermen and Inhabitants of the Towne of Tenby* (Oxford, 1643). See also *The Welch Mercury*, 1 (21–28 Oct. 1643), p. 3.
16. *Mercurius Aulicus*, 39 (25 Sept.–1 Oct. 1643), p. 540.
17. *Some Particular Animadversions*, p. 15; John Poyer, *Poyer's Vindication* (London, 1649), pp. 5–6.
18. Worc. Coll., Clarke MS 16, fo. 89v; Poyer, *Poyer's Vindication*, p. 3.
19. Poyer, *Poyer's Vindication*, p. 2.
20. Eliot, *An Answer*, p. 4.
21. NLW, Great Sessions 4/786/3/63.
22. [John Eliot], *A Declaration of Divers Gentlemen of Wales Concerning Collonell Poyer* (London, 1648), p. 2.
23. [John Eliot], *A Short Comment Upon the Grounds and Reasons of Poyers Taking up Armes* (London, 1649), pp. 1–2.
24. [Eliot], *A Short Comment*, pp. 2–3.
25. *The Perfect Weekly Account* (11–18 Apr. 1649), p. 446.
26. Poyer, *Poyer's Vindication*, p. 4.
27. [Thelwall], *A True Relation*, p. 2.
28. Elaine Murphy, *Ireland and the War at Sea, 1641–1653* (Woodbridge, 2012), pp. 38–40.
29. Bodl. Lib., Tanner MS 62, fo. 315.
30. [Thelwall], *A True Relation*, p. 3.
31. [Thelwall], *A True Relation*, p. 3.
32. Bodl. Lib., Tanner MS 62, fo. 315.

33. TNA, SP16/492, fo. 264.
34. For some discussion of perceptions of financial corruption among the parliamentarians, see Jason Peacey, *Print and Public Politics during the English Revolution* (Cambridge, 2013), pp. 152–4.
35. *Mercurius Aulicus*, 43 (22–28 Oct. 1643), p. 606.
36. [Eliot], *An Answer*, p. 3.
37. [Thelwall], *A True Relation*, p. 2.
38. *Mercurius Aulicus* (31 Dec. 1643–6 Jan. 1644), p. 752; (21–27 Jan. 1644), pp. 796–7.
39. *Mercurius Civicus*, 37 (1–8 Feb. 1644), pp. 392–4.
40. *Mercurius Civicus*, 37 (1–8 Feb. 1644), pp. 392–4. See also *The Spie*, 3 (5–13 Feb. 1644), p. 22.
41. Noticeably, it was John Eliot, the author of these allegations, who later repeated the claim in a legal deposition that Poyer 'then Mayor of Pembrooke and others of the chiefe of that towne' subscribed this 'instrument': TNA, HCA 13/60, pt 2, fo. 274.
42. [Thelwall], *A True Relation*, p. 3; *Mercurius Civicus*, 37 (1–8 Feb. 1644), p. 392.
43. Hostile sources describe Poyer as 'deputy mayor', but in a petition to parliament in Dec. 1645, Poyer related that 'for these three years last past [he] hath borne the office of mayor': *LJ*, VIII, p. 22.
44. *Mercurius Aulicus* (21–27 Jan. 1644), p. 796.
45. *Mercurius Civicus*, 37 (1–8 Feb. 1644), p. 392.
46. Murphy, *Ireland and the War at Sea*, pp. 38–40.
47. William Smith, *A True and Exact Relation of the Proceedings* (London, 1644), pp. 2–3.
48. TNA, HCA 13/60, pt 2, fo. 274.
49. Smith, *A True and Exact Relation*, p. 3.
50. [Eliot], *An Answer in Just Vindication*, p. 5.
51. Somerset Heritage Centre, DD/WO/55/1/17. Other copies can be found at Bodl. Lib., Tanner MS 62, fo. 539r–v; Smith, *A True and Exact Relation*, pp. 10–11; Thelwall, *A True Relation*, pp. 14–15.
52. Somerset Heritage Centre, DD/WO/55/1/17. See also the response by Sir Henry Vaughan in Bodl. Lib., Tanner MS 62, fo. 540v.
53. See Hutton, *Royalist War Effort*, esp. pp. 68–75.
54. A very full account of proceedings can be found in Simon Thelwall's relation to the Speaker: [Thelwall], *A True Relation*, pp. 1–16. It can also be followed in Leach, *Pembrokeshire*, pp. 62–86.
55. [Thelwall], *A True Relation*, p. 7.
56. [Thelwall], *A True Relation*, pp. 7–8. The others were Rowland Laugharne, Arthur Owen, Rice Powell, Thomas Laugharne, Walter Cuny, Rowland Wogan, John Wogan, John Powell and John Gunter.
57. *Some Particular Animadversions*, p. 24.
58. 'Original Letters', *Archaeologia Cambrensis*, new series, 13 (1853), 63.
59. For more detail, see Lloyd Bowen, 'Faction and Connection in Pembrokeshire Politics, 1640–9' (forthcoming).
60. *Some Particular Animadversions*, p. 16; Lambeth Palace Library, MS 679, pp. 155–6.
61. *CJ*, III, pp. 570, 590; *LJ*, VI, p. 670.
62. *The Kingdomes Weekly Intelligencer*, 51 (16–25 Apr. 1644), p. 413.
63. TNA, SP19/118/16, SP19/21/28; BL, Add. MS 18,981, fo. 97.
64. *Some Particular Animadversions*, p. 27.
65. *Some Particular Animadversions*, p. 28.
66. Bodl. Lib., Tanner MS 61, fo. 25.

67. *Some Particular Animadversions*, p. 28. For another report of royalist outrages in the county, see *The Kingdomes Weekly Intelligencer*, 77 (15–23 Oct. 1644), p. 618.
68. *The Kingdomes Weekly Intelligencer*, 77 (15–23 Oct. 1644), pp. 618–19.
69. Poyer, *Poyer's Vindication*, p. 3.
70. TNA, SP19/126/105.
71. Bodl. Lib., Tanner MS 61, fo. 25.
72. Andrew Thrush, 'Lewis Powell', in J. P. Ferris and Andrew Thrush (eds), *History of Parliament: The House of Commons, 1604–29*: https://www.historyofparliamentonline.org/volume/1604-1629/member/powell-lewis-1576-1636 (accessed 24 Oct. 2019).
73. [Eliot], *Declaration of Divers Gentlemen*, p. 4.
74. Bodl. Lib., Tanner MS 60, fo. 21.
75. TNA, HCA 13/247.
76. *Some Particular Animadversions*, p. 42.
77. Bodl. Lib., Tanner MS 60, fo. 21.
78. Bodl. Lib., Tanner MS 60, fo. 23.
79. Bodl. Lib., Tanner MS 60, fo. 22.
80. TNA, HCA 13/60, pt 2, fo. 355v.
81. *Heads of Chiefe Passages in Parliament*, 2 (12–19 Jan. 1649), p. 11. For their positions in the town, see 'Mayors of Pembroke', *WWHR*, 5 (1915), 121; NLW, SD1674/193; TNA, C5/611/210; E134/15ChasI/Mich41.
82. Bodl. Lib., Tanner MS 60, fo. 45.
83. A later pamphlet acknowledged that the Pembrokeshire committee had ordered Poyer to relinquish possession of Carew to Philipps: [Eliot], *An Answer in Just Vindication*, p. 8.
84. Somerset Heritage Centre, DD/TB/41/5/23. I am most grateful to Prof. Mark Stoyle for furnishing me with images of this and other documents from the Carew MSS.
85. Somerset Heritage Centre, DD/TB/41/5/22.
86. Somerset Heritage Centre, DD/TB/41/5/21.
87. Somerset Heritage Centre, DD/TB/41/5/24.
88. *Some Particular Animadversions*, p. 45.
89. *The Parliaments Post*, 1 (6–13 May 1645), pp. 2–3.
90. *Some Particular Animadversions*, pp. 34–5.
91. [Eliot], *An Answer in Just Vindication*, p. 7.
92. [Eliot], *A Declaration of Divers Gentlemen*, p. 4.
93. Bodl. Lib., Tanner MS 60, fo. 115.
94. *Mercurius Aulicus* (20–27 Apr. 1645), pp. 1564–5; *Mercurius Aulicus* (4–11 May 1645), pp. 1578–80.
95. *The Kingdomes Weekly Intelligencer*, 100 (13–20 May 1645), p. 804; *Mercurius Aulicus* (4–11 May 1645), pp. 1578–80.
96. *An Exact and Humble Remonstrance* (London, 1645), p. 5.
97. *Mercurius Aulicus* (4–11 May 1645), p. 1579. Cf. Bodl. Lib., Carte MS 14, fo. 609.
98. John Lewis, *Contemplations on these Times, Or, The Parliament Explained to Wales* (London, 1646), p. 9.
99. *CJ*, IV, p. 154.
100. *CJ*, IV, p. 231; *LJ*, VII, p. 526.
101. TNA, SP21/8, fos 349, 358, 364; SP21/21, fos 47, 56–7.
102. TNA, SP21/21, fo. 57.
103. *An Exact and Humble Remonstrance*, p. 4; Granville Penn (ed.), *Memorials of the Professional Life and Times of Sir William Penn* (2 vols, London, 1883), I, pp. 110–12. Cf. Parliamentary Archives, HL/PO/JO/10/1/225.

104. [Rowland Laugharne], *A True Relation of the Late Successe of the Kings and Parliaments Forces in Pembroke-Shire* (London, 1645), p. 5.

105. *CJ*, IV, pp. 288, 290.

106. *Some Particular Animadversions*, p. 45.

Chapter 4: The Struggle for Supremacy: Poyer and Post-War Politics, 1646–1647

1. David Como, *Radical Parliamentarians and the English Civil War* (Oxford, 2018), pts I–II.

2. Ann Hughes, *Gangraena and the Struggle for the English Revolution* (Oxford, 2004).

3. Ethan Shagan, 'Constructing Discord: Ideology, Propaganda, and English Responses to the Irish Rebellion of 1641', *Journal of British Studies*, 36 (1997), 4–34.

4. Not all prayer book Protestants were milquetoast moderates, of course: Isaac Stephens, 'Confessional Identity in Early Stuart England: The "Prayer Book Puritanism" of Elizabeth Isham', *Journal of British Studies*, 50 (2011), 24–47.

5. Kenneth Fincham and Stephen Taylor, 'Episcopalian Identity, 1640–1662', in Anthony Milton (ed.), *The Oxford History of Anglicanism, Vol. I* (Oxford, 2016), pp. 457–81.

6. *The Declaration of Col. Poyer and Col. Powell* (London, 1648), pp. 4–5.

7. *Declaration of Col. Poyer and Col. Powell*, p. 6.

8. John Poyer, *Poyer's Vindication* (London, 1649), p. 2.

9. *The Declaration and Speech of Colonell John Poyer* (London, 1649), p. 3.

10. *Heads of Chiefe Passages in Parliament*, 2 (12–19 Jan. 1648), pp. 10–11.

11. J. T. Evans, *The Church Plate of Pembrokeshire* (London, 1905), pp. 74–5, and plate IX.

12. John Morrill, 'The Church in England, 1642–1649', in *idem*, *The Nature of the English Revolution* (London, 1991), pp. 89–114; Judith Maltby, '"The Good Old Way": Prayer Book Protestantism in the 1640s and 1650s', *Studies in Church History*, 38 (2004), 233–56; Fincham and Stephen Taylor,' Episcopalian Identity, 1640–1662', pp. 457–81.

13. See p. 98.

14. E. D. Jones, 'The Gentry of South Wales in the Civil War', *National Library of Wales Journal*, 11 (1959), 143.

15. Pembrokeshire Archives, HBORO/541; 'Sampson Lort', History of Parliament unpublished biography, 1640–1660. I am very grateful to Stephen Roberts for allowing me to see this prior to publication.

16. For White, see Jacqueline Eales, 'John White', *Oxford Dictionary of National Biography*: <https://doi-org.abc.cardiff.ac.uk/10.1093/ref:odnb/29254> (accessed 22 Sept. 2019).

17. William Smith, *A True and Exact Relation* (London, 1644), pp. 2–4.

18. Smith, *A True and Exact Relation*, p. 4.

19. See, for example, *Mercurius Civicus*, 46 (4–11 Apr. 1644), p. 468.

20. For Swanley's poor relations with Rowland Laugharne, see Granville Penn (ed.), *Memorials of the Professional Life and Times of Sir William Penn* (2 vols, London, 1883), I, p. 116.

21. [John Eliot], *An Answer in Just Vindication of Some Religious and Worthy Gentlemen of Pembrokeshire* (London, 1646), p. 10.

22. *CJ*, III, p. 517.

23. [Eliot], *An Answer in Just Vindication*, p. 6.

24. [Eliot], *An Answer in Just Vindication*, p. 10.

25. TNA, HCA 13/60, pt 2, fos 256r–v, 274, 275, 282.

26. TNA, HCA 13/60, pt 2, fos 320, 355v.

27. *Lords Journals*, VII, p. 517; Parliamentary Archives, HL/PO/JO/10/1/190.

28. The proceedings were brought in the name of Augustine Baxter, chaplain to Captain William Smith, but it seems he had made common cause with Poyer and his allies, and it is difficult to ascertain whether Poyer was also joined in this as a collusive action: *The Kingdomes Weekly Intelligencer*, 143 (24–31 Mar. 1646), p. 60; TNA, HCA 13/60, pt 3, fo. 320.

29. TNA, HCA 13/60, pt 2, fo. 273v.

30. TNA, HCA 13/60, pt 2, fo. 265.

31. TNA, HCA 13/60, pt 3, fo. 319.

32. TNA, HCA 13/60, pt 2, fo. 273v–75.

33. TNA, HCA 13/60, pt 2, fo. 275.

34. TNA, HCA 13/60, pt 2, fos 355v–7v.

35. For Poyer's collection of such examinations, see TNA, HCA 13/247. One is endorsed, 'Testimony that severall parliament ships have brought provision & c to Dublyn'. He told the court that he had the examinations with him in London 'to shew', and their presence among the court archive suggests that this is exactly what he did.

36. *The Kingdomes Weekly Intelligencer*, 143 (24–31 Mar. 1646), p. 57. See also William Penn's letter to Swanley rejoicing at his 'free and fair acquittance from those foul and false imputations by which enemies of goodness imagined to obfuscate the radiant beams of your resplendent virtues': Penn, *Memorials of Sir William Penn*, I, p. 222.

37. Leach suggests Poyer was in London from Dec. 1645 until June 1647, a position followed by subsequent commentators: Leach, *Pembrokeshire*, pp. 118–19; Mathias, 'The Second Civil War and Interregnum', in *Pembs. Co. Hist.*, pp. 198–9.

38. Parliamentary Archives, HL/PO/JO/10/1/199.

39. [Eliot], *An Answer in Just Vindication*, p. 8.

40. [Eliot], *An Answer in Just Vindication*, p. 9.

41. *LJ*, VIII, pp. 22–3.

42. John Poyer, *Poyer's Vindication* (London, 1649), p. 4.

43. Parliamentary Archives, HL/PO/JO/10/1/199. For his petition to Lenthall, see Bodl. Lib., Nalson MS 5, fo. 192.

44. A hostile letter from Pembroke dated 28 Oct. 1645 reported that Poyer 'is going for London to get to be governour of this towne': [Eliot], *An Answer in Just Vindication*, p. 17.

45. There were reports that the Pembroke committee had attacked Laugharne after his loss at Newcastle Emlyn in Apr. 1645: *Some Particular Animadversions of Marke for Satisfaction of the Contumatious Malignant* (London, 1646), p. 34.

46. Poyer, *Poyer's Vindication*, p. 4.

47. *LJ*, VIII, p. 90.

48. Poyer, *Poyer's Vindication*, p. 4.

49. John Cook, *The Vindication of the Professors & the Profession of the Law* (London, 1646), sig. A4v.

50. For these aspects, see Michael Braddick, *The Common Freedom of the People: John Lilburne and the English Revolution* (Oxford, 2018).

51. Bodl. Lib., Nalson MS 5, fo. 203.

52. Bodl. Lib., Nalson MS 5, fo. 203.

53. Parliamentary Archives, HL/PO/JO/10/1/199.

54. M. A. E. Green (ed.), *Calendar of the Proceedings of the Committee for Compounding, 1643–1660* (5 vols, London, 1889–92), I, p. 791.

55. Poyer, *Poyer's Vindication*, p. 4.
56. Stephen Roberts, 'How the West was Won', *Welsh History Review*, 21 (2003), 664–5.
57. *The Moderate Intelligencer*, 74 (30 July–6 Aug. 1646), p. 583.
58. Parliamentary Archives, HL/PO/JO/1/10/199.
59. [Eliot], *An Answer in Just Vindication*, p. 4.
60. Jason Peacey, *Print and Public Politics during the English Revolution* (Cambridge, 2013), and the literature cited.
61. Joad Raymond, *The Invention of the Newspaper: English Newsbooks, 1641–1649* (Oxford, 1996).
62. For the date of publication, we can cross-reference the comments made in the preface to Eliot's *Answer* and the supportive discussion Poyer's text received in a parliamentary newsbook of late February to early March: [Eliot], *An Answer in Just Vindication*, sig. A2r–v; *The Moderate Intelligencer*, 52 (26 Feb.–5 Mar. 1646), p. 320.
63. This is [Eliot], *An Answer in Just Vindication*.
64. [Eliot], *An Answer in Just Vindication*, p. 3.
65. For such publishing strategies, see Peacey, *Print and Public Politics*, pp. 267–97, 307–30.
66. I am grateful to Mark Stoyle for drawing my attention to Weare's case. On Weare, see Andrew Hopper, *Turncoats and Renegadoes: Changing Sides during the English Civil Wars* (Oxford, 2012), pp. 167–8.
67. John Weare, *The Apologie of Colonell John Were* (London, 1644), p. 1.
68. *The Moderate Intelligencer*, 52 (26 Feb.–5 Mar. 1646), p. 320.
69. Lloyd Bowen, 'Faction and Connection in Pembrokeshire Politics, 1640–9' (forthcoming).
70. [Eliot], *An Answer in Just Vindication*, sig. A2.
71. Thomas Richards, *A History of the Puritan Movement in Wales* (London, 1920), pp. 40, 43, 66.
72. Parliamentary Archives, HL/PO/JO/10/1/248.
73. Richards, *History of the Puritan Movement*, p. 282.
74. John Venn (ed.), *A Biographical Dictionary of Gonville and Caius College, 1396–1897* (4 vols, 1897–1912), I, p. 216.
75. [John Eliot], *A Declaration of Divers Gentlemen of Wales Concerning Collonell Poyer* (London, 1648), p. 5; Worc. Coll., Clarke MS 110, fo. 131; *Heads of Chiefe Passages in Parliament*, 2 (12–19 Jan. 1649), p. 11; [John Eliot], *A Short Comment upon the Grounds and Reasons of Poyers Taking up Armes* (London, 1649), p. 1.
76. Poyer, *Poyer's Vindication*, p. 4.
77. *The Kingdomes Weekly Intelligencer*, 160 (4–11 Aug. 1646), pp. 195–6.
78. As early as Oct. 1645 some elements were counselling that south Wales would be better served by appointing 'one hole commander in cheife appointed by his excellencie [Fairfax]': Bodl. Lib., Nalson MS 4, fo. 280.
79. Bodl. Lib., Tanner MS 60, fo. 578.
80. Roger Lort, *Epigrammatum Rogeri Lort* (London, 1646).
81. Parliamentary Archives, HL/PO/JO/10/1/211.
82. 'Mayors of Pembroke', *WWHR*, 5 (1916), 121; Edward Laws, *History of Little England Beyond Wales* (London, 1888), p. 334n; NLW, SD1683/202.
83. A splendid analysis of the growing power of the New Model and political Independency in south Wales can be found in Roberts, 'How the West was Won', 646–74.
84. Parliamentary Archives, HL/PO/JO/10/1/225.

85. Poyer, *Poyer's Vindication*, p. 2.
86. [Eliot], *An Answer in Just Vindication*, p. 8.
87. Parliamentary Archives, HL/PO/JO/10/1/225; *LJ*, IX, p. 14.
88. *CJ*, V, p. 125.
89. [John Eliot], *A Short Comment upon the Grounds and Reasons of Poyers Taking up Armes* (London, 1649), p. 3.
90. *CJ*, V, p. 137.
91. Bowen, 'Faction and Connection'.
92. [Eliot], *A Declaration of Divers Gentlemen*, p. 4; Worc. Coll., Clarke MS 110, fo. 131.
93. Poyer, *Poyer's Vindication*, p. 4.
94. [Eliot], *A Declaration of Divers Gentlemen*, p. 4. These were possibly the charges devised by Eliot and Sir Richard Philipps and sent to Sir Thomas Fairfax which are found at Worc. Coll., Clarke MS 110, fo. 131.

Chapter 5: The Road to Rebellion, August 1647–March 1648

1. On this, see Robert Ashton, *Counter-Revolution: The Second Civil War and its Origins, 1646–8* (New Haven and London, 1992).
2. Ashton, *Counter-Revolution*, pp. 48–80.
3. Ashton, *Counter-Revolution*, pp. 241–5; Ann Hughes, *Gangraena and the Struggle for the English Revolution* (Oxford, 2002).
4. Ashton, *Counter-Revolution*, pp. 229–66; John Morrill, 'The Church in England, 1642–9', in John Morrill (ed.), *Reactions to the English Civil War, 1642–1649* (London, 1982), pp. 89–114.
5. Ashton, *Counter-Revolution*, pp. 81–116; Robert Ashton, 'From Cavalier to Roundhead Tyranny', in Morrill, *Reactions to the English Civil War*, pp. 185–207. Cf. Clive Holmes, 'Centre and Locality in Civil-War England', in John Adamson (ed.), *The English Civil War: Conflict and Contexts, 1640–49* (Basingstoke, 2009), pp. 153–74.
6. For an equally intriguing reorientation of political allegiances across the first civil war which has some parallels, albeit in a very different context, see David Scott, 'The Barwis Affair: Political Allegiance and the Scots during the British Civil Wars', *English Historical Review*, 115 (2000), 843–63.
7. John Poyer, *Poyer's Vindication* (London, 1649), p. 4.
8. Worc. Coll., Clarke MS 16, fo. 87v; Bodl. Lib., Tanner MS 58, fo. 721.
9. BL, Add. MS 46,391B, fo. 180.
10. *Heads of Chiefe Passages in Parliament*, 2 (12–19 Jan. 1648), p. 11.
11. [John Eliot], *A Short Comment upon the Grounds and Reasons of Poyers Taking up Armes* (London, 1649), p. 2.
12. Although he would later claim that he released them 'in obedience to the General's letter': HMC, *Leyborne-Popham MSS*, p. 15.
13. Valerie Pearl, 'London's Counter-Revolution', in Gerald Aylmer (ed.), *The Interregnum: The Quest for Settlement, 1646–1660* (London, 1977), pp. 29–56; Ian Gentles, *The New Model Army* (Oxford, 1992), pp. 185–9; Ashton, *Counter-Revolution*, pp. 279–89.
14. See, for example, Bodl. Lib., Clarendon MS 30, fo. 46; BL, Stowe MS 189, fo. 39v; TNA, SP21/9, pp. 3, 5; Keith Lindley and David Scott (eds), *The Journal of Thomas Juxon, 1644–1647* (Camden Society, 5th series, 13, 1999), p. 159.
15. Lloyd Bowen, 'Faction and Connection in Pembrokeshire Politics, 1640–9' (forthcoming).

16. Lambeth Palace Library, MS 679, p. 55.
17. Bodl. Lib., Tanner MS 60, fo. 22; *Heads of Chiefe Passages in Parliament*, 2 (12–19 Jan. 1648), p. 11.
18. *Heads of Chiefe Passages in Parliament*, 2 (12–19 Jan. 1648), p. 11.
19. Edward Laws, *The History of Little England Beyond Wales* (London, 1888), p. 334. Laws is incorrect in asserting that Poyer was 're-elected mayor'.
20. Worc. Coll., Clarke MS 110, fo. 131.
21. *Perfect Occurrences*, 118 (30 Mar.–5 Apr. 1649), p. 929.
22. Worc. Coll., Clarke MS 16, fo. 88.
23. Although this was unattributed, the style and substance of the editorial and its close relationship with the 'Grievances' submitted to Fairfax, means that it was unquestionably Eliot's.
24. *Heads of Chiefe Passages in Parliament*, 2 (12–19 Jan. 1648), pp. 10–11. Cf. Worc. Coll. Clarke MS 110, fo. 131.
25. *Heads of Chiefe Passages in Parliament*, 2 (12–19 Jan. 1648), p. 12.
26. *Heads of Chiefe Passages in Parliament*, 2 (12–19 Jan. 1648), p. 12.
27. Poyer, *Poyer's Vindication*, p. 4.
28. TNA, SP21/24, p. 8; *Perfect Occurrences of Every Daie Iournall in Parliament*, 57 (28 Jan.–4 Feb. 1648), p. 400.
29. TNA, SP21/9, p. 13.
30. Worc. Coll., Clarke MS 16, fo. 88r–v.
31. TNA, SP21/24, p. 8; SP21/9, p. 13.
32. Poyer would claim that he was besieged in Pembroke suddenly by his local enemies who had 'no commission, either from the parliament or generall to warrant them in that action'. In the same pamphlet, however, he also alleged that it was Fleming who began the siege: Worc. Coll., Clarke MS 16, fos 87v–88.
33. Lambeth Palace Library, MS 679, p. 163.
34. *CJ*, V, p. 454. On Scawen, see John Adamson, 'Of Armies and Architecture: The Employments of Robert Scawen', in Ian Gentles, John Morrill and Blair Worden (eds), *Soldiers, Writers and Statesmen of the English Revolution* (Cambridge, 1998), pp. 36–67.
35. *The Kingdoms Weekly Account*, 7 (16–23 Feb. 1648), p. 50.
36. *The Kingdoms Weekly Account*, 4 (25 Jan.–4 Feb. 1648), pp. 30–1.
37. *The Kingdoms Weekly Account*, 6 (9–16 Feb. 1648), p. 41.
38. On these royalist newsbooks, see Jason McElligott, *Royalism, Print and Censorship in Revolutionary England* (Woodbridge, 2007).
39. *Mercurius Bellicus*, 4 (14–20 Feb. 1648), sig. D4v (irregular pagination).
40. Bodl. Lib., Tanner MS 58, fo. 721; Worc. Coll., Clarke MS 110, fo. 233v.
41. *The Kingdomes Weekly Intelligencer*, 250 (29 Feb.–7 Mar. 1648), p. 861.
42. See also Poyer's later claim that his soldiers refused to disband 'without any security for their arrears, supplies for ther present necessities or indempnities for what past', especially because Lort and his associates had set themselves against Poyer and any forces not of the New Model: Poyer, *Poyer's Vindication*, p. 8.
43. Bodl. Lib., Tanner MS 58, fo. 724.
44. TNA, SP29/440, fo. 78r–v; NLW, SD1665/142.
45. Bodl. Lib., Tanner MS 60, fo. 22; *Heads of Chiefe Passages in Parliament*, 2 (12–19 Jan. 1648), p. 11; Laws, *History of Little England Beyond Wales*, p. 334n.
46. Bodl. Lib., Tanner MS 60, fo. 22; Lambeth Palace Library, MS 679, p. 55; Poyer, *Poyer's Vindication*, p. 2. In a lawsuit of May 1649 over cattle taken by Cuny from Lort to supply Pembroke garrison, Cuny maintained that in 1643 Lort was 'in actuall

armes against the parliament of England and . . . made a stronge garrison of his dwelling howse against the parliament': TNA, C8/93/152.

47. *CJ*, V, p. 477; TNA, SP21/24, pp. 19–20.

48. *LJ*, X, p. 89; *CJ*, V, pp. 477–8.

49. *The Moderate Intelligencer*, 155 (2–9 Mar. 1648), p. 1197.

50. *The Kingdomes Weekly Intelligencer*, 250 (29 Feb.–7 Mar. 1648), p. 861.

51. *The Kingdomes Weekly Post*, 9 (2–9 Mar. 1648), p. 63.

52. See the discontented petition from Laugharne's officers of 25 Feb. 1648 which claimed that they were owed two-and-a-half years' back pay and lamented that the debentures which they received in lieu of pay would be 'subiect to cavills and exceptions by their adversaries', which meant the commissioners from the Lort–Eliot group appointed in Dec. 1647: *A Perfect Diurnall*, 239 (21–28 Feb. 1648), pp. 1926–7.

53. John Eliot, *A Just Vindication on the Behalf of Iohn Eliot, Esq* (London, 1648), pp. 6–7.

54. Worc. Coll., Clarke MS 114, fo. 10v.

55. Bodl. Lib., Nalson MS 6, fo. 166.

56. Bodl. Lib., Nalson MS 22, fo. 275.

57. TNA, SP28/50, fos 233–7, 266.

58. *A Perfect Diurnall*, 239 (21–28 Feb. 1648), pp. 1926–7.

59. Bodl. Lib., Clarendon MS 30, fo. 301. Cf. TNA, SP21/24, p. 12. This is an interesting side note given the connections which were said to have been established between Poyer's rebellion and north Wales in May 1648: see pp. 133, 138, 140.

60. Bodl. Lib., Tanner MS 58, fo. 735. The petition was printed in *The Kingdomes Weekly Post*, 9 (2–9 Mar. 1648), pp. 68–9, and also *A Letter of a Sad Tragedy by Prince Griffin* (London, 1648), pp. 3–6. Cf. *The Kingdomes Weekly Intelligencer*, 249 (22–29 Feb. 1648), p. 854.

61. Eliot, *A Just Vindication*, p. 1.

62. Eliot, *A Just Vindication*, p. 3.

63. Eliot, *A Just Vindication*, p. 8.

64. *A Perfect Diurnall of Some Passages in Parliament*, 243 (20–27 Mar. 1648), p. 1956. This was also printed in *The Declaration and Resolution of Col. Iohn Poyer* (London, 1648), pp. 4–5, *Prince Charles his Letter* (London, 1648), pp. 1–3 and John Rushworth, *Historical Collections* (8 vols, London, 1721–2), VII, p. 1034.

65. David Como, *Radical Parliamentarians and the English Civil War* (Oxford, 2018), p. 17.

66. For example, Ashton, *Counter-Revolution*, p. 417, and see pp. 207–12. This was a trait of even royalist Restoration histories too, as in John Davies's observation that 'the first effects of their discontents appeared in Wales [in 1647–8], though at first, I suppose, begun by the chiefs more out of self-interest than heavy well-wishing to the king': John Davies, *The Civill Warres of Great Britain and Ireland* (Glasgow, 1664), p. 231.

67. Poyer, *Poyer's Vindication*, p. 8.

68. *The Declaration and Resolution of Col. Iohn Poyer*, p. 5.

69. *A Perfect Diurnall of Some Passages in Parliament*, 243 (20–27 Mar. 1648), p. 1955. The use of the term 'bullies' for Poyer's men turns up in both Roger Lort's and Eliot's writings.

70. It was, for example, repeated *in extensio* in Whitelocke, *Memorials*, II, p. 287.

71. *Calendar of State Papers, Venetian, 1647–52*, p. 52. See also the royalist newsletter which predicted 'ere long there wilbe an appearance for the king in Pembrocke & the other southerne parts of Walles, being much encouraged by the resolute deteynure of Pembrocke Castle in despight of the late ordinance of both houses': Bodl. Lib., Clarendon MS 31, fo. 6v.

72. Worc. Coll., Clarke MS 110, fo. 296.

73. *CJ*, V, p. 506; TNA, SP21/15, pp. 16–17; *A Perfect Diurnall of Some Passages in Parliament*, 243 (20–27 Mar. 1648), p. 1957. Annesley was acting as Lort's intermediary for receiving army pay at this time: TNA, SP28/53, fo. 132.

74. For the following, see *A Perfect Diurnall of Some Passages in Parliament*, 243 (20–27 Mar. 1648), pp. 1958–9.

75. Although these payments had been authorised on 12 Jan. the money was not received until early March: TNA, SP28/50, fos 233v, 266v. James Philipps, one of the treasurers, later claimed that some of the money had been 'taken up by Collonell Powells forces dureing the late rebellion before it was payed unto the high Collector': TNA, SP28/52, fo. 167.

76. Worc. Coll. Clarke MS 110, fo. 296; *A Bloody Slaughter at Pembrooke-Castle in Wales* (London, 1648), pp. 1–3; TNA, SP21/24, p. 25; *Heads of Chiefe Passages in Parliament*, 11 (15–22 Mar. 1648), p. 88; *Mercurius Melancholicus*, 30 (20–27 Mar. 1648), p. 178; *Mercurius Pragmaticus*, 28 (21–28 Mar. 1648), sig. D4v.

77. On Ibbitson, see John Morrill and Philip Baker, 'The Case of the Armie Truly Re-Stated', in Michael Mendle (ed.), *The Putney Debates of 1647: The Army, The Levellers and the English State* (Cambridge, 2001), p. 110; Jason Peacey, 'Print, Publicity, and Popularity: The Projecting of Sir Balthazar Gerbier, 1642–1662', *Journal of British Studies*, 51 (2012), 297–300.

Chapter 6: Poyer, Powell and the Prince, March–April 1648

1. The standard study of the Second Civil War is Robert Ashton, *Counter-Revolution: The Second Civil War and its Origins, 1646–8* (New Haven and London, 1994).

2. David Stevenson, *Revolution and Counter-Revolution in Scotland, 1644–1651* (London, 1977).

3. Laura A. M. Stewart, *Rethinking the Scottish Revolution: Covenanted Scotland, 1637–1651* (Oxford, 2016), pp. 256–302.

4. Ashton, *Second Civil War, passim.*

5. *Mercurius Pragmaticus*, 25 (29 Feb.–7 Mar. 1648), sig. A4v.

6. Bodl. Lib., Clarendon MS 31, fo. 38; *The Declaration and Resolution of Col. Iohn Poyer* (London, 1648), pp. 1–2.

7. Bodl. Lib., Clarendon MS 31, fo. 38; *Declaration and Resolution of Col. Iohn Poyer*, p. 2.

8. John Eliot, *A Just Vindication on the Behalf of Iohn Eliot, Esq* (London, 1648), p. 10; *A Perfect Diurnall of Some Passages in Parliament*, 144 (27 Mar.–3 Apr. 1648), p. 1651 (irregular pagination); Worc. Coll., Clarke MS 114, fo. 8v.

9. *Declaration and Resolution of Col. Iohn Poyer*, p. 3. For the loss of Tenby, see also Bodl. Lib., Clarendon MS 31, fo. 41v; TNA, SP21/24, p. 29.

10. *Prince Charles his Letter* (London, 1648), p. 3.

11. *The Kingdomes Weekly Intelligencer*, 253 (21–28 Mar. 1648), p. 881. Cf. *Declaration and Resolution of Col. Iohn Poyer*, p. 1.

12. *A Perfect Diurnall of Some Passages in Parliament*, 144 (27 Mar.–3 Apr. 1648), p. 1658.

13. Bodl. Lib, Clarendon MS 31, fo. 38v.

14. *A Perfect Diurnall of Some Passages in Parliament*, 144 (27 Mar.–3 Apr. 1648), p. 1658; *CJ*, V, p. 515.

15. *Mercurius Pragmaticus*, 28 (21–28 Mar. 1648), sig. D4v.

16. *Mercurius Melancholicus*, 31 (27 Mar.–3 Apr. 1648), p. 180.

17. *Mercurius Aulicus Againe*, 6 (2–9 Mar. 1648), sig. F4v.

18. Mark Stoyle, *Soldiers and Strangers: An Ethnic History of the English Civil Wars* (New Haven and London, 2005), pp. 11–32, 153–72; Lloyd Bowen, 'Representations of

Wales and the Welsh during the Civil Wars and Interregnum', *Historical Research* 77 (2004), 358–76.

19. *Mercurius Elencticus*, 19 (29 Mar.–5 Apr. 1648), p. 148.
20. *A Perfect Diurnall of Some Passages in Parliament*, 144 (27 Mar.–3 Apr. 1648), p. 1658.
21. Bodl. Lib., Nalson MS 4, fo. 279v.
22. *Perfect Occurrences*, 64 (24–31 Mar. 1648), p. 538.
23. *A Perfect Diurnall of Some Passages in Parliament*, 144 (27 Mar.–3 Apr. 1648), p. 1658.
24. *The Perfect Weekly Account*, 2 (29 Mar.–5 Apr. 1648), pp. 12–13.
25. *The Perfect Weekly Account*, 2 (29 Mar.–5 Apr. 1648), p. 13; S. R. Gardiner (ed.), *The Hamilton Papers* (Camden Society, new series, 27, 1880), p. 174; Bodl. Lib., Clarendon MS 31, fo. 56v.
26. Bodl. Lib., Clarendon MS 31, fos 38v, 56v, 87.
27. Gardiner, *Hamilton Papers*, p. 170; *Calendar of State Papers, Venetian, 1647–52*, p. 52.
28. *CJ*, V, p. 521; TNA, SP21/24, p. 18.
29. TNA, SP21/24, pp. 17–18; *CJ*, V, p. 519.
30. Gardiner, *Hamilton Papers*, p. 174.
31. Bodl. Lib., Tanner MS 57, fo. 62.
32. Worc. Coll., Clarke MS 114, fo. 1.
33. *The Declaration and Resolution of Divers Officers and Soldiers* (London, 1648), pp. 2–3; *The Kingdomes Weekly Intelligencer*, 255 (4–11 Apr. 1648), pp. 901–2; *Mercurius Poeticus*, 1 (5–13 May 1648), p. 8; *Mercurius Bellicus*, 12 (11–18 Apr. 1648), p. 6.
34. *The Declaration and Resolution of Divers Officers*, pp. 1–2. Cf. Worc. Coll., Clarke MS 114, fo. 1.
35. Worc. Coll., Clarke MS 114, fo. 1.
36. Bodl. Lib., Clarendon MS 31, fo. 42.
37. *The Declaration and Resolution of Divers Officers and Soldiers under the Command of Major General Laughorn* (London, 1648), pp. 4–5. One slightly hysterical report of Apr. 1648 claimed that Poyer and Powell had '40,000 in armes'!: Gardiner, *Hamilton Papers*, p. 182.
38. *The Declaration and Resolution of Divers Officers and Soldiers*; Whitelocke, *Memorials*, II, p. 301.
39. *The Declaration and Resolution of Divers Officers and Soldiers*, p. 5.
40. See also Bodl. Lib., Clarendon MS 31, fo. 87.
41. Bodl. Lib., Clarendon MS 31, fo. 44.
42. *The Declaration of Col. Poyer and Col. Powell and the Officers and Soldiers under their Command* (London, 1648). Parts of this tract were reproduced under the title 'A Declaration of Colonel Powell', in *The Moderate Intelligencer*, 177 (3–10 Aug. 1648), pp. 1474–5.
43. It may be worth recalling here Laugharne's efforts to have Pembrokeshire spared from the excise in 1645: Bodl. Lib., Nalson MS 5, fo. 203v.
44. Lloyd Bowen, 'Preaching and Politics in the Welsh Marches, 1643–1663: The Case of Alexander Griffith', *Historical Research* (forthcoming, 2021); Stephen K. Roberts, 'How the West was Won: Parliamentary Politics, Religion and the Military in South Wales, 1642–1649', *Welsh History Review*, 21 (2003), 663, 666.
45. See *English Short Title Catalogue*: <*http://estc.bl.uk/R203201*> (accessed 2 Oct. 2019).
46. *Mercurius Bellicus*, 13 (18–25 Apr. 1648), pp. 4–5.
47. Gardiner, *Hamilton Papers*, p. 181.
48. Bodl. Lib., Clarendon MS 31, fo. 51.

49. See also the notice taken of the *Declaration* by a parliament supporter in Swansea on 17 Apr., who believed that Powell's 'declaring absolutely for the king' would diminish rather than augment the insurgents' forces, although they noted the 'commonalty [are] . . . chiefly for them': *The Kings Maiesties Last Speech* (London, 1648), pp. 5–6.

50. Bodl. Lib., Clarendon MS 31, fo. 51.

51. *LJ*, X, pp. 189–90; Whitelocke, *Memorials*, II, pp. 298–9; Gardiner, *Hamilton Papers*, pp. 171, 175, 177, 184; Bodl. Lib., Clarendon MS 31, fo. 43.

52. *Mercurius Veridicus*, 1 (14–21 Apr. 1648), sig. A3v. See also *Mercurius Veridicus*, 2 (21–28 Apr. 1648), sigs. B1, B2v; *Mercurius Melancholicus*, 34 (17–24 Apr. 1648), pp. 201–2; Bodl. Lib., Clarendon MS 31, fos 56, 68.

53. Rushworth, *Historical Collections*, VII, p. 1051.

54. Such an invasion by Inchiquin's forces through Milford Haven was mooted again later in the year: *A Letter Sent from Newport to a Gentleman in London* (London, 1648), p. 5.

55. On this, see Ian Gentles's observation when discussing the Second Civil War that '"Personal treaty with the king" were the code words by which royalists knew one another and attempted to bring moderate opinion to their side': *The New Model Army* (Oxford, 1992), p. 236.

56. Bodl. Lib., Clarendon MS 31, fo. 55.

57. R. N. Worth (ed.), *The Buller Papers* (Plymouth, 1895), pp. 101–2; Mark Stoyle, '"The Gear Rout": The Cornish Rising of 1648 and the Second Civil War', *Albion*, 32 (2000), 54. I am most grateful to Mark Stoyle for providing me with a transcript of this letter.

58. *Calendar of State Papers, Venetian, 1647–52*, p. 55.

59. Folger Shakespeare Library, X.d. 483(20); Stoyle, '"Gear Rout"', 54.

60. Thomas Carte (ed.), *The Life of James Duke of Ormonde* (6 vols, Oxford, 1851), VI, p. 553. A manuscript copy of the *Declaration* ended up among Clarendon's papers: Bodl. Lib., Clarendon MS 31, fo. 46r–v.

61. *A Perfect Diurnall*, 247 (17–24 Apr. 1648), p. 1992.

62. *The Moderate Intelligencer*, 176 (27 July–3 Aug. 1648), p. 1469.

63. *The Moderate Intelligencer*, 177 (3–10 Aug. 1648), p. 1477.

64. *Mercurius Veridicus*, 1 (14–21 Apr. 1648), sig. A3v. Cf. *Mercurius Pragmaticus*, 6 (5–9 May 1648), sig. F4r–v.

65. *The Declaration and Protestation of the Kings Army in South-Wales* (London, 1648). Thomason dated his copy '4 Aprill', but this is a mistake for 4 May: BL, E.438(13).

66. *Declaration and Protestation of the Kings Army in South-Wales*, p. 6. This formulation, and the text of the oath itself, is repeated in *A Declaration of Divers Gentlemen and others in the Principality of Wales* (London, 1648), p. 4.

67. *A Declaration of the Kings Maiesties Army in the North of England* (London, 1648), pp. 3–4.

68. For this, see John Walter's brilliant *Covenanting Citizens: The Protestation Oath and Popular Political Culture in the English Revolution* (Oxford, 2017).

69. *Declaration of the Kings Maiesties Army in the North of England*, title page.

70. *Declaration and Protestation of the Kings Army in South-Wales*, title page.

71. Samuel Lewis, *A Topographical Dictionary of Wales* (2 vols, London 1854), I, p. 38.

72. Gardiner, *Hamilton Papers*, p. 193. See also the report after the Battle of St Fagans that 'the [Welsh] countrys [are] so well associated': Bodl. Lib., Clarendon MS 31, fo. 85v; *Mercurius Pragmaticus*, 8 (16–23 May 1648), sig. H5.

73. *The Perfect Weekly Account*, 6 (12–19 Apr. 1648), p. 37.

74. *A Perfect Diurnall*, 247 (17–24 Apr. 1648), p. 1992.

75. *A Declaration by Major General Laughorn* (London, 1648), p. 3; *Declaration and Protestation of the Kings Army in South-Wales*, p. 6.

76. *Declaration of Divers Gentlemen*, p. 4; *The Moderate Intelligencer*, 177 (3–10 Aug. 1648), p. 1477.

77. *Perfect Occurrences of Every Daies Iournall*, 68 (14–21 Apr. 1648), p. 582 (paginated as '482').

78. *A Perfect Diurnall*, 247 (17–24 Apr. 1648), p. 1992.

79. *A Fight. The Lord Goring Beaten at Coulchester in Essex* (London, 1648).

80. *A Fight*, p. 4. We can identify the newsbook as *Perfect Occurrences*, 75 (2–9 June 1648), p. 542.

81. *A Fight*, p. 5.

82. *Strange and Terrible Newes from the North* (London, 1648), p. 1; *The Kingdomes Weekly Intelligencer*, 257 (18–25 Apr. 1648), p. 915; *The Perfect Weekly Account*, 7 (19–29 Apr. 1648), sig. G3v.

83. [John Eliot], *A Declaration of Divers Gentlemen of Wales Concerning Collonell Poyer* (London, 1648).

84. Patrick Ludolph, 'An Anatomy of the London Agent', *Parliamentary History*, 33 (2014), 291–9; Laura A. M. Stewart, *Rethinking the Scottish Revolution: Covenanted Scotland, 1637–1651* (Oxford, 2016), p. 275. A royalist newspaper noted that the pamphlet was produced by Mabbott, 'the rebells owne lycencer': *Mercurius Elencticus*, 22 (19–26 Apr. 1648), p. 170.

85. *Mercurius Elencticus*, 22 (19–26 Apr. 1648), p. 170.

86. [Eliot], *A Declaration of Divers Gentlemen of Wales*, p. 1.

87. *Mercurius Elencticus*, 22 (19–26 Apr. 1648), p. 170.

88. *The Declaration and Resolution of Col. John Poyer* (London, 1648), p. 3.

89. *Colonell Powell and Col. Poyers Letter to his Highnesse the Prince of Wales* (London, 1648). The London bookseller George Thomason obtained his copy of this pamphlet on 20 Apr. 1648: BL, E.436(14).

90. *Mercurius Bellicus*, 13 (18–25 Apr. 1648), pp. 4–6.

91. Sean Kelsey, '"King of the Sea": The Prince of Wales and the Stuart Monarchy', *History*, 92 (2007), 428–48; *idem*, '"A No-King, or a New": Royalists and the Succession, 1648–1649', in Jason McElligott and David Smith (eds), *Royalists and Royalism during the English Civil Wars* (Cambridge, 2007), pp. 192–213.

92. On London in this period, see Ian Gentles, 'The Struggle for London in the Second Civil War', *Historical Journal*, 26 (1983), 277–305.

93. *A Declaration of Divers Gentlemen and others of the Principality of Wales* (London, 1648). George Thomason obtained his copy on 4 Aug.: BL, E456(32). Although the provenance of these 'instructions' in the printed pamphlet is unclear, they do seem genuine and agree with abstracts of the originals among the Prince's papers in the Pepys manuscripts at Magdalen College, Cambridge: HMC, *Pepys MSS*, pp. 245–6, 281–2.

94. Hugh Peter, *A Copy of his Highnesse Prince Charles his Letter* (London, 1648), pp. 4–5; *The Moderate Intelligencer*, 176 (27 July–3 Aug. 1648), pp. 1469–70.

95. Peter, *Prince Charles his Letter*, p. 3.

96. See also the Prince's letter to the rebel leaders dated 28 Apr. 1648, which thanked them for their 'expressions of your affections, kindnesse and fidelity to the interest and service of the king . . . in a season wherein soe many others have departed from the duties of their allegiance': TNA, SP29/417, fo. 550.

97. See also Clarendon's description of Henry Jermyn's positive response to Laugharne's entreaties: Edward Hyde, earl of Clarendon, *The History of the Rebellion and Civil Wars*, ed. W. D. Macray (6 vols, Oxford, 1888), VI, p. 42.

98. Bodl. Lib., Clarendon MS 31, fos 60, 69v; HMC, *Pepys MSS*, p. 282.
99. Gardiner, *Hamilton Papers*, p. 193.
100. *The Desires and Propositions of the Lord Inchequin* (London, 1648), p. 4. Thomas Horton also referred to the circulation of disinformation by Powell and Poyer ('divided by faire tales to ruine themselves') to persuade the people to support them: *A Great Fight in Wales* (London, 1648), p. 2.
101. TNA, SP21/24, p. 31.
102. Gardiner, *Hamilton Papers*, p. 188.
103. *Perfect Occurrences*, 70 (28 Apr.–4 May 1648), p. 494.
104. *Desires and Propositions of the Lord Inchequin*, p. 5.
105. TNA, SP21/9, pp. 43, 45–7.
106. TNA, SP21/24, pp. 30–1.
107. TNA, SP21/24, p. 31.
108. *A Great Fight in Wales* (London, 1648); Bodl. Lib., Clarendon MS 31, fo. 64.
109. Bodl. Lib., Clarendon MS 31, fo. 64r–v.
110. Whitelocke, *Memorials*, II, p. 306.
111. *Calendar of State Papers, Venetian, 1647–52*, p. 59.
112. TNA, SP21/24, p. 40.
113. Bodl. Lib., Tanner MS 57, fo. 27.
114. TNA, SP21/24, p. 101; *The Moderate Intelligencer*, 163 (27 Apr.–4 May 1648), p. 1302.
115. Bodl. Lib., Clarendon MS 31, fo. 67. Cf. Gardiner, *Hamilton Papers*, p. 195.
116. *The Moderate Intelligencer*, 163 (27 Apr.–4 May 1648), p. 1302.
117. Bodl. Lib., Clarendon MS 31, fo. 69. Noticeably, however, Laugharne challenged Horton's presence on the basis of his appointment as commander by parliamentary ordinance.
118. Hyde, *History of the Rebellion*, VI, p. 42. For the composition of his *History*, see Ronald Hutton, 'Clarendon's "History of the Rebellion"', *English Historical Review*, 97 (1982), 70–88; C. H. Firth, 'Clarendon's "History of the Rebellion"', *English Historical Review*, 19 (1904), 25–54, 246–62, 464–83.
119. Hyde, *History of the Rebellion*, VI, p. 42.
120. Bodl. Lib. Clarendon MS 31, fo. 60. This newsletter of 25 Apr. 1648 mentions 'the agent from the south Wales men', a construction which indicates Poyer and Powell. It also mentioned that this 'agent' had waited at Paris for a fortnight, which suggests that it may have been William Culpepper who was described as leaving for the West Country and later France in late March. The agent was 'dispatched' by 5 May, which would have given Culpepper plenty of time to return to south Wales and be taken at Tenby by late May: Bodl. Lib., Clarendon MS 31, fo. 68v. Cf. *The Kingdomes Weekly Intelligencer*, 256 (11–18 Apr. 1648), p. 909.
121. See his letter dated 6 May 1648 at Worc. Coll., Clarke MS 114, fo. 10v.
122. *A Declaration by Major General Laughorn* (London, 1648), p. 1.
123. *Declaration by Major General Laughorn*, p. 4.
124. *Declaration by Major General Laughorn*, pp. 5–6.
125. For reports of Stradling's ill-judged assault 'in the heate of blood', see Bodl. Lib., Clarendon MS 31, fo. 85r–v.
126. *LJ*, X, p. 253.
127. For the battle, see Robert Matthews, *'A Storme Out of Wales': The Second Civil War in South Wales, 1648* (Newcastle upon Tyne, 2012), pp. 75–100.
128. *A List of the Prisoners Taken . . . by Collonell Horton* (London, 1648), p. 8.
129. *The Moderate Intelligencer*, 165 (11–18 May 1648), p. 1318.

Chapter 7: The Siege of Pembroke, May–July 1648

1. *The Moderate Intelligencer*, 165 (11–18 May 1648), p. 1318.
2. Worc. Coll., Clarke MS 114, fo. 12.
3. TNA, SP21/24, p. 54.
4. *Mercurius Urbanicus*, 1 (2–9 May 1648), title page.
5. *Mercurius Melancholicus*, 39 (15–22 May 1648), p. 235.
6. *The Declaration of Lieutenant-Generall Cromwell Concerning his Present Design and Engagement against Col. Poyer* (London, 1648).
7. *CJ*, V, p. 556; *LJ*, X, p. 253. The famous puritan divine Stephen Marshall preached the thanksgiving sermon to parliament on 17 May, while William Strong preached to senior London officials in St Paul's: Stephen Marshall, *Emmanuel, A Thanksgiving Sermon Preached to the . . . Commons* (London, 1648); William Strong, *The Vengeance of the Temple* (London, 1648).
8. *The Moderate Intelligencer*, 165 (11–18 May 1648), p. 1318. Cf. Bodl. Lib., Clarendon MS 31, fo. 80; *Mercurius Bellicus*, 17 (16–23 May 1648), pp. 1–2.
9. *A Perfect Diurnall*, 251 (15–22 May 1648), p. 2021.
10. Bodl. Lib., Clarendon MS 31, fo. 83. A libel was also distributed in Covent Garden satirising the forthcoming 17 May thanksgiving, which concluded 'God save Kinge Charles and hange all his enemies!': Worc. Coll., Clarke MS 114, fo. 13.
11. *A Declaration by Major General Laughorn* (London, 1648), p. 8.
12. *The Desires and Propositions of the Lord Inchequin* (London, 1648), pp. 3–4; *The Perfect Weekly Account*, 6 (12–19 Apr. 1648), p. 40; Mark Stoyle, '"The Gear Rout": The Cornish Rising of 1648 and the Second Civil War', *Albion*, 32 (2000), 37–58.
13. TNA, SP21/24, p. 54.
14. Robert Ashton, *Counter-Revolution: The Second Civil War and its Origins, 1646–8* (New Haven and London, 1994), pp. 423–38.
15. One report of the rebels' actions in Wales before St Fagans noted that they were full of 'force and vigour' but lacked arms and ammunition which they expected from the Prince of Wales: S. R. Gardiner (ed.), *The Hamilton Papers* (Camden Society, new series, 27, 1880), p. 200.
16. Gardiner, *Hamilton Papers*, p. 197.
17. Gardiner, *Hamilton Papers*, p. 198.
18. Edward Hyde, earl of Clarendon, *The History of the Rebellion*, ed. W. D. Macray (6 vols, Oxford, 1888), VI, pp. 42–3.
19. Bodl. Lib., Clarendon MS 31, fo. 79v. Cf. *Mercurius Pragmaticus*, 8 (16–23 May 1648), sig. H5.
20. Bodl. Lib., Clarendon MS 31, fo. 82.
21. *A Perfect Diurnall*, 215 (15–22 May 1648), p. 2024. Cf. Whitelocke, *Memorials*, II, p. 316.
22. Bodl. Lib., Tanner MS 57, fo. 62.
23. TNA, SP21/9, p. 49.
24. S. A. Raymond, 'The Glamorgan Arraymen, 1642–1645', *Morgannwg*, 24 (1980), 24–5.
25. Stephen K. Roberts, 'How the West was Won: Parliamentary Politics, Religion and the Military in South Wales, 1642–9', *Welsh History Review*, 21 (2003), 659; Bodl. Lib., Nalson MS 4, fo. 238; M. A. E. Green (ed.), *Calendar of the Proceedings of the Committee for Advance of Money, 1642–1656* (3 vols, London, 1888), II, p. 889.
26. Lloyd Bowen, 'Faction and Connection in Pembrokeshire Politics, 1640–9' (forthcoming).
27. Bodl. Lib., Tanner MS 57, fo. 67. These were Captain Richard Jones of Nanteos, Captain Thomas Vaughan, Captain Thomas Lloyd of Llanllyr, Colonel James

Lewis of Abernantbychan. All were suggested as committeemen for Cardiganshire. Cf. Rushworth, *Historical Collections*, VII, p. 1121.

28. *Perfect Occurrences*, 75 (2–9 June 1648), p. 544; *A Perfect Diurnall*, 254 (5–12 June 1648), p. 2035; *Mercurius Pragmaticus*, 7 (9–16 June 1648), sig. G4v; Whitelocke, *Memorials*, II, p. 326; *CJ*, V, p. 587.

29. *An Ordinance of the Lords and Commons . . . for Sequestration of the Estates of Major Generall Laughorne* (London, 1648); *LJ*, X, pp. 332, 333–4. This ordinance is omitted from C. H. Firth and R. S. Rait (eds), *Acts and Ordinances of the Interregnum* (3 vols, London, 1911).

30. *Exceeding Good Newes from South-Wales* (London, 1648), p. 2.

31. *Two Great Victories* (London, 1648), p. 2.

32. *Exceeding Good Newes from South-Wales*, p. 2.

33. Leach, *Pembrokeshire*, pp. 190, 239.

34. TNA, SP25/72, fo. 23.

35. *A Perfect Diurnall*, 254 (5–12 June 1648), p. 2044; *Dangerous Fight at Pembrooke Castle*, p. 6.

36. Whitelocke, *Memorials*, II, p. 326; *The Moderate Intelligencer*, 170 (15–22 June 1648), p. 1406.

37. TNA, SP29/25, fo. 37.

38. TNA, SP21/24, p. 101.

39. *Perfect Occurrences*, 75 (2–9 June 1648), p. 542.

40. *The Last Newes from Kent* (London, 1648), sig. A4v.

41. Hugh Peter, *A Copy of his Highnesse Prince Charles his Letter* (London, 1648), p. 4.

42. S. C. Lomas (ed.), *The Letters and Speeches of Oliver Cromwell* (3 vols, London, 1904), I, p. 320.

43. Lomas, *Letters and Speeches*, I, p. 321.

44. *A Message Agreed upon by the Lords and Commons Assembled in Parliament* (London, 1648), p. 3.

45. Lomas, *Letters and Speeches*, I, p. 313.

46. Lomas, *Letters and Speeches*, I, p. 313; Whitelocke, *Memorials*, II, pp. 335–6.

47. *Dangerous Fight at Pembrooke Castle*, p. 6.

48. Lomas, *Letters and Speeches*, I, p. 313.

49. *A Perfect Diurnall*, 254 (5–12 June 1648), p. 2044.

50. *The Moderate Intelligencer*, 168 (1–8 June 1648), p. 1383.

51. *Perfect Occurrences*, 76 (9–16 June 1648), p. 334.

52. Laugharne's health did rally and he was sufficiently recovered to participate in a cavalry charge against the besiegers in mid-June: *Dangerous Fight at Pembrooke Castle*, p. 6.

53. TNA, SP29/39, fo. 272.

54. HMC, *Pepys MSS*, p. 208.

55. Lomas, *Letters and Speeches*, I, p. 314.

56. *Perfect Occurrences*, 75 (2–9 June 1648), p. 542; *Exceeding Good Newes*, p. 4.

57. This was the reading offered by a letter, almost certainly penned by Eliot, printed in a hostile pamphlet a few days later. This described the positions related in the diurnals as 'very untrue' and having been spread by 'some of Poyers agents' in London 'to extenuate the foulenesse of his rebellion': *A Fight. The Lord Goring Beaten at Coulchester* (London, 1648), p. 4.

58. *The Moderate*, 172 (29 June–6 July 1648), p. 1431.

59. TNA, SP21/24, pp. 148–9. Colonel Ewer's troop had already been sent to Coventry along with two troops of Thornhagh's horse: TNA, SP21/24, p. 97.

60. Lomas, *Letters and Papers*, I, p. 320.

61. *The Moderate*, 172 (29 June–6 July 1648), p. 1431.
62. *The Moderate*, 172 (29 June–6 July 1648), p. 1431.
63. *Perfect Occurrences*, 80 (7–14 July 1648), p. 391.
64. TNA, SP29/39, fo. 272.
65. On the conventions of surrender and their application in the civil wars, see Barbara Donagan, *War in England, 1642–1649* (Oxford, 2008), esp. ch. 17.
66. *The Moderate Intelligencer*, 174 (13–20 July 1648), p. 1453.
67. Peter, *A Copy of his Highnesse Prince Charles his Letter*, p. 4.
68. *The Moderate*, 1 (11–18 July 1648), p. 6.
69. *Perfect Occurrences*, 81 (14–21 July 1648), p. 593 (paginated as 580), reprinted in Lomas, *Letters and Papers*, III, p. 386.
70. *The Moderate*, 1 (11–18 July 1648), p. 6. For surrendering to parliament's mercy at Colchester, see Donagan, *War in England*, pp. 357–8, 364.
71. *Perfect Occurrences*, 81 (14–21 July 1648), p. 593 (paginated as 580); *The Moderate Intelligencer*, 174 (13–20 July 1648), p. 1453.
72. *Perfect Weekly Account*, 19 (19–29 July 1648), sig. T1.

Chapter 8: Revenge and Revolution: Poyer, Print and Parliamentary Justice, August 1648–April 1649

1. *Perfect Weekly Account*, 19 (19–29 July 1648), sig. T4v.
2. *CJ*, V, p. 588.
3. *Perfect Occurrences*, 75 (2–9 June 1648), p. 545.
4. *CJ*, V, p. 642; *Perfect Occurrences*, 82 (21–28 July 1648), p. 407.
5. Patricia Crawford, 'Charles Stuart, that Man of Blood', *Journal of British Studies*, 16 (1977), 41–61.
6. For these, see Barbara Donagan, 'Codes and Conduct in the English Civil War', *Past & Present*, 118 (1988), 65–95.
7. Barbara Donagan, *War in England, 1642–1649* (Oxford, 2008), pp. 312–88; *idem*, 'Myth, Memory and Martyrdom: Colchester 1648', *Essex Archaeology and History*, 34 (2004), 172–80.
8. S. C. Lomas (ed.), *Letters and Speeches of Oliver Cromwell* (3 vols, London, 1903), I, p. 321.
9. Blair Worden, 'Oliver Cromwell and the Sin of Achan', in Derek Beales and Geoffrey Best (eds), *History, Society and the Churches* (Cambridge, 1985), pp. 125–45.
10. Lomas, *Letters and Speeches*, I, p. 324.
11. *Duke Hamiltons Conditions for Surrendring Himself* (London, 1648), pp. 3–4.
12. Lomas, *Letters and Speeches*, III, pp. 386–8.
13. Cromwell's impression of Matthews as a ringleader of the rebellion likely came from Thomas Wogan: Bodl. Lib., Tanner MS 57, fo. 62.
14. M. A. E. Green (ed.), *Calendar of the Proceedings of the Committee for Compounding, 1643–1660* (5 vols, London, 1889–92), III, pp. 1855–6. The order for his composition was made on 25 Sept. 1648: *CJ*, VI, p. 31.
15. Quoted in Donagan, *War in England*, p. 356.
16. Donagan, *War in England*, p. 382.
17. *CJ*, V, p. 670; *The Moderate*, 5 (8–15 Aug. 1648), p. 40.
18. For Peter, see R. P. Stearns, *The Strenuous Puritan: Hugh Peter, 1598–1660* (Urbana, 1954); Alexandra Walsham, 'Phanaticus: Hugh Peter, Antipuritanism and the Afterlife of the English Revolution', *Parergon*, 32 (2015), 65–97.
19. Hugh Peter, *A Copy of his Highnesse Prince Charles his Letter* (London, 1648). Thomason obtained his copy on 3 Aug.: BL, E.456(24).

20. Peter, *A Copy of his Highnesse Prince Charles his Letter*, pp. 4–5.

21. *The Moderate Intelligencer*, 176 (27 July–3 Aug. 1648), pp. 1469–70; 177 (3–10 Aug. 1648), p. 1478.

22. *The Moderate Intelligencer*, 176 (27 July–3 Aug. 1648), p. 1469.

23. Peter, *A Copy of his Highnesse Prince Charles his Letter*, p. 5.

24. BL, Egerton MS 2618, fo. 27; Add. MS 19,399, fo. 58; *A Perfect Diurnall*, 264 (14–21 Aug. 1648), p. 2128; *The Bloudy Battel at Preston in Lancashire* (London, 1648), pp. 8–9.

25. *A Perfect Diurnall*, 264 (14–21 Aug. 1648), p. 2128; BL, Add. MS 19,399, fo. 60; Whitelocke, *Memorials*, II, p. 384.

26. The classic study of this period is David Underdown, *Pride's Purge: Politics in the Puritan Revolution* (Oxford, 1971).

27. *A Copie of Two Letters, Sent from Divers Officers of the Army in the North to … Lord Fairfax* (London, 1648); *The Articles and Charge of the Officers and Souldiers in the Armie* (London, 1648), p. 1.

28. *CJ*, VI, p. 73.

29. *CJ*, VI, p. 94.

30. Sean Kelsey, 'The Trial of Charles I', *English Historical Review*, 118 (2003), 583–616.

31. *The Declaration of His Highnesse the Prince of Wales* (London, 1649), pp. 5–6.

32. Bodl. Lib., Clarendon MS 34, fo. 19.

33. Although at least one history believed they did, in fact, escape: John Dauncey, *An Exact History of the Several Changes of Government in England* (London, 1660), p. 3.

34. *A Perfect Diurnall*, 288 (29 Jan.–5 Feb. 1649), p. 2318; Whitelocke, *Memorials*, II, p. 517.

35. *CJ*, VI, p. 126.

36. TNA, SP16/515, fo. 141. This letter is dated in the calendar as '?1647' and this dating has generally been followed in the scholarship. However, as Chapter 4 demonstrates, Poyer was not incarcerated in London for months on end in 1647 as was previously thought, and it seems much more likely that the two women were together in and around Windsor or London while their husbands were awaiting trial.

37. *An Act Concerning the Sequestration of South-Wales and the County of Monmouth* (London, 1649), printed in C. H. Firth and R. S. Rait (eds), *Acts and Ordinances of the Interregnum* (3 vols, London, 1911), II, pp. 14–16.

38. *A Perfect Diurnall*, 294 (12–19 Mar. 1649), p. 2363; Whitelocke, *Memorials*, II, p. 552.

39. *The Kingdomes Weekly Intelligencer*, 303 (13–20 Mar. 1649), p. 1291; *CJ*, VI, p. 165. The text is also produced in *Perfect Occurrences*, 115 (9–16 Mar. 1649), p. 901.

40. *The Kingdomes Weekly Intelligencer*, 303 (13–20 Mar. 1649), p. 1293.

41. TNA, SP19/123/105–8; M. A. E. Green (ed.), *Calendar of the Proceedings of the Committee for Advance of Money, 1642–1656* (3 vols, London, 1888), II, pp. 1020–1.

42. Worc. Coll., Clarke MS 16, fos 87v–90v.

43. The only reference I have seen to Eliot's pamphlet is in Andrew Hopper, *Turncoats and Renegadoes: Changing Sides during the English Civil Wars* (Oxford, 2012), p. 143.

44. Francis Jones, 'Griffith of Penybenglog: A Study in Pembrokeshire Genealogy', *Transactions of the Honourable Society of Cymmrodorion* (1938), 140–4. It is possible that the author was George William Griffith, another antiquary and father of William Griffith, although he seems not to have signed himself simply 'William Griffith'.

45. Worc. Coll., Clarke MS 16, fo. 87v.

46. Worc. Coll., Clarke MS 16, fo. 88.

47. Worc. Coll., Clarke MS 16, fo. 88v.

48. Worc. Coll., Clarke MS 16, fo. 89.

49. Worc. Coll., Clarke MS 16, fo. 89v.

50. [John Eliot], *A Short Comment upon the Grounds and Reasons of Poyers Taking up Armes* (London, 1649), p. 1. My italics.
51. For Cuny in this period, see Bodl. Lib., Tanner MS 58, fo. 724; TNA, SP23/167, p. 691; SP24/85, unfol.; NLW Great Sessions 4/788/1/18.
52. [Eliot], *Short Comment*, p. 2.
53. [Eliot], *Short Comment*, p. 5.
54. John Poyer, *Poyer's Vindication* (London, 1649). Thomason dated his copy 29 Mar. 1649: BL, E.548(31).
55. Poyer, *Poyer's Vindication*, p. 8.
56. I am very grateful to Mark Bainbridge of Worcester College Library for confirming that the pamphlet is indeed missing.
57. W. Carew Hazlitt, *Second Series of Bibliographical Collections and Notes on English Literature, 1474–1700* (London, 1882), p. 192.
58. J. C. Morrice, *Wales in the Seventeenth Century: its Literature and Men of Letters and Action* (Bangor, 1918), p. 38.
59. For such discrete publishing efforts, see Jason Peacey, *Print and Public Politics in the English Revolution* (Cambridge, 2013).
60. Poyer, *Poyer's Vindication*, p. 8.
61. *Perfect Occurrences*, 118 (30 Mar.–6 Apr. 1649), p. 923. Bowen was the man sent by Laugharne to the earl of Essex in the spring of 1642. He had been a captain in Laugharne's regiment but it is not known why he was selected by Cromwell after the siege of Pembroke for particular punishment: *Some Particular Animadversions of Marke for Satisfaction of the Contumatious Malignant* (London, 1646), pp. 11–12; Bodl. Lib., Tanner MS 58, fo. 735.
62. *The Articles and Charge Exhibited by the Court-Marshall at Whitehall Against Major Generall Laughorn, Col. Poyer, Col. Powell and Captain Bowen* (London, 1649): Trinity College Library, Cambridge, classmark Y.8.59. I am most grateful to James Kirwan and Sandy Paul for obtaining a reproduction of this unique text for me.
63. *The Kingdomes Weekly Intelligencer*, 307 (10–17 Apr. 1649), p. 1326.
64. The following is based on John M. Collins, 'Hidden in Plain Sight: Martial Law and the Making of the High Courts of Justice, 1642–60', *Journal of British Studies*, 53 (2014), 859–84 and Donagan, *War in England*, pp. 169–90.
65. *Perfect Occurrences*, 118 (30 Mar.–6 Apr. 1649), p. 926.
66. *The Articles and Charge . . . Against . . . Col. Poyer*, p. 2. Cf. *Perfect Occurrences*, 118 (30 Mar.–6 Apr. 1649), p. 926; *The Kingdomes Weekly Intelligencer*, 306 (3–10 Apr. 1649), pp. 1316–18.
67. *The Articles and Charge . . . Against . . . Col. Poyer*, p. 2. Cf. Poyer, *Poyer's Vindication*, p. 2.
68. Again, this response is lifted from Poyer, *Poyer's Vindication*, p. 2.
69. *Perfect Occurrences*, 118 (30 Mar.–6 Apr. 1649), p. 926.
70. *The Articles and Charge . . . Against . . . Col. Poyer*, p. 3; *Perfect Occurrences*, 118 (30 Mar.–6 Apr. 1649), p. 927.
71. *The Articles and Charge . . . Against . . . Col. Poyer*, p. 3; *Perfect Occurrences*, 118 (30 Mar.–6 Apr. 1649), p. 929.
72. *Mercurius Pragmaticus*, 49 (3–10 Apr. 1649), sig. Nnn3v.
73. *Perfect Occurrences*, 119 (6–13 Apr. 1649), p. 959.
74. See also the fact that Ann Laugharne lodged with Sir Hugh at his house in Dean's Yard near Westminster Abbey: TNA, SP19/118, fo. 27.
75. *A Modest Narrative of Intelligence*, 2 (7–14 Apr. 1649), p. 11.
76. *A Perfect Diurnall*, 298 (9–16 Apr. 1649), p. 2423; *The Perfect Weekly Account* (11–18 Apr. 1649), p. 446.

77. *A Perfect Diurnall*, 298 (9–16 Apr. 1649), pp. 2423–4; *The Kingdomes Faithfull and Impartiall Scout*, 11 (6–13 Apr. 1649), pp. 84–5.
78. For the name of the president, see *A Modest Narrative of Intelligence*, 2 (7–14 Apr. 1649), p. 11.
79. *The Perfect Weekly Account* (11–18 Apr. 1649), p. 446.
80. *Perfect Occurrences*, 119 (6–13 Apr. 1649), p. 964.
81. *A Perfect Diurnall*, 298 (9–16 Apr. 1649), p. 2424; Whitelocke, *Memorials*, III, p. 12.
82. *The Moderate*, 40 (10–17 Apr. 1649), p. 422; *A Modest Narrative of Intelligence*, 2 (7–14 Apr. 1649), p. 16.
83. *Mercurius Pragmaticus*, 50 (10–17 Apr. 1649), sig. Ooo3.
84. *A Modest Narrative of Intelligence*, 2 (7–14 Apr. 1649), p. 16; *A Modest Narrative of Intelligence*, 3 (14–21 Apr. 1649), pp. 20–1; Whitelocke, *Memorials*, III, p. 13. *The Declaration and Resolution of the Irish Army* (London, 1648), p. 6.
85. *A Modest Narrative of Intelligence*, 2 (7–14 Apr. 1649), p. 16.
86. *The Moderate*, 40 (10–17 Apr. 1649), p. 423; *The Perfect Weekly Account* (11–18 Apr. 1649), p. 449.
87. *A Modest Narrative of Intelligence*, 3 (14–21 Apr. 1649), p. 18.
88. HMC, *Leyborne-Popham MSS*, pp. 14–15.
89. HMC, *Leyborne-Popham MSS*, p. 17. None of these petitions are to be found among the Leyborne-Popham deposit at Worcester College, Oxford, and their present whereabouts are not known. I am grateful to Mark Bainbridge, librarian at Worcester College, for this information.
90. *Calendar of State Papers, Venetian, 1647–1652*, p. 99.
91. James Heath, *Chronicle of the Late Intestine Warr* (London, 1663), p. 427.
92. *Continued Heads of Perfect Passages in Parliament*, 2 (20–27 Apr. 1649), pp. 10–11.
93. Donagan, *War in England*, p. 192.
94. *The Moderate*, 41 (17–24 Apr. 1649), p. 434; Whitelocke, *Memorials*, III, p. 20.
95. HMC, *Leyborne-Popham MSS*, p. 15.
96. *Perfect Occurrences*, 121 (20–27 Apr. 1649), pp. 993–4; *Continued Heads of Perfect Passages in Parliament*, 2 (20–27 Apr. 1649), p. 13.
97. *The Moderate*, 41 (17–24 Apr. 1649), p. 434. These are also briefly enumerated in *The Declaration and Speech of Colonell John Poyer* (London, 1649), pp. 1–2.
98. *Perfect Occurrences*, 121 (20–27 Apr. 1649), p. 988.
99. *Declaration and Speech of . . . John Poyer*, p. 2.
100. Bodl. Lib., Clarendon MS 34, fo. 7r–v.
101. Bodl. Lib., Clarendon MS 37, fo. 89v.
102. *Declaration and Speech of . . . John Poyer*, pp. 2–3.
103. *Perfect Occurrences*, 121 (20–27 Apr. 1649), p. 999.
104. *Declaration and Speech of . . . John Poyer*, p. 3.
105. *Perfect Occurrences*, 121 (20–27 Apr. 1649), p. 999; *A Modest Narrative of Intelligence*, 4 (21–28 Apr. 1649), p. 30.
106. *Perfect Occurrences*, 121 (20–27 Apr. 1649), p. 999; *The Kingdomes Faithfull and Impartiall Scout*, 13 (20–27 Apr. 1649), pp. 103–4; *Declaration and Speech of . . . John Poyer*, p. 3.
107. *Perfect Occurrences*, 121 (20–27 Apr. 1649), p. 999.

Chapter 9: Afterlives

1. *List of Sheriffs for England and Wales* (London, 1898), p. 266; J. R. S. Phillips (ed.), *Justices of the Peace in Wales and Monmouthshire, 1541–1689* (Cardiff, 1975), pp. 219–21.

2. TNA, SP19/126, fos 105–8.
3. TNA, C5/33/64.
4. *Truth Manifest, Or, A Modest Reply to a Paper Lately Printed* (London, 1659).
5. Philip Jenkins, 'Wales and the Order of the Royal Oak', *National Library of Wales Journal*, 24 (1985–6), 349.
6. Richard Burton Archives, Swansea University, Cawdor (Lort) MS 23/911; *Calendar of State Papers, Domestic, 1661–2*, p. 260.
7. E. D. Jones, 'The Gentry of South Wales in the Civil War', *National Library of Wales Journal*, 11 (1959–60), 143.
8. TNA, PROB 11/315, fos 362–63v.
9. TNA, C5/46/43; C5/518/73; C8/158/5; E134/24and25Chas2/Hill6; PROB 28/518; Lambeth Palace Library, Arches MSS A4, fos 15, 29, 34, 63; A5, fos 314–22; Bbb 84, 97, 98; Ee 12/6.
10. Pembrokeshire Archives, HBORO 371.
11. 'Sampson Lort', History of Parliament unpublished biography, 1640–60. I am very grateful to Stephen Roberts for allowing me to see this prior to publication.
12. Jones, 'Gentry of South Wales', 144.
13. Pembrokeshire Archives, HBORO 371, 541.
14. 'Mayors of Pembroke', *WHHR*, 5 (1913), 121, 128; *Truth Manifest*.
15. 'Sampson Lort', History of Parliament unpublished biography, 1640–60.
16. Richard Burton Archives, Swansea University, Cawdor (Lort) MS 23/912; TNA, SP29/3, fo. 91.
17. TNA, PROB 11/324, fos 59–61v.
18. C. H. Firth and R. S. Rait (eds), *Acts and Ordinances of the Interregnum* (3 vols, London, 1911), II, pp. 314, 108, 1336.
19. TNA, SP29/440, fo. 78.
20. NLW, SD1673/20.
21. Firth and Rait, *Acts and Ordinances*, II, pp. 15, 47, 314, 1087, 1336, 1384.
22. [William Beech], *A New Light-House at Milford* (London, 1650), p. 2 (first pagination).
23. [John Eliot], *The Humble Petition of Iohn Elliot of the County of Pembrook* (London, *c*.1650). See also Worc. Coll., shelfmark G.5.11(58), *Iohn Elliot Esquire, his Reply to the Registers Scandalous and Deceitfull Observations upon his Petition* (London, *c*.1650).
24. William Beech, *To Mr John Eliot, an Esq.; At (or Near) the Doores of the Right Honorable the Parliament of England* (London, 1650).
25. NLW, Eaton Evans & Williams (Solicitors) Records 1298.
26. Richard Burton Archives, Swansea University, Cawdor (Lort) MS 20/784.
27. TNA, C8/325/118.
28. *CJ*, VIII, p. 86; *Statutes of the Realm*, V, p. 223.
29. TNA, SP19/118, fo. 27.
30. B. Weiser, 'Access and Petitioning during the Reign of Charles II', in E. Cruickshanks (ed.), *The Stuart Courts* (Stroud, 2000), pp. 203–13.
31. TNA, SP29/25, fo. 37.
32. TNA, SP19/83, fo. 69.
33. Hugh Peter, *A Copy of his Highnesse Prince Charles his Letter* (London, 1648), p. 3.
34. On this, see Stewart Beale, 'Royalist Widows and the Crown, 1660–70', *Historical Research*, 92 (2019), 746.
35. TNA, SP29/37, fo. 271.
36. On widows' sufferings following the wars, there is now a substantial scholarship, but see especially Beale, 'Royalist Widows and the Crown'; *idem*, 'War Widows and

Revenge in Restoration England', *The Seventeenth Century*, 32 (2018), 195–217; Imogen Peck, 'The Great Unknown: The Negotiation and Narration of Death by English War Widows, 1647–60', *Northern History*, 53 (2016), 220–35; Hannah Worthen, 'Supplicants and Guardians: The Petitions of Royalist War Widows during the Civil Wars and Interregnum, 1642–60', *Women's History Review*, 26 (2016), 528–40.

37. TNA, SP29/37, fo. 271.
38. TNA, SP29/37, fo. 272.
39. *CJ*, VIII, p. 309.
40. *Calendar of State Papers, Domestic, 1663–4*, p. 254.
41. TNA, SP44/18, p. 75.
42. TNA, SP29/142B, fo. 75.
43. TNA, SP29/103/160; SP29/125/57; *Calendar of State Papers, Domestic, 1668–9*, p. 204; Yale University, Beineke Library, Osborn MS 17210.
44. 'Mayors of Pembroke', *WWHR*, 5 (1915), 123; NLW, MS 1370B, no. 28.
45. J. Carpenter Smith, *History of St George's Parish, Flushing, Long Island* (Flushing, 1897), pp. 24–7; Henry Onderdonk (ed.), *Record Kept by Rev. Thomas Poyer, Rector of Episcopal Churches at Jamaica, Newtown & Flushing, Long Island* (Brooklyn, 1913).
46. Jones, 'Gentry of South Wales', 142–7.
47. *A Perfect Diurnall*, 300 (23–30 Apr. 1649), p. 2460.
48. Whitelocke, *Memorials*, III, p. 22.
49. Contrast this with the gushing royalist memorials to the 'martyrs' of Colchester: Barbara Donagan, 'Myth, Memory and Martyrdom: Colchester 1648', *Essex Archaeology and History*, 34 (2004), 172–80.
50. *Mercurius Elencticus*, 1 (24 Apr.–1 May 1649), p. 4.
51. For the character of the royalist press, see Jason McElligott, *Royalism, Print and Censorship in Revolutionary England* (Woodbridge, 2007).
52. *Mercurius Elencticus*, 1 (24 Apr.–1 May 1649), p. 4.
53. *Mercurius Pragmaticus* (23–30 Apr. 1649), sig. A2v.
54. This was echoed in a royalist manuscript newsletter which described him as dying 'with singular courage & contempt of death': Bodl. Lib., Clarendon MS 37, fo. 89v.
55. *The Man in the Moon*, 3 (23–30 Apr. 1649), p. 23.
56. 'Pembrokeshire Parsons', *WWHR*, 3 (1912–13), 234, 236.
57. William Beech, *More Sulphure for Basing* (London, 1645); Ann Laurence, *Parliamentary Army Chaplains, 1642–1651* (Woodbridge, 1990), p. 98.
58. See also TNA, SP19/123, fo. 170. I discuss Eliot and Beech further in a forthcoming publication.
59. Beech, *A New Light-House at Milford*.
60. Beech, *A New Light-House at Milford*, p. 4 (first pagination).
61. A 'gin' was a snare for catching game.
62. *The Turne of Time* (?London, ?1653).
63. Thomas May, *A Breviary of the History of the Parliament of England* (London, 1650), p. 191.
64. May, *A Breviary of the History of the Parliament*, p. 192.
65. May, *A Breviary of the History of the Parliament*, p. 202.
66. M. H., *The History of the Union of the Four Famous Kingdoms* (London, 1659), title page.
67. Mark Stoyle, *Soldiers and Strangers: An Ethnic History of the English Civil Wars* (New Haven and London, 2005).

68. M. H., *History of the Union*, pp. 75–6.

69. M. H., *History of the Union*, pp. 76–81.

70. M. H., *History of the Union*, p. 81.

71. Although see Mark Stoyle, '"The Gear Rout": The Cornish Rising of 1648 and the Second Civil War', *Albion*, 32 (2000), 37–58.

72. Matthew Neufeld, *The Civil Wars after 1660: Public Remembering in Late Stuart England* (Woodbridge, 2013); Erin Peters, *Commemoration and Oblivion in Royalist Print Culture* (London, 2017).

73. Wendy A. Maier, 'Heath, James', *Oxford Dictionary of National Biography*: <https://doi-org.abc.cardiff.ac.uk/10.1093/ref:odnb/12836> (accessed 19 Sept. 2019).

74. James Heath, *A Brief Chronicle of the Late Intestine Warr* (London, 1663), p. 310.

75. Heath, *Brief Chronicle*, p. 311.

76. Heath, *Brief Chronicle*, p. 427.

77. James Heath, *A New Book of Loyal English Martyrs* (London, 1665), p. 143.

78. David Lloyd, *Memoires of the Lives, Actions, Sufferings & Deaths* (London, 1668).

79. William Winstanley, *The Loyall Martyrology* (London, 1665), pp. 15–16.

80. This can be seen on the National Portrait Gallery's website: Ref: NPG D26783, at <https://www.npg.org.uk/collections/search/portrait/mw131293/> (accessed 10 Oct. 2019).

81. Thomas Hobbes, *History of the Civil Wars of England* (London, 1679), pp. 208–9.

82. Richard Fenton, *A Historical Tour through Pembrokeshire* (London, 1811), pp. 369–71.

83. On its influence, see Blair Worden, 'Thomas Carlyle and Oliver Cromwell', *Proceedings of the British Academy*, 105 (2000), 131–70; *idem*, *Roundhead Reputations* (London, 2002), pp. 264–95.

84. S. C. Lomas (ed.), *The Letters and Speeches of Oliver Cromwell* (3 vols, London, 1904), I, p. 311.

85. Lomas, *Letters and Speeches*, I, p. 312.

86. Lomas, *Letters and Speeches*, I, pp. 324–5.

87. See, for example, the novelist John Buchan's description of Poyer as 'an alcoholic presbyter' in his 1934 biography of Oliver Cromwell: John Buchan, *Oliver Cromwell* (London, 1934), p. 271. I am grateful to Mark Stoyle for drawing my attention to this reference.

88. John Rushworth, *Historical Collections* (8 vols, London, 1721–2), VII, p. 1033; *A Perfect Diurnall of Some Passages in Parliament*, 243 (20–27 Mar. 1648), p. 1955.

89. Edward Laws, *The History of Little England Beyond Wales* (London, 1888).

90. NLW, MS 1377B. His notes are to be found in NLW, MSS 1370B–1371B.

91. Laws, *Little England Beyond Wales*, p. 322.

92. Laws, *Little England Beyond Wales*, p. 334.

93. R. T. Jenkins, E. D. Jones and Brynley F. Roberts (eds), *The Dictionary of Welsh Biography, 1941–1970* (London, 2001), pp. 154–5.

94. Leach, *Pembrokeshire*, p. 7.

95. Leach, *Pembrokeshire*, pp. 7, 83, 103–4: 'Most of Poyer's ... misfortunes, even perhaps his disastrous participation in the second civil war, appear to be traceable to antagonisms arising out of his seizure of Carew Castle' (p. 83).

96. Leach, *Pembrokeshire*, p. 162.

97. Andrew Hopper, *Turncoats and Renegadoes: Changing Sides during the English Civil Wars* (Oxford, 2012), pp. 9, 160.

98. Rowland Mathias, 'The First Civil War' and 'The Second Civil War and Interregnum', in *Pembs. Co. Hist.*, pp. 159–224.

99. Ronald Hutton, *The Royalist War Effort, 1642–1646* (London, 1982; 2nd edn, 1999).

100. Hutton, *Royalist War Effort*, p. 68.
101. Peter Gaunt, *A Nation Under Siege: The Civil War in Wales, 1642–48* (London, 1991).
102. Stephen Roberts, 'How the West was Won: Parliamentary Politics, Religion and the Military in South Wales, 1642–9', *Welsh History Review*, 21 (2003), 646–74.
103. Robert Ashton, *Counter-Revolution: The Second Civil War and its Origins, 1646–8* (New Haven and London, 1994).
104. Ashton, *Counter-Revolution*, pp. 416–17. See also Ian Gentles's description of Poyer as 'turning increasingly to the bottle to stiffen his courage': *The New Model Army* (Oxford, 1992), p. 242.
105. Ashton, *Counter-Revolution*, p. 417.
106. Robert Matthews, *'A Storme Out of Wales': The Second Civil War in South Wales, 1648* (Newcastle upon Tyne, 2012).
107. Matthews, *'Storme Out of Wales'*, pp. 182–3.
108. Cf. John Morrill, *The Revolt in the Provinces: The People of England and the Tragedies of War, 1630–1648* (London, 1999).
109. Matthews, *'Storme Out of Wales'*, pp. 183–7.

Bibliography

Manuscripts

Beineke Library, Yale University, New Haven
Osborn MS 17210

Bodleian Library, Oxford
Carte MSS 3, 4, 16
Clarendon MSS 30–37
Nalson MSS 2–6, 22
Rawlinson A221
Tanner MSS 57–62

British Library, London
Additional MSS 18,981, 19,399, 46,391B
Egerton MS 2618
Stowe MS 189

Folger Shakespeare Library, Washington D.C.
X.d. 483 (20)

Huntington Library, San Marino, Los Angeles
Ellesmere MSS 7135, 1443, 7598, 7600A

Lambeth Palace Library, London
Arches MSS
MS 679

Longleat House
Devereux MS 4
DE/Box VIII/112

The National Archives of the United Kingdom, Kew
C2, C3, C5, C8, C219
E112, E134, E179

HCA 13
PC2
PROB 11, PROB 28
SP16, SP19, SP21, SP23, SP24, SP25, SP28, SP29, SP44
STAC 5, STAC 8

National Library of Wales, Aberystwyth
Bronwydd MS 3360
Dynevor MSS A97, B348
Eaton Evans & Williams (Solicitors) Records
Great Sessions 4
Muddlescombe Deeds 1787
NLW MSS 1370B, 1371B, 1377B
Picton Castle Estate MS 1897
Pontfaen Estate Records MS 58
SD (St David's Probate)

Parliamentary Archives, London
HL/PO/JO/10/1/190, 199, 211, 225

Pembrokeshire Archives, Haverfordwest
HBORO 73/4–6; 371, 541

Plymouth and West Devon Record Office, Plymouth
1/359/72

Richard Burton Archives, Swansea University
Cawdor (Lort) MSS 6/258; 13/619; 20/784; 23/912

Somerset Heritage Centre, Taunton
DD/TB/41/5/21–4
DD/WO/55/1/17
Q/SR

Tenby Museum
TEM/Box 16

Trinity College, Dublin
MS 838

Worcester College, Oxford
Clarke MSS 16, 41, 110, 114

Contemporary Printed Works

An Act Concerning the Sequestration of South-Wales and the County of Monmouth (London, 1649).

The Agreement of the Major, Aldermen and Inhabitants of the Towne of Tenby (Oxford, 1643).

The Articles and Charge Exhibited by the Court-Marshall at Whitehall Against Major Generall Laughorn, Col. Poyer, Col. Powell and Captain Bowen (London, 1649).

The Articles and Charge of the Officers and Souldiers in the Armie (London, 1648).

Beech, William, *More Sulphure for Basing* (London, 1645).

— *To Mr John Eliot, an Esq.; At (or Near) the Doores of the Right Honorable the Parliament of England* (London, 1650).

— *A New Light-House at Milford* (London, 1650).

A Bloody Slaughter at Pembrooke-Castle in Wales (London, 1648).

The Bloudy Battel at Preston in Lancashire (London, 1648).

Cook, John, *The Vindication of the Professors & the Profession of the Law* (London, 1646).

A Copie of Two Letters, Sent from Divers Officers of the Army in the North to . . . Lord Fairfax (London, 1648).

Dauncey, John, *An Exact History of the Several Changes of Government in England* (London, 1660).

Davies, John, *The Civill Warres of Great Britain and Ireland* (Glasgow, 1664).

The Declaration of His Highnesse the Prince of Wales (London, 1649).

A Declaration of the Kings Maiesties Army in the North of England (London, 1648).

The Declaration of Lieutenant-Generall Cromwell Concerning his Present Design and Engagement against Col. Poyer (London, 1648).

The Declaration and Protestation of the Kings Army in South-Wales (London, 1648).

The Declaration and Resolution of Divers Officers and Soldiers under the Command of Major General Laughorn (London, 1648).

The Declaration and Resolution of the Irish Army (London, 1648).

The Desires and Propositions of the Lord Inchequin (London, 1648).

Duke Hamiltons Conditions for Surrendring Himself (London, 1648).

[Eliot, John], *An Answer in Just Vindication of Some Religious and Worthy Gentleman of Pembrokeshire* (London, 1646).

— *A Declaration of Divers Gentlemen of Wales Concerning Collonell Poyer* (London, 1648).

— *A Just Vindication on the Behalf of Iohn Eliot, Esq* (London, 1648).

— *A Short Comment upon the Grounds and Reasons of Poyers Taking up Armes* (London, 1649).

— *The Humble Petition of Iohn Elliot of the County of Pembrook* (London, c.1650)

— *Iohn Elliot Esquire, his Reply to the Registers Scandalous and Deceitfull Observations upon his Petition* (London, c.1650)

An Exact and Humble Remonstrance (London, 1645).

Exceeding Good Newes from South-Wales (London, 1648).

A Fight. The Lord Goring Beaten at Coulchester in Essex (London, 1648).

A Great Fight in Wales (London, 1648).

Heath, James, *A Chronicle of the Late Intestine Warr* (London, 1663).

— *A New Book of Loyal English Martyrs* (London, 1665).

Hobbes, Thomas, *History of the Civil Wars of England* (London, 1679).

The Kings Maiesties Last Speech (London, 1648).

The Last Newes from Kent (London, 1648).

[Laugharne, Rowland], *A True Relation of the Late Successe of the Kings and Parliaments Forces in Pembroke-Shire* (London, 1645).

— *A Declaration by Major General Laughorn* (London, 1648).

A Letter of a Sad Tragedy by Prince Griffin (London, 1648).

A Letter Sent from Newport to a Gentleman in London (London, 1648).

Lewis, John, *Contemplations on these Times, Or, The Parliament Explained to Wales* (London, 1646).

A List of the Prisoners Taken . . . by Collonell Horton (London, 1648).

Lloyd, David, *Memoires of the Lives, Actions, Sufferings & Deaths* (London, 1668).

Lort, Roger, *Epigrammatum Rogeri Lort* (London, 1646).

Marshall, Stephen, *Emmanuel, A Thanksgiving Sermon Preached to the . . . Commons* (London, 1648).

May, Thomas, A *Breviary of the History of the Parliament of England* (London, 1650).

A Message Agreed upon by the Lords and Commons Assembled in Parliament (London, 1648).

'M. H.', *The History of the Union of the Four Famous Kingdoms* (London, 1659).

An Ordinance of the Lords and Commons . . . for Sequestration of the Estates of Major Generall Laughorne (London, 1648)

Peter, Hugh, *A Copy of his Highnesse Prince Charles his Letter* (London, 1648).

Poyer, John, *Poyer's Vindication* (London, 1649).

— *The Declaration and Speech of Colonell John Poyer* (London, 1649).

[Poyer, John and Powell, Rice], *The Declaration of Col. Poyer and Col. Powell* (London, 1648).

[Poyer, John and Powell, Rice], *Colonell Powell and Col. Poyers Letter to his Highnesse the Prince of Wales* (London, 1648).

Prince Charles his Letter (London, 1648).

Rushworth, John, *Historical Collections* (8 vols, London, 1721–2).

Smith, William, *Severall Letters of Great Importance and Good Successe* (London, 1643).

Some Particular Animadversions of Marke for Satisfaction of the Contumatious Malignant (London, 1646).

Speed, John, *The Theatre of the Empire of Great Britain* (London, 1611).

Strange and Terrible Newes from the North (London, 1648).

Strong, William, *The Vengeance of the Temple* (London, 1648).

[Thelwall, Simon], *A True Relation of the Routing of His Majesties Forces in the County of Pembroke* (London, 1644).

The Turne of Time (?London, ?1653).

Truth Manifest, Or, A Modest Reply to a Paper Lately Printed (London, 1659).

Two Great Victories (London, 1648).

Weare, John, *The Apologie of Colonell John Were* (London, 1644).

Winstanley, William, *The Loyall Martyrology* (London, 1665).

Newsbooks

Continued Heads of Perfect Passages in Parliament
Heads of Chiefe Passages in Parliament
The Kingdomes Faithfull and Impartiall Scout
The Kingdomes Weekly Intelligencer
The Kingdomes Weekly Post
The Man in the Moon
Mercurius Aulicus
Mercurius Aulicus Againe
Mercurius Bellicus
Mercurius Civicus
Mercurius Elencticus
Mercurius Melancholicus
Mercurius Poeticus
Mercurius Pragmaticus
Mercurius Urbanicus
Mercurius Veridicus
The Moderate
The Moderate Intelligencer
A Modest Narrative of Intelligence
The Parliaments Post
A Perfect Diurnall
A Perfect Diurnall of Some Passages in Parliament
Perfect Occurrences of Every Daie Iournall in Parliament
The Perfect Weekly Account
The Spie
The Welch Mercury

General Printed Primary Works

Acts of the Privy Council of England, 1630–1 (London, 1964).

British History Online, High Court of Chivalry Proceedings: *https://www. british-history.ac.uk/no-series/court-of-chivalry*.

Broadway, Jan, Cust, Richard and Roberts, Stephen K., (eds), A *Calendar of the Docquets of Lord Keeper Coventry, 1625–1640* (London, 2004).

Calendar of State Papers, Domestic.

Calendar of State Papers, Venetian.

Carte, Thomas (ed.), *The Life of James Duke of Ormonde* (6 vols, Oxford, 1851).

Coates, Wilson H., Young, Anne Steele and Snow, Vernon F. (eds), *The Private Journals of the Long Parliament* (3 vols, New Haven and London, 1982–92).

Commons Journals.

Dwnn, Lewis, *Visitations of Wales*, ed. S. R. Meyrick (2 vols, Llandovery, 1846).

Firth, C. H. and Rait, R. S. (eds), *Acts and Ordinances of the Interregnum* (3 vols, London, 1911).

Gardiner, S. R. (ed.), *The Hamilton Papers* (Camden Society, new series, 27, 1880).

Green, M. A. E. (ed.), *Calendar of the Proceedings of the Committee for Advance of Money, 1642–1656* (3 vols, London, 1888).

— (ed.), *Calendar of the Proceedings of the Committee for Compounding, 1643–1660* (5 vols, London, 1889–92).

Hazlitt, W. Carew, *Second Series of Bibliographical Collections and Notes on English Literature, 1474–1700* (London, 1882).

HMC, *Leyborne-Popham MSS.*

HMC, *Pepys MSS.*

HMC, *Salisbury MSS, Vol. XXI.*

Hyde, Edward, earl of Clarendon, *The History of the Rebellion and Civil Wars*, ed. W. D. Macray (6 vols, Oxford, 1888).

Jones, E. D., 'The Gentry of South Wales in the Civil War', *National Library of Wales Journal*, 11 (1959).

Jones, John Gwynfor (ed.), *The Dialogue of the Government of Wales (1594)* (Cardiff, 2010).

Lawrence, Thomas B., *The Thomas Book, giving the Genealogies of Sir Rhys ap Thomas* (New York, 1896).

Lewis, E. A. (ed.), *Welsh Port Books, 1550–1603* (London, 1927).

Lindley, Keith and Scott, David (eds), *The Journal of Thomas Juxon, 1644–1647* (Camden Society, 5th series, 13, 1999).

Lomas, S. C. (ed.), *The Letters and Speeches of Oliver Cromwell* (3 vols, London, 1904).

Lords Journals.

Miles, Dilwyn (ed.), *The Description of Pembrokeshire* (Llandysul, 1994).

Onderdonk, Henry (ed.), *Record Kept by Rev. Thomas Poyer, Rector of Episcopal Churches at Jamaica, Newtown & Flushing, Long Island* (Brooklyn, 1913).

'Original Letters', *Archaeologia Cambrensis*, new series, 13 (1853).

Owen, George, *A Description of Penbrokshire*, ed. H. Owen (4 vols, London, 1898–1933).

Penn, Granville (ed.), *Memorials of the Professional Life and Times of Sir William Penn* (2 vols, London, 1883).

Roots, Ivan (ed.), *Speeches of Oliver Cromwell* (London, 1989).

'Tenby in 1621', *Cambrian Journal*, 2nd ser., 5 (1862).

Venn, John (ed.), *A Biographical Dictionary of Gonville and Caius College, 1396–1897* (4 vols, London, 1897–1912).

Whitelocke, Bulstrode, *Memorials of the English Affairs* (4 vols, Oxford, 1853).

Worth, R. N. (ed.), *The Buller Papers* (Plymouth, 1895).

Secondary Literature

Adamson, John, 'Of Armies and Architecture: The Employments of Robert Scawen', in Ian Gentles, John Morrill and Blair Worden (eds), *Soldiers, Writers and Statesmen of the English Revolution* (Cambridge, 1998).

— *The Noble Revolt* (London, 2007).

Ashton, Robert, 'From Cavalier to Roundhead Tyranny', in John Morrill (ed.), *Reactions to the English Civil War, 1642–49* (Harlow, 1982).

— *Counter-Revolution: The Second Civil War and its Origins, 1646–8* (New Haven and London, 1992).

Beale, Stewart, 'War Widows and Revenge in Restoration England', *The Seventeenth Century*, 32 (2018).

— 'Royalist Widows and the Crown, 1660–70', *Historical Research*, 92 (2019).

Bowen, Lloyd, 'Representations of Wales and the Welsh during the Civil Wars and Interregnum', *Historical Research*, 77 (2004).

— 'Wales and Religious Reform in the Long Parliament, 1640–42', *Transactions of the Honourable Society of Cymmrodorion*, 12 (2006).

— *The Politics of the Principality: Wales, c.1603–1642* (Cardiff, 2007).

— 'Faction and Connection in Pembrokeshire Politics, 1640–9' (forthcoming).

— 'Preaching and Politics in the Welsh Marches, 1643–1663: The Case of Alexander Griffith', *Historical Research* (forthcoming, 2021).

Braddick, Michael, *The Common Freedom of the People: John Lilburne and the English Revolution* (Oxford, 2018).

Buchan, John, *Oliver Cromwell* (London, 1935).

C[lark], G. T. and R. O. J., 'Some Account of the Parishes of St Nicholas and St Lythan, co. Glamorgan', *Archaeologia Cambrensis*, 3rd series, 30 (1862).

Collins, John M., 'Hidden in Plain Sight: Martial Law and the Making of the High Courts of Justice, 1642–60', *Journal of British Studies*, 53 (2014).

Como, David, *Radical Parliamentarians and the English Civil War* (Oxford, 2018).

Crawford, Patricia, 'Charles Stuart, that Man of Blood', *Journal of British Studies*, 16 (1977).

Cressy, David, *England on Edge: Crisis and Revolution, 1640–42* (Oxford, 2006).

Crouch, Henry, *A Complete Guide to the Officers of His Majesty's Customs in the Out-Ports* (London, 1732).

Cust, Richard, *Charles I and the Aristocracy, 1625–1642* (Cambridge, 2013).

Darcy, Eamon, *The Irish Rebellion of 1641 and the Wars of the Three Kingdoms* (Woodbridge, 2013).

Dodd, A. H., 'Nicholas Adams', in J. P. Ferris (ed.), *The House of Commons, 1558–1603*: <https://www.historyofparliamentonline.org/volume/1558-1603/member/adams-nicholas-1565-1628>.

Donagan, Barbara, 'Codes and Conduct in the English Civil War', *Past & Present*, 118 (1988).

— 'Myth, Memory and Martyrdom: Colchester 1648', *Essex Archaeology and History*, 34 (2004).

— *War in England, 1642–1649* (Oxford, 2008).

Donald, Peter, *An Uncounselled King: Charles I and the Scottish Troubles, 1637–1641* (Cambridge, 1990).

Eales, Jacqueline, 'White, John', *Oxford Dictionary of National Biography*: https://doi-org.abc.cardiff.ac.uk/10.1093/ref:odnb/29254.

Evans, J. T., *The Church Plate of Pembrokeshire* (London, 1905).

Fincham, Kenneth and Taylor, Stephen, 'Episcopalian Identity, 1640–1662', in Anthony Milton (ed.), *The Oxford History of Anglicanism, Vol. I* (Oxford, 2016).

Fincham, Kenneth and Tyacke, Nicholas, *Altars Restored: The Changing Face of English Religious Worship, c.1547–c.1700* (Oxford, 2007).

Firth, C. H., 'Clarendon's "History of the Rebellion"', *English Historical Review*, 19 (1904).

Fissel, Mark, *The Bishops' Wars: Charles I's Campaigns against Scotland, 1638–1640* (Cambridge, 1994).

Fuidge, N. M., 'Gelly Meyrick', in J. P. Ferris (ed.), *The History of Parliament: The House of Commons, 1558–1603*: <http://www.histparl.ac.uk/volume/1558-1603/member/meyrick-(merrick)-gelly-1556-1601/>.

Gaunt, Peter, *A Nation Under Siege: The Civil War in Wales, 1642–48*
  (London, 1991).
Gentles, Ian, 'The Struggle for London in the Second Civil War', *Historical*
  Journal, 26 (1983).
— *The New Model Army* (Oxford, 1992).
— *The English Revolution and the Wars in the Three Kingdoms, 1638–1652*
  (Harlow, 2007).
Holmes, Clive, 'Centre and Locality in Civil-War England', in John
  Adamson (ed.), *The English Civil War: Conflict and Contexts, 1640–49*
  (Basingstoke, 2009).
Hopper, Andrew, 'Meyrick, Sir John', *Oxford Dictionary of National*
  Biography: https://doi-org.abc.cardiff.ac.uk/10.1093/ref:odnb/18642.
— *Turncoats and Renegadoes: Changing Sides during the English Civil Wars*
  (Oxford, 2012).
Hore, Herbert F., 'Mayors and Bailiffs of Tenby', *Archaeologia Cambrensis*,
  new series, 14 (April 1853).
Howells, Brian, 'Land and People, 1536–1642', in *Pembs. Co. Hist.*
— 'The Economy, 1536–1642', in *Pembs. Co. Hist.*
— (ed.), *Pembrokeshire County History, Volume III: Early Modern*
  Pembrokeshire, 1536–1815 (Haverfordwest, 1987).
Howells, John, 'The Boroughs of Medieval Pembrokeshire: Pembroke', in
  R. F. Walker (ed.), *Pembrokeshire County History, Volume II: Medieval*
  Pembrokeshire (Haverfordwest, 2002).
Hughes, Ann, *Gangraena and the Struggle for the English Revolution*
  (Oxford, 2004).
Hunneyball, Paul M., 'The Development of Parliamentary Privilege,
  1604–29', *Parliamentary History*, 34 (2015).
Hutton, Ronald, 'Clarendon's "History of the Rebellion"', *English*
  Historical Review, 97 (1982).
— *The Royalist War Effort, 1642–1646* (2nd edn, London, 1999).
Jenkins, J. G., *The Welsh Woollen Industry* (Cardiff, 1969).
Jenkins, Philip, 'Wales and the Order of the Royal Oak', *National Library of*
  Wales Journal, 24 (1985–6).
Jones, E. D., 'The Gentry of South Wales in the Civil War', *National*
  Library of Wales Journal, 11 (1959–60).
Jones, Francis, 'Griffith of Penybenglog: A Study in Pembrokeshire Genealogy',
  Transactions of the Honourable Society of Cymmrodorion (1938).
Kelsey, Sean, 'The Trial of Charles I', *English Historical Review*, 118 (2003).
— '"King of the Sea": The Prince of Wales and the Stuart Monarchy',
  History, 92 (2007).
— '"A No-King, or a New": Royalists and the Succession, 1648–1649', in
  Jason McElligott and David Smith (eds), *Royalists and Royalism during*
  the English Civil Wars (Cambridge, 2007).

Laurence, Ann, *Parliamentary Army Chaplains, 1642–1651* (Woodbridge, 1990).

Laws, Edward, *History of Little England Beyond Wales* (London, 1888).

Leach, A. L., *The History of the Civil War (1642–1649) in Pembrokeshire and on its Borders* (London, 1937).

Lewis, Samuel, *A Topographical Dictionary of Wales* (2 vols, London 1854).

Lindley, Keith, 'Impact of the 1641 Rebellion upon England and Wales', *Irish Historical Review*, 18 (1972).

Ludolph, Patrick, 'An Anatomy of the London Agent', *Parliamentary History*, 33 (2014).

Maltby, Judith, '"The Good Old Way": Prayer Book Protestantism in the 1640s and 1650s', *Studies in Church History*, 38 (2004).

Mathew, David, *The Celtic Peoples and Renaissance Europe. A Study of the Celtic and Spanish Influences on Elizabethan History* (London, 1933).

Mathias, Roland, 'The First Civil War', in *Pembs. Co. Hist.*

Matthews, Robert, *'A Storme out of Wales': The Second Civil War in South Wales, 1648* (Newcastle upon Tyne, 2012).

'Mayors of Pembroke', *WWHR*, 5 (1915).

McElligott, Jason, *Royalism, Print and Censorship in Revolutionary England* (Woodbridge, 2007).

Milton, Anthony, 'Arminians, Laudians, Anglicans, and Revisionists: Back to Which Drawing Board?', *Huntington Library Quarterly*, 78 (2015).

Morrice, J. C., *Wales in the Seventeenth Century: Its Literature and Men of Letters and Action* (Bangor, 1918).

Morrill, John, 'The Church in England, 1642–1649', in *idem, The Nature of the English Revolution* (London, 1993).

— 'The Attack on the Church of England in the Long Parliament, 1640–1642', in *idem, The Nature of the English Revolution* (London, 1993).

— 'The Unweariableness of Mr Pym: Influence and Eloquence in the Long Parliament', in S. D. Amussen and M. A. Kishlansky (eds), *Political Culture and Cultural Politics in Early Modern England* (Manchester, 1995).

— *The Revolt in the Provinces: The People of England and the Tragedies of War, 1630–1648* (London, 1999).

— and Baker, Philip, 'The Case of the Armie Truly Re-Stated', in Michael Mendle (ed.), *The Putney Debates of 1647: The Army, The Levellers and the English State* (Cambridge, 2001).

Murphy, Elaine, *Ireland and the War at Sea, 1641–1653* (Woodbridge, 2012).

Neufeld, Matthew, *The Civil Wars after 1660: Public Remembering in Late Stuart England* (Woodbridge, 2013).

Ó hannracháin, Tadhg, 'Counter Reformation: The Catholic Church, 1550–1641', in Jane Ohlmeyer (ed.), *The Cambridge History of Ireland* (Cambridge, 2018).

O'Hara, David A., *English Newsbooks and the Irish Rebellion, 1641–49* (Dublin, 2005).

Peacey, Jason, *Print and Public Politics in the English Revolution* (Cambridge, 2013).

—— 'Print, Publicity, and Popularity: The Projecting of Sir Balthazar Gerbier, 1642–1662', *Journal of British Studies*, 51 (2012).

Pearl, Valerie, 'London's Counter-Revolution', in G. E. Aylmer (ed.), *The Interregnum: The Quest for Settlement, 1646–1660* (London, 1977).

Peck, Imogen, 'The Great Unknown: The Negotiation and Narration of Death by English War Widows, 1647–60', *Northern History*, 53 (2016).

'Pembrokeshire Parsons', *WWHR*, 3 (1912–13).

Perceval-Maxwell, M., *The Outbreak of the Irish Rebellion of 1641* (Dublin, 1994).

Peters, Erin, *Commemoration and Oblivion in Royalist Print Culture* (London, 2017).

Raymond, Joad, *The Invention of the Newspaper: English Newsbooks, 1641–1649* (Oxford, 1996).

—— *Pamphlets and Pamphleteering in Early Modern Britain* (Cambridge, 2003).

Raymond, S. A., 'The Glamorgan Arraymen, 1642–1645', *Morgannwg*, 24 (1980).

Richards, Thomas, *A History of the Puritan Movement in Wales* (London, 1920).

Roberts, Stephen, 'How the West was Won', *Welsh History Review*, 21 (2003).

Russell, Conrad, *The Fall of the British Monarchies, 1637–1642* (Oxford, 1991).

Scott, David, 'The Barwis Affair: Political Allegiance and the Scots during the British Civil Wars', *English Historical Review*, 115 (2000).

Shagan, Ethan, 'Constructing Discord: Ideology, Propaganda, and English Responses to the Irish Rebellion of 1641', *Journal of British Studies*, 36 (1997).

Sharpe, Kevin, *The Personal Rule of Charles I* (New Haven and London, 1992).

Smith, J. Carpenter, *History of St George's Parish, Flushing, Long Island* (Flushing, 1897).

Stearns, R. P., *The Strenuous Puritan: Hugh Peter, 1598–1660* (Urbana, 1954).

Stephens, Isaac, 'Confessional Identity in Early Stuart England: The "Prayer Book Puritanism" of Elizabeth Isham', *Journal of British Studies*, 50 (2011).

Stevenson, David, *The Scottish Revolution, 1637–1644: The Triumph of the Covenanters* (Newton Abbot, 1973).

— *Revolution and Counter-Revolution in Scotland, 1644–1651* (London, 1977).

Stewart, Laura A. M., *Rethinking the Scottish Revolution: Covenanted Scotland, 1637–1651* (Oxford, 2016).

Stoyle, Mark, '"The Gear Rout": The Cornish Rising of 1648 and the Second Civil War', *Albion*, 32 (2000).

— *Soldiers and Strangers: An Ethnic History of the English Civil Wars* (New Haven and London, 2005).

Thrush, Andrew, 'Hugh Owen', in J. P. Ferris and Andrew Thrush (eds), *The History of Parliament: The House of Commons, 1604–29*: <*https://www.historyofparliamentonline.org/volume/1604-1629/member/owen-hugh-1604-1671*>.

— 'Lewis Powell', in J. P. Ferris and Andrew Thrush (eds), *History of Parliament: The House of Commons, 1604–29*: <*https://www.historyofparliamentonline.org/volume/1604-1629/member/powell-lewis-1576-1636*>.

Tyacke, Nicholas, *Anti-Calvinists: The Rise of English Arminianism*, c.*1590–1640* (Oxford, 1990).

Underdown, David, *Pride's Purge: Politics in the Puritan Revolution* (Oxford, 1971).

Walsham, Alexandra, 'Phanaticus: Hugh Peter, Antipuritanism and the Afterlife of the English Revolution', *Parergon*, 32 (2015).

Walter, John, *Covenanting Citizens: The Protestation Oath and Popular Political Culture in the English Revolution* (Oxford, 2017).

Weiser, B., 'Access and Petitioning during the Reign of Charles II', in E. Cruickshanks (ed.), *The Stuart Courts* (Stroud, 2003).

Worden, Blair, 'Oliver Cromwell and the Sin of Achan', in Derek Beales and Geoffrey Best (eds), *History, Society and the Churches* (Cambridge, 1985).

— 'Thomas Carlyle and Oliver Cromwell', *Proceedings of the British Academy*, 105 (2000).

— *Roundhead Reputations* (London, 2002).

Worthen, Hannah, 'Supplicants and Guardians: The Petitions of Royalist War Widows during the Civil Wars and Interregnum, 1642–60', *Women's History Review*, 26 (2016).

Index